DATE DUE			
MAR – 4 1993			
7/12/93			
OCT 1 2 1993			
FEB 2 1 1994			
MAY 1 2 1995			
MAR 15 2006			

SEX,
DEATH
and GOD
in L.A.

SEX,
DEATH
and GOD
in L.A.

*Edited and with an Introduction
by David Reid*

Pantheon Books / New York

"On the Edge of the Pacific Century," by Alexander Cockburn,
was originally published in *Interview* Magazine (August 1989).

"*Chinatown*, Revisited? The 'Internationalization' of Downtown
Los Angeles," by Mike Davis, first appeared in *New Left Review*
(July–August 1987).

Photographs on pages 266, 286 and 294 courtesy of Dion Neutra,
Architect and Neutra Papers—UCLA Special Collections; pages
268, 270, 274, 278, 279, 308, and 312 courtesy of Thomas S. Hines.

Library of Congress Cataloging-in-Publication Data
Sex, death and God in L.A./edited and with an introduction by
David Reid.
p. cm.
ISBN 0-394-57321-8
1. Los Angeles (Calif.)—Civilization. I. Reid, David, 1946–   .
F869.L85S48   1992
979.4'94—dc20   90-52578

Book Design by Chris Welch

Now shall I praise the cities, those long-surviving (I watched them in awe) great constellations of earth.

Rainer Maria Rilke, "Fragment of an Elegy"

"LA." I loved the way she said "LA"; I love the way everybody says "LA" on the Coast; it's their one and only golden town when all is said and done.

Jack Kerouac, *On the Road*

Quadrangular, reticulated cities (Los Angeles, for instance) are said to produce a profound uneasiness: they offend our synesthetic sentiment of the City, which requires that any urban space have a center to go to, to return from, a complete site to dream of and in relation to which to advance or retreat; in a word, to invent oneself.

Roland Barthes, *Empire of Signs*

Back in Los Angeles, we missed Los Angeles.

Randall Jarrell, "Thinking of the Lost World"

CONTENTS

NOTE AND ACKNOWLEDGMENTS

Explaining why he had given a collection of his essays the title *Sex, Death and Money*, Gore Vidal observed that the "vivid triad" after all comprehended "the essential interests of the naked ape." There is a similar rationale for the title—very like—of this collection of original essays and memoirs about a large city in Southern California (all but Alexander Cockburn's essay and the first of Mike Davis's were written for this book, and they have been brought up to date). The city with the impossibly resonant name, the Town of Our Lady the Queen of the Angels, has been one of the supreme urban spectacles of the world ever since it became a metropolis in the early years of this century—a sprawling, dispersed, "fragmented" metropolis (as Robert M. Fogelson called it in a noted study) that the world recognized almost at once as representing something new under the sun, an unprecedented and possibly sinister mutation of the idea of a city. The early rise of Los Angeles was bracketed by the closing of the frontier and the arrival of the movies—a fateful symmetry, as Norman Mailer once observed, and one that has shaped and shadowed the region's entire development.

The plan of this book is to consider the character and customs of Los Angeles in relation to the fundamental things: sex, death, and religion, but also politics and race, love and marriage, the cult of youth and beauty, architecture, movies, the sense of the past. Charles Péguy said,

"Everything begins in mysticism and ends in politics." Rereading, I see how fitting it is that Alexander Cockburn's evocation of the Pacific Century, which opens the book, should commence with a shaman's-eye view of megalopolis, and that Jeremy Larner's closing story should include the apotheosis of a movie producer.

In a very general way, this approach was suggested by studies of past sensibilities such as LeRoy Ladurie's *Love, Money, and Death in the Pays d'Oc* and Theodore Zeldin's great history of the "passions and illusions" of France between 1848 and 1945. There was obviously no way of encompassing the thousand worlds of Los Angeles, but inviting an array of distinguished and venturesome writers to explore its range of sense and sensibilities seemed to promise access into a great many of them.

By the same token, the range of voices, styles, and forms to be found here, from learned scholarship to reportage to confession, was calculated. The real name of the City of Angels is legion, and it does not sing in chorus.

It is a pleasure to thank Sara Bershtel, formerly of Pantheon Books, who asked me to edit a book about Los Angeles and who can finally see what has come of her asking. Fred Jordan did not allow this book to be orphaned, and for some months it was sustained by Robert Cloud, who offered many valuable suggestions. Brief portions of the introduction appeared in *University Publishing* and *Vanity Fair* in a different form. I wish to thank Christine Taylor and Patricia Towers, respectively, who proposed and edited the original pieces. Sandra Dijkstra has been my resourceful agent and dear friend. Her assistants, Laurie Fox and Katherine Goodwin, were unfailingly helpful. I am grateful to Leonard Michaels for his shrewd advice and generous heart. Ernest W. Machen III kindly read my essay and saved me from several embarrassments.

Many of the contributors were asked to write under uncomfortable deadlines, and all of them bore with utmost patience and professionalism various alarums and excursions on the way to publication. Though grateful to all, I owe a special debt to Mike Davis both for his constant encouragement and the pleasure of his company and for introducing me to Lynell George and Rubén Martínez at *L.A. Weekly*.

To Shelley Wanger, who firmly, calmly, and kindly brought the book to completion, and to her able and surpassingly patient assistant, Hellyn Sher, I am also grateful indeed.

My wife, Jayne Walker, has been my collaborator and the trimmer of my prose, and this book is as much hers as mine. Our son, Stephen, watched the compiling of this book, as he has witnessed the writing of others, indulgently. Finally, I dedicate this book to my mother and father, whose kindness and generosity I can acknowledge but never repay.

David Reid
Berkeley, California
September 1991

FOR MAX AND ANTONIA REID

INTRODUCTION

In every age there is a capital city, an absolute theater of ambition. Paris was "the capital of the nineteenth century." After 1945 New York City became indisputably "the supreme metropolis of the present." In the strange new postmodern imperium we live in, Los Angeles, at the very least, has become the American city the world watches for signs and portents. The night flight over Southern California country replaces the skyline of Manhattan as the up-to-date epiphany of limitlesss urban power and sweep; soaring vertical vista is exchanged for measureless sprawl, Faustian stone and steel for a vast shimmering electronic labyrinth. "There is nothing to match flying over Los Angeles by night," according to the airborne French oracle, Jean Baudrillard.

Greater Los Angeles, as Alexander Cockburn writes in these pages, is "the only megalopolis of the First World growing at a rate comparable to those of the supercities—São Paulo, Cairo, and Canton—of the Third World." These cities are, respectively, 450, 1,000, and 2,000 years old. At 210, Los Angeles is young for such a vast and terrible town. By 2001, only four of the world's twenty-three biggest cities, each claiming a population upwards of 10 million, will be in the so-called developed nations: Greater New York, Tokyo-Yokohoma, Moscow, and the Consolidated Metropolitan Statistical Area of Los Angeles–Anaheim–Riverside. The population of this last city-state, whose passions and illusions are the subject of this book, is already in the neighborhood of 14.5 million. Compare these multitudes to the 1,610 souls discovered in the frowzy and isolated Pueblo de Nuestra Señora la Reina de Los Angeles de Porciúncula, the Town of Our Lady the Queen of the Angels, by the United States census in 1850, two years after the Yankee leviathan embraced Manifest Destiny and plundered Upper California from Mexico.

This formerly remote coast lies at the cusp of a half-dozen world cultures, among them Asian, Pacific, Ibero-American, Anglo-American. Historically, the place to look for mixed multitudes in California was San Francisco. During the decades of white immigration from the Midwest, from 1880 to 1930, indeed almost to the mid-1960s, it was not the diversity of Los Angeles's population that struck observers, rather its uniformity.

"Though Spanish in name, and Spanish in the name of hundreds of its streets," Oliver Carlson's *A Mirror for Californians* reassured readers in 1941, "Los Angeles is an American city—perhaps the most American of all our great cities." As Carey McWilliams wrote only a few years later in his classic *Southern California Country* (1946), Los Angeles had always been an "archipelago" of races and ethnic groups—but the substantial African-American, Mexican, and Asian (Japanese, Chinese, Filipino) islands were reduced to peonage. As recently as 1960, 85 percent of the population of Greater Los Angeles—Orange, Ventura, Riverside, San Bernardino, L.A., and Imperial counties—was still "Anglo," as non-Hispanic European-Americans are taxonomized in Southern California. Today, after a congeries of demographic happenings mostly unexpected by the futurists at RAND or anywhere else, including fallout from the lost crusade in South Asia, the figure for Anglos hovers at about 50 percent; by 2010 the *Los Angeles Times* projects it will be about 42 percent, almost the same figure as for Latinos. African-Americans and slightly more numerous

Asian-Americans will account for most of the remainder. The *Times*, having shed its reactionary ways and become, on some days of the week, the best big-city daily in the country, now invokes diversity as religiously as it used to hymn the virtues of the Open Shop and the Criminal Syndicalism Act.

A recent anatomy of the Forty-Sixth Assembly District, described as "the Ellis Island of California," was eloquent on this shift in editorial sensibility, and as interesting for that as for any of the facts and figures it adduced about the "human laboratory of racial, ethnic and cultural diversity that stretches from the Downtown skyscrapers to the teeming apartments of Mid-Wilshire; from the drug and gang turf of Pico and Vermont on the south to million-dollar hillside homes abutting Griffith Park on the north. Into the district's melting pot come daily arrivals from El Salvador, Guatemala, Mexico, the Philippines, Korea, Thailand, Vietnam, Soviet Armenia, and elsewhere." If the Forty-sixth, with its alarming death rate and other social ills, is not exactly the promised land—only its anteroom—the diligent and the lucky can aspire to Eagle Rock and West Covina.

In *Postmodern Geographies*, one of the best books about the city, Edward W. Soja evokes the multitudinous "metro-sea" of Los Angeles in terms of the "Aleph," the magical object in the story by Jorge Luis Borges that reflects the images of, literally, everything in the world. "One finds in Los Angeles not only the high technology complexes of the Silicon Valley and the erratic sunbelt economy of Houston, but also the far-reaching industrial decline and bankrupt urban neighborhoods of rust-belted Detroit or Cleveland . . . ," he writes. "There is a Boston in Los Angeles, a Lower Manhattan and a South Bronx, a São Paulo and a Singapore." There are factories "producing parts which are stamped 'Made in Brazil' and clothing marked 'Made in Hong Kong.' " Signs in Old English lettering lead into Westminster's Little Saigon. Like the Aleph, the city has become as compendious as a studio back lot in the old days when Tod Hackett, in Nathanael West's *The Day of the Locust*, could wonder at the juxtaposition of a Dutch windmill with the bones of a dinosaur.

"The film industry has never portrayed California," David Hockney said to me several years ago at his house on the top of a Hollywood hill. "For good reason, probably. Even today I don't think there's one building you could show in a backdrop and instantly know it's L.A., as you could with New York. The city itself is not that well known. Certainly not in paintings," he added modestly. Yet, in terms of a standard repertoire of icons and auratic images, what city in the world does the world think it knows better than the City of Angels?

A frieze of coppery bodies posed against white volumes, like Camus's description of Algiers; the calligraphic purity of elements in the print advertisements of *L.A. Story*: amphibious palm tree, ocean, childlike Californian (Steve Martin) doing a cartwheel; young Proteus rising from the sea in a wet suit on the predictable jacket of *A Day in the Life of California*; the what-now-seem overdressed golden-age movie stars in Jean Howard's photographs, and the godlike grease monkeys in those of Herb Ritts; the HOLLYWOOD, originally HOLLYWOODLAND, sign which, in common with so many of California's beloved monuments, was never intended to last and merely languished into permanence; Hockney's own painted palms and pools, enveloped in stillness, seeming always to have been painted in a spell of "earthquake weather." In John Updike's novel *Bech Is Back*, Jerusalem reminds Henry Bech of Southern California. "Here were the same low houses and palm fronds, the same impression of staged lighting, exclusively frontal, as if the backs of these buildings dissolved into unpainted slats and rotting canvas, into weeds and warm air—that stagnant, balmy, expectant air of Hollywood when the sun goes down." Pauline Kael, praising Sarah Jessica Parker's portrayal of a "bouncy nymph": "She's the spirit of L.A.: she keeps saying yes."

Peter Conrad, disrespecting L.A. in *Imagining America*, delivers what is intended to be a knockdown verdict: "Physique, in this bronzed paradise, has taken over from character as the source of identity." Other philosophical tourists are more taken with this society of spectacles that concentrates the pleasures and perplexities we have agreed to call "postmodern": Fredric Jameson luxuriating in the "hyperspaces" of the Westin Bonaventure Hotel, Jean-François Lyotard rhapsodizing about the campus of the University of California at San Diego and its handsome students ("infinite languor of green-blond hair"), Umberto Eco enthusiastically discovering one kitschy display after another, Baudrillard coming down for a landing on Mulholland Drive. But then, the "unreality" (lately, "hyperreality") of American life (and is not California America's America?) has been an article of faith for European intellectuals since existentialism was in flower. Christopher Isherwood put a long complaint about this credo in his novel *A Single Man* almost thirty years ago: "My God, you sound like some dreary French intellectual who's just set foot in New York for the first time! That's exactly the way they talk! *Unreal!* . . . The truth is, our way of life is too austere for them."

The countermyth to the bronzed paradise, cold current to its warm current, is *noir* L.A., as in the canonical novels by James M. Cain and Raymond Chandler and their movie adaptations: Los Angeles as a sleepless city of night, where neon glows like radium and three o'clock in the morning comes sooner than you think. Jack Kerouac, though he worked a very different vein of Americana, recognized the place when he saw it in 1947 (the year *film noir* was named by the French critic Nino Frank). "What brutal, hot, siren-whining nights there are! LA is the loneliest and most brutal of American cities. . . . The beatest characters in the country swarmed on the sidewalks—all of it under those soft Southern California stars that are lost in the brown halo of the huge desert encampment LA really is."

Roman Polanski's film of Robert Towne's script for *Chinatown* showed how satisfyingly *noir*'s mood of fatality answered to a detailed knowledge of Los Angeles's conspiratorial past. The polar division of sunshine and *noir*, as Mike Davis demonstrates in *City of Quartz*, is the fault line separating all Los Angeles mythologies, and this is no parochial issue: it is Los Angeles's complex fate to figure in the contemporary imagination of the city as both utopia and Great Wrong Place.

Long before the last drought, some uncanny spirit of place whispered that civilization on this coast is bound to be impermanent and unsustainable in the long run. The imagination of disaster has always been vivid in Southern California, and from towering infernos to marauding "supergangs," many of the direst forebodings are regularly fulfilled. Gore Vidal writes of an occasion when "Los Angeles had been on fire for three days. As I took a taxi from the studio I asked the driver, 'How's the fire doing?' 'You mean,' said the Hollywoodian, 'the holocaust.' The style, you see, must come as easily and naturally as that."

Such grim vistas contradict the received mythology of blithe bronzed youth, but then, the modern City of Angels was born old and has only gradually grown young. Even twenty-five years ago, Pauline Kael's undressed vision of Los Angeles was no bouncy nymph; it was grim survivalists around the pool at the Beverly Hills Hotel, not young but "ageless like crocodiles." It is difficult to say how much of Los Angeles's air of fatalism and baffled expectancy lingers from the decades between 1880 and 1930 when Southern California lured mostly the unyoung and infirm, and the care and housing of invalids ranked as a leading industry.

These new argonauts were nothing like the hairy-chested 'Forty-Niners, whose lost beauty and virility Mark Twain mourned in *Roughing It*. Many of the later arrivals actually dropped dead just as their train pulled into the promised land. At the turn of the century, boosters like Charles Fletcher Lummis could only regret that the Southland had so few blond beasts to show compared with San Francisco. As regards the cult of youth in Southern California, there has always been more than a hint of the whited sepulcher to all that (and on this subject see Eve Babitz's essay in this volume).

"The California sky, so like the Egyptian, smiled on my work," Thomas Mann wrote, remembering how he had settled into his house on Amalfi Drive in Pacific Palisades to wait out the war and finish the Joseph novels. Even after Los Angeles was canopied with smog (a wartime plague that descended in 1942 and never lifted), some trick of light, air, and setting continued to put travelers in mind of ancient cities and antique lands. Evelyn Waugh was reminded of Addis Ababa, the newly arrived David Hockney of Cavafy's Alexandria. "The hot climate's near enough to Alexandria, sensual: and this downtown was sleazy, a bit dusty, very masculine . . . all tacky and everything," he wrote in *My Early Years*.

Los Angeles often brings to mind the big cities of the "crowded and cosmopolitan" centuries between Alexander and Augustus. I wonder if there is another city in history Los Angeles more resembles than Alexandria in the bright pagan world, another "self-advertising megalopolis" and for most of a thousand years the global capital of science, scholarship, mass media, mystery religions, occultism, advanced sensuality, and avant-garde schools of asceticism. Alexandria concentrated all those features of the Hellenistic world which (as the classical historian Peter Green lists them) make that lost world seem so uncannily like our own—"the same obsessive pursuit of affluence, exotic religious cults, fads in astrology and magic, offbeat eroticism, gourmet food," even the same kind of military-industrial-academic complex.

"Shall I tell you what is my highest ambition?" Dr. Mulge asks in Aldous Huxley's *After Many a Summer Dies the Swan*. "It is to make of Tarzana the living Center of the New Civilization that is coming to blossom here in the West. The Athens [but he might as well have said the Alexandria or Pergamon] of the twentieth century is on the point of emerging here, in the Los Angeles Metropolitan Area. I want Tarzana to be its Parthenon and its Art, Philosophy, Science— I want them all to find their home in Tarzana, to radiate their influence from our campus, to. . . ."

Until the end of the eighteenth century, there were no cities in the West that compared in size, population, or wealth to the giant cities of Asia or the metropolises of antiquity. As Europe entered into the age of revolution, only London counted more than 1 million inhabitants. By 1900 Paris, Berlin, and Vienna had passed the million mark, and cities were growing in North America at the fastest rate in history—but how late Los Angeles joined the procession! In 1880, when Chicago was a strapping metropolis of 1 million and threatening to overtake New York—or London— Los Angeles was a hundred-year-old town of 11,000, slightly smaller (according to Oliver Carlson) than Logansport, Indiana, and Chicopee, Massachusetts.

Not simply late to bloom, Los Angeles was the last world city to arise out of the relatively brief period (roughly corresponding to what historians call the "long nineteenth century," from 1789 to 1914) when the biggest cities were to be found in the come-lately West rather than in the ancient East. (Houston, Texas, and Sydney, Australia, are not world cities.) By the same token, Los Angeles was the last metropolis to reach such magnitude when the biggest urban centers in the New World were boasted by the United States rather than (as in 1780 and again approaching 2000) by Mexico and South America. Not geography (Puget Sound, where Raymond Chandler once set a story, is farther west) but historical belatedness would be the key to its mythologies.

In the notes for his unfinished "Arcades" project, Walter Benjamin wrote that the secret of the immense modern cities—"their most hidden aspect"—is how "this historical object of the new metropolis with its uniform streets and incalculable rows of houses has realized the architecture dreamed of by the ancients: the laybrinth." However baffling (a dictionary definition of a laybrinth is "a devious arrangement of linear patterns forming a design"), a proper labyrinth becomes entirely logical when seen from the proper angle (as in a night flight over Los Angeles), or whenever its principle of connectedness is found. Thus, a mid-century visitor to the Los Angeles labyrinth, the Spanish philosopher Julián Marias, was amazed by the gigantic, geometrical sea of houses. "When one is in a residential area, for miles around there is nothing other than *homes*," he wrote with evident horror. Happily, the good European needed only to peer inside a few picture windows to see the phosphor glow that connected them. Only apparently turned in on themselves, the houses were little domestic monads linked by the "preordained harmony of television."

This touristic epiphany, which appears in Marias's book *America in the Fifties*, simply confirmed what the exiled scholars of the Frankfurt School, Theodor Adorno and Max Horkheimer, had already discerned from their wartime redoubt in Pacific Palisades: that the American "culture industry," manufacturing lowbrow dreams from coastal factories, was "a system uniform and whole in every part," like a web, a net, a certain kind of labyrinth. In *The Pacific Wall* Jean-François Lyotard, another oracle overcome by Los Angeles, reconfigures the maze: "Los Angeles is the capital *(la capitale)* of the world because it is not a metropolis by European or East Coast standards," i.e., not a solid city arranged around something, but a game of chess, whose usually vacant diagonals are forty miles long and lead nowhere.

From its beginning, Los Angeles has been arranging itself into the logical grids that Oswald Spengler said are the infallible mark of late, wintry world cities. Alexandria, the prototype of Los Angeles, was laid out in a chessboard pattern approved by Alexander the Great himself, who was buried in a glass coffin at the crossroads of the city. No doubt it is a sign of Los Angeles's postmodernity that it radiates from nothing at all. The architectural historian Reyner Banham, who rather despised Downtown, pointed out with evident satisfaction that even the site of the original plaza has been lost, "and thus leaves a mystery at the very heart of the city."

No place has masqueraded so profitably as other places than Southern California, and no city has paraded its self-regard so remorselessly as Los Angeles: what confirms L.A.'s status as cosmopolis is how brazenly it has begun to portray itself as the place where stories end, destinies are decided, ancient quarrels are resumed and concluded. And with such good reason. How many mental maps must be rearranged to accommodate the sober fact that George Bush once lived in Compton? On screen warlocks are resurrected from the seventeenth century, and cyborgs arrive from the twenty-first. Alternative universes, corresponding to the different quarters of the city, are conjured and spun off into oblivion. Sizing up the punks in *Terminator 1* and the bikers in *Terminator 2*, Arnold Schwarzenegger's computer brain automatically classifies them in terms of Sheldonian body-types, as efficiently as Aldous Huxley, who used to ride the escalator at Ohrbach's department store downtown and point out to his companions here a tubby endormorph, there a hunky mesomorph. In this bronzed paradise, physique is character *and* destiny. Oscar Wilde said that everybody reported missing is sooner or later seen in San Francisco. Like so many distinctions, this one has migrated down the coast. In a poem by Mark Strand, Gregor Samsa has been metamorphosed again. No longer an insect, merely writing to a friend, he is "an ordinary man, living in Los Angeles, trying to get by as best I can."

One autumn day at mid-century—November 4, 1951, according to his journal—the diplomat and cold warrior George Kennan sat in a garden overlooking the leafy affluence of Pasadena and wondered why the fine prospect should fill him with so much unease. Of course he knew that beneath the foliage of the eucalyptus trees and the shrubbery the land was barren. In reality, Southern California was a remote and desert place, the water naturally available in the basin sufficient to supply a good-sized town, never the Babylonish metropolis sprawling to the west. And Hollywood itself was uneasy, disturbed by fear of communism in some quarters of the industry (Ronald Reagan, the president of the Screen Actors Guild, carried a gun), of anticommunist crusaders in others; fear of television and the fickleness of the domestic audience that had begun to desert the movie palaces even before television. Ben Hecht would remember his friend David O. Selznick raving at dawn in the deserted streets of Tinseltown: "Hollywood's like Egypt. Full of crumpled pyramids. It'll never come back. It'll just keep on crumbling until finally the wind blows the last studio prop across the sands."

Taking the long view, which the atomic age encouraged, Kennan brooded on the vulnerability of Los Angeles, of all American cities the most abjectly dependent on the automobile, its lifelines stretched taut across the desert to the turbines on the Colorado. "Here the helplessness is greatest, but also the thoughtlessness . . . ," he wrote. "There is really a subtle but profound difference between people here and what Americans used to be, and still partly are, in other parts of the country." Free from want and oppression, the average

Californian became childlike, "fun-loving, quick to laughter and enthusiasm, unanalytical, unintellectual, outwardly expansive, preoccupied with physical beauty and prowess, given to sudden and unthinking seizures of aggressiveness, driven constantly to protect his status in the group by an eager conformism—yet not unhappy." When the day of reckoning comes, "values will suddenly prove to have been lost that were forged slowly and laboriously in the more rugged experience of Western political development elsewhere."

By 1950 the most important politician to come out of Southern California had manifested himself, in fact, had been elected to the United Sates Senate. Two other California politicians have become president, Ronald Reagan and the Dour Engineer, Herbert Hoover; but they were not born and raised in the golden land. They had not taken the Happy Road to Heaven with Sister Aimee at Angelus Temple or sweated in the citrus groves. Richard Nixon emerged from the half-Atlantean, half-Iowan demi-metropolis of the twenties and thirties. When he first ran for Congress in 1946, the effects of the Depression were still being felt. "It was not easy," our lost leader writes in his latest memoir, *In the Arena*. Briskly, he dismisses the calumny, circulated by "some 'historians,' " that he accused his opponent, "a liberal with a socialist background," of communism. No, "The main difficulty was that our neighbors [next to the house he rented from his barber in Whittier] raised minks for a living. Minks make beautiful coats," he concedes judiciously, "but as animals they are repulsive because they eat their young. I can still remember working on speeches late at night and hearing the screaming of the young minks next door." Night after night, he had to endure those terrible screams while he wrote speeches that did not accuse Jerry Voorhis of being a Communist.

The habit of reporting Southern California as the new

utopia persisted as late as the mid-sixties, when the American century turned giddy (and Richard Nixon moved to New York). The June 28, 1966 issue of *Look* magazine declared: "Now, it turns out, everybody's whole life can be led as a work of art, California shows us a wide and brilliant spectrum of possibilities. . . . It is quite safe to say that the *average* student of the year 2000 would be considered, in today's terms, a genius."

The lost war in Asia had the incidental effects of breaking the old liberal consensus that made California, on a good day, look like a laboratory for the nation, flooding its schools with Vietnamese, Cambodian, Hmong, and other South Asian children, many of whom actually perform at "genius" levels, if they can negotiate the overcrowded, understaffed classrooms of an increasingly penurious Sunbelt state. (Opulent California spends less per student than any other industrial state, and the city of Los Angeles, which is richer than most states, spends less than that.)

If Los Angeles is no longer plausible as utopia, then perhaps it can be rehabilitated as cautionary lesson. For example, is Los Angeles, in the spring of 1991, accused of having a brutish, racist police force? "Critics of L.A.," says *Newsweek*, quoting Kevin Starr, "should know that Los Angeles is a massive experiment in what the American republic will be in in the 21st century."

In fact, no one knows what or if the American republic will be in 2076, but if the past is any guide at all, it will not be much like Southern California. The immense number of fashions and follies that it incubates, ranging in the recent decades from psychedelia to the Reagan Revolution to Michael Milken's junk bonds, does not make it any more a model for the alien continent east of the Sierras. In 1945, as the country was about to become abruptly younger, Angelenos were older than the national average. Today, as America's population ages and its families diminish in size, Los

Angeles's households are larger, its birthrate higher, and its average citizen younger than the norms for the rest of the country, and these differences are increasing. Predominantly Caucasian even thirty years ago, it is now the most racially diverse metropolis in the country, if not the world. Just as the world's fascination with California was most intense forty years ago, the "Californization" of American life, as the historian John Lukacs call it, was mostly a phenomenon of the Nixon years. Even Ronald Reagan gave the White House less of a Los Angeles coloration than Richard Nixon, whose inner circle sometimes looked to be a cabal requiring a degree from USC for admission.

That enduring myth of Southern California as Tomorrowland shows how tenacious journalistic habit can be; it is a classic locus of what Arthur Dubin in a remarkable new book calls "futurehype," or the "tyranny of prophecy." Rather than a prophecy, a laboratory, or (least of all!) a microcosm, Los Angeles is the Burgess Shale of American life, crowded with the fossilized remains of tomorrows that never arrived, but swarming with wonderful life. Edmund Wilson had it right fifty years ago when he wrote, "But California, since we took it away from the Mexicans, has always presented itself to Americans as one of the strangest and most exotic of our adventures." Only now it is no longer, if it ever was, merely one of "our" American exploits.

In this book, Alexander Cockburn, the Post-Modern-day Juvenal, looks at the new Downtown, and the historian Mike Davis ventures into the postindustrial "empty quarter."

Carolyn See, whose novel, *Golden Days*, boldly went one day beyond apocalypse, explores an interracial world. Another remarkable Los Angeles novelist, Eve Babitz, writes about the erotics of asceticism. Two extraordinary young writers for *L.A. Weekly*, one of the nation's liveliest weeklies, contribute essays combining reportage with personal witness, Lynell George writing about death at an early age,

Rubén Martínez about holy politics. My own essay describes how every faith from "Theosophistry to Christian Sirens" came to flourish in Southern California.

David Thomson, whose novels *Suspects* and *Silver Light* make up one of the great secret histories, muses on the topography of a celebrated street. Jeremy Larner, an Academy Award winner for his original screenplay, *The Candidate*, numbers the rules of the game in movieland.

Thomas S. Hines, the biographer of Richard Neutra, analyzes modernism (and Post-Modernism, since it has come to that) in Los Angeles architecture from Irving Gill to Frank O. Gehry.

Here is how they threaded the labyrinth that lies at the end of the American road.

POWER

ON THE RIM OF
THE PACIFIC
CENTURY

C hange yourself into a condor, as did shamans of the
Chumash, who lived in these parts for ten millennia, and you can soar toward the sun, winning the
whole view from Point Conception to San Clemente Island.
Look south across the town-house gridlock of Orange
County to the tank trails of Camp Pendleton, east to the residential land rush of Riverside and San Bernardino counties'
"Inland empire," north toward the "supervalley" that now
sprawls from Burbank to Ventura, and west to the Pacific's
rim, where our destiny reputedly lies: in sum, the nation-state of Greater Los Angeles, with 14 million individuals, 132
incorporated cities, and an economy bigger than India's.

But what's a bird's-eye view worth when all you can see is haze? Drop back to Earth instead and assume the form of late-twentieth-century man standing on the roof of a concrete parking tower on the corner of Alameda and the Hollywood Freeway downtown, within eyeshot of the sometimes drab but transfiguring moments of Los Angeles's history: La Placita, where a handful of black and Indian *pobladores* planted the seeds of the megalopolis just over two centuries ago; the hillside of Chavez Ravine, where Edward Doheny tapped his first gusher and started an entire cycle of greed and corruption; the decayed glory of the old Beaux-Arts business district, where real-estate speculators kept their offices; and, in a growing crescent, from north-by-northwest to the south, the confusion of caissons, girders, spires, battlements, and corporate logos that herald the twenty-first century. The shape of things to come rises before our eyes.

From our parking-garage perch, my friend Mike Davis and I were trying to decipher the patterns of growth and decay, change and persistence. Mike, author of a fine book about L.A.—*City of Quartz*—was born sixty miles east of here in a gritty blue-collar town, Fontana, about the same time— 1946—that the first cell of the Hell's Angels was organized there; his love-hate relationship with Los Angeles comes from years spent as a student at UCLA, a truck driver and political organizer.

Mike pointed north, showing me the old Gray Line Bus terminal at Third and Beaudry (now one of the most valuable sites in the development wars west of the Harbor Freeway). Twenty years ago, for the traditional *tour d'horizon*, visitors would have boarded their tour bus and headed straight up the Hollywood Freeway to Grauman's Chinese, Universal Studios, and Forest Lawn. Downtown was little more than skid row and a few residual old-time hotels. Its faded glory was best monumentalized by the virtually empty Union Station, the last great palace of the Age of Rail (built in 1939, the same year that the Pasadena Freeway was opened). If Downtown preserved any virtue it was the ambience of leisurely decay and the provision of time capsules, like Blair's tearoom (now gone) or Philippe's (currently the last citadel of ten-cent coffee in America), where one could linger in *temps perdu*.

Over the last generation, however, Los Angeles has come back to Downtown, as tax-driven redevelopment and a flood of offshore investment have positioned its new high-rise citadel to become, with Tokyo, twin capital of the long-awaited Pacific Century. Los Angeles, in fact, is the only megalopolis of the First World growing at a rate comparable to those of the supercities—São Paulo, Cairo, and Canton—of the Third World.

But the city that invented urban sprawl has a new economic geometry: "outer cities," or suburban downtowns, in Encino, Glendale, Pasadena, Century City, Santa Monica, Long Beach, and at LAX, held in subordinate orbit to the recentered supremacy of the financial megastructures that march down Figueroa from Bunker Hill to South Park and leap illicitly over the moat of the Harbor Freeway to Central City West. Dominating the scene is the puissant cylinder of Maguire Thomas Partners Library Tower, the tallest building west of the Rockies, surrounded by thirty new skyscrapers built since 1969, the majority foreign-owned. Up to 90 percent of recent Downtown building has been financed from abroad.

This is the pride and glory. But within a five-mile radius of this overweening skyscape is a second city of nearly a million poor immigrants from Mexico, Central America, and the Pacific Basin, whose sweated labor reproduces the economies of Manila, Guatemala City, and Singapore. In the last quarter-century commercial redevelopment has erased whole neighborhoods, such as Bunker Hill and Chavez Ravine (now Dodger Stadium), but this may have been a mere prelude to the scale of residential displacement that will result from offshore capital's prospective invasion of the crowded tenement districts that ring Downtown from Boyle Heights to Chinatown, Temple-Beaudry to Westlake, Pico-Union to Central-Avalon.

At the same time, Downtown is a Monopoly board of political intrigues and development rivalries. Mike again pointed to the amiable Spanish Colonial and Moderne bulk of Union Station, where construction crews are working twenty-four hours a day to excavate an underground home terminal for Los Angeles's pharaonically expensive subway system (which will be under construction for the remainder of this century). In the next few years the idyllically lethargic station will spring back to life as the resurrected center of rail and bus mass transit. With traffic mitigation built into the site, Union Station instantly becomes the potential generator of windfall profits for all new developments in its immediate radius.

Thus the chronically ambitious councilman Richard Alatorre, who plans to become the city's first Mexican mayor since the nineteenth century, is hoping to make a megadevelopment centered on Union Station and encompassing Olvera Street and the old Terminal Annex Post Office, the cash cow that will pay his way into City Hall. Meanwhile, Olympia and York, the giant Toronto-based developer, is locked in a protracted battle to take over the property interests of Southern Pacific–Santa Fe. If the alloyed efforts of Alatorre and Olympia and York are eventually successful, that will have shifted the center of gravity for Downtown redevelopment.

A similar liturgy celebrating the eternal coupling of political hubris and the developer's cashbox is being sung a few blocks to our southwest in Little Tokyo. The neighborhood dates back to the turn of the century, when Japanese farmworkers and nurserymen created a tiny downtown niche where they could eat and gamble for bed and board. After Pearl Harbor the Nisei were forcibly relocated, and Little Tokyo temporarily became "Bronzeville," an overcrowded dormitory and juke district for black war workers. After an arduous struggle to reclaim their neighborhood in the postwar years, the retired farmworkers and petty merchants ultimately lost control of it—somewhat ironically—to the big Tokyo developers and banks seeking to expand southward into skid row.

Over the past decade Little Tokyo forces and City Hall have essayed various blueprints to eliminate the troublesome denizens of the "Nickel" (so called because Fifth Street is skid row's main axis). The homeless have been scheduled for deportation to Newhall or to the top of the Santa Monica Mountains, and it has even been proposed—an innovative notion of Councilman Gilbert Lindsay, self-proclaimed "Emperor of Downtown"—that they be put on ferries in the harbor, in the manner of New York's plan to locate its homeless on islets on the East River.

Temporarily foiled in their march south by bleeding-heart liberals and skeptical city council members (who worry that the homeless may be dumped in their districts), Little Tokyo's developers, like Sumitomo Bank, have turned eastward, where the 1987 earthquake providentially cleared a corridor for development. Scarcely had the ground stopped heaving before the developers had sent in teams of surveyors and engineers, all intent to prove that Nature herself approved the demolition of the old brick industrial buildings standing between San Pedro Street and the Los Angeles River. Indeed, as Mike and I scanned a 190-degree arc south and east of Little Tokyo, in the quadrant of its prospective expansions, there were only three buildings over eight stories in height. For a developer it must be as it was for Moses, gazing down from Mount Nebo across the Promised Land, counting the shekels and the yen.

Even northward, thirty years ago the skyline would have risen little higher than Tacoma's or Omaha's. Until 1959 the only structures over 150 feet tall were City Hall and the Braly Building, on the corner of Fourth and Spring. Both, along with Union Station and the Olympic Coliseum, were designed by the tireless architect John Parkinson, Los Angeles's forgotten Christopher Wren. He built the Beaux-Arts Braly Tower in 1904, and at thirteen stories, it was the city's first genuine skyscraper. Anxious to perpetuate this achievement, Parkinson took advantage of his membership in and influence on the Municipal Art Commission (the city's embryonic planning agency) to set a building-height limitation at 150 feet, leaving Braly preeminent forever, or at least until 1928, when he collaborated in the design of the twenty-seven-story City Hall.

What would that early Municipal Art Commission, which conceived a vast, only partially completed City Beautiful design for Los Angeles (including the Civic Center and Union Station), have thought of the contemporary art jury that recently endorsed the design for a huge, floating metal cloud to be suspended over the Hollywood Freeway in the Civic Center slot? This wacky structure was meant to be Los Angeles's latter-day equivalent of the Statue of Liberty, responding to Shuwa Investment Corporation's offer to help Mayor Bradley finance a monument to Pacific amity. Shuwa, which received deluxe treatment from City Hall in a Downtown high-rise buying spree, had good reason to celebrate; but other forces, like the citizens of East Los Angeles, took a different view of historical commemoration. Some of them suggested, as an alternative to the $115 million metal cloud, a statue on the north bank of the freeway of Tiburcio Vásquez, the *Californio* outlaw and folk hero, hanged by the gringos in the 1870s.

Anglo justice in late-imperial Los Angeles is represented by an extraordinary contemporary structure. Mike and I descended to ground level and crossed Alameda for a closer look at the Metropolitan Detention Center, a high-rise jail for federal prisoners which was designed by Ellerbe Becket of Pasadena and passed into the hands of the Bureau of Prisons in November 1988. Life being mostly a matter of resting up after coming from somewhere while waiting to go someplace else, the airport terminals, hotels, and jails of the twenty-first century will all blend into one form, very well evinced in this particular ten-story jailhouse. An inmate sweeping the flagstones of the nicely landscaped patio said the place wasn't so bad. Inside, in the main lobby, there were furnishings of such lobbies everywhere: planes of flat pastels and glass; well-tended interior shrubbery; a reception desk with two chic young black women in miniskirts, fingertips resting on computer keyboards, asking for your name and for what this is in reference to; a tactful security gate on the alert for unwelcome metal objects. You wouldn't be ashamed to have your mother come looking for you here, not the way you would at the old county jail a mile to the east, one of the largest and most overcrowded facilities in the county, where the L.A. gangs have their own special isolation wings.

In fact, the new federal detention center is the sixth jail within three miles of City Hall. Downtown and East L.A. house the largest incarcerated population in the United States—some 25,000 inmates. Mike and I had a decorous conversation with Lynden Croasmun, executive assistant to the prison's warden, Margaret Hambrick. Croasmun was vexed that no one had told her about a UCLA Planning Department exhibit in honor of the bicentennial of the French Revolution, in which there is a model of the Bastille blending into the Bonaventure Hotel and also some very beautiful night shots of the detention center.

We walked east, past the gaping foundation holes scheduled to accommodate a new federal building and a VA hospital, toward the Parker Center, headquarters of the LAPD. We were talking about the militarization of life and, indeed, space in Los Angeles, the ARMED RESPONSE signs planted in West Side lawns, the architectural policing of social boundaries which forms the master narrative of newly built Los Angeles. One such social boundary was a few blocks north of us: the apartments rising under the brow of Bunker Hill below the Museum of Contemporary Art. There was no way that the dangerous classes could get from down here, where we were, to up there, where the proud possessors of these new dwellings were conducting their affairs.

In the interval of a couple of blocks we could see the class war fought out at the level of the built environment. Amid the corporate towers of the prime redevelopment zones there were pleasant little spaces, gardens, bowers amid the reflecting glass, along with avant-garde street furniture inviting you to linger and repose. Move toward skid row, and the destitute urban nomad pushing his purloined shopping cart finds himself the object of low-intensity civic warfare: rounded bus seats he can't lie down on, sprinkler systems drenching areas where he might sleep, spikes and bars guarding trash he might try to sort through.

There's a division of labor in the vast structure of security, invigilation, and swift and deadly response up to and including helicopter gunships in the LAPD's air force. Private security guards hold down the labor-intensive roles of electronic surveillance, guard duty, and so forth, while the police govern the capital-intensive macro-systems of surveillance, from data systems to the paramilitary tac squads. We were in fact walking right over the digitalized brain of the great beast; on our left was Parker Center, the police headquarters named for Ed Parker, the psychotic 1950s architect of the modern LAPD, and on our right was City Hall East. At the fourth and fifth sublevels beneath our feet, earthquake-proof, was the hardware of the Emergency Command

and Control Communications System, the most elaborate police command system in the world, conceptualized by Hughes Aerospace at the end of the 1960s, refined by the Jet Propulsion Lab, developed by System Development Corporation of Santa Monica, paid for by a $42 million tax override in 1977, and finally put into operation in time for the 1984 Olympics. Down in the bunker they talk to the cars and to the helicopters that fly over the city nineteen hours a day.

A block later we came upon St. Vibiana's Cathedral, where Pope John Paul II stayed. Next door, besieged by the routinely desperate, was the Union Rescue Mission, which the Catholic archdiocese was trying to get moved. Archbishop Mahony's reputation as a social liberal is somewhat in eclipse after his attempt to break the gravediggers' union in his archdiocese, which earned him the enmity of organized labor. The trusty ally these days of this man of God is Richard Riordan, legal eagle, developer, corporate lawyer, maestro of the leveraged buyout. Riordan and several other rich friends recently bought Mahony a jet-powered helicopter so that never again will the archbishop be caught in terrestrial gridlock.

Rising up behind St. Vibiana's is the mass of the Ronald Reagan State Office Building, first in a horrible series of such-named structures intended to be the primary anchor for the gentrification of the Spring Street–Broadway corridor. The office building houses some eight thousand people, mustered to spend their disposable income in the boutiques and malls intended to replace the tackier and more colorful bazaars which make Broadway the busiest such retail thoroughfare north of Mexico City.

Unlike many cities, Los Angeles has preserved most of its 1900–1925 Beaux-Arts commercial core, a fossil Downtown revived in recent years as the retail and cultural center of the Spanish-speaking inner city. Meanwhile, the banks and enterprises that had lodged there until the 1950s, forming the financial heart of Southern California, pulled up stakes and marched west five blocks to the Figueroa-Flower corridor, now flanked on either side by the World Trade Center, the Bonaventure (now partly owned by the Japanese), ARCO, the Bank of Montreal, and so forth. They leaped clear of the old core, reckoning that scorched earth would be the consequence of their departure. Instead, these are the liveliest blocks in the whole of Downtown.

We stood on the corner of Third and Broadway. On the southeast corner is the Bradbury Building, the famous old utopian socialist structure whose architect followed the instructions of his dead brother via Ouija board. The building was intended to prefigure Edward Bellamy's imagining of socialist America in the year 2000. Across the street is the Million Dollar Theater, raised in 1918. In the 1940s it was the great venue for rhythm-and-blues and for big bands, and today it is host to thriving Spanish-language vaudeville, floor shows, movies, and bingo. Next to it is the spectacular Grand Central Market. All three of these famous structures are now owned by the real-estate speculator Ira Yellin, who proposes to make them the cornerstones of the gentrification provoked by the eight thousand consumers soon to be pent in the Reagan office building. Yellin, together with Bruce Corwin, who owns or controls all the theaters along Broadway and a handful of others, has sponsored "Miracle on Broadway," a publicly subsidized scheme for "reviving the Broadway–Spring Street corridor." It's hardly necessary to point out that Broadway is already revived as a great Latino-American shopping zone, with a retail turnover higher than that of Rodeo Drive.

Will the flavors of Broadway be subdued by the decorum of genteel consumption by those buyers from the Reagan complex and the Maguire "library tower," where 10,000 units of human purchasing power will soon reside? The developers' original plan had been to tear down the old library, ravaged by fire. Public outcry reminded the developers that it was the most distinguished building in the city. Maguire magnanimously agreed to help renovate the old library, simultaneously acquiring the air rights above it, thus enabling him to send his own "library tower" rushing toward the heavens. It may be that gentrification will, to an extent, be held at bay.

We wandered back to the parking garage opposite the federal jail and toured the cityscapes bordering on this puissant heart. First we headed straight east toward the Los Angeles River. Once, before it was turned into a concrete sewer by the Army Corps of Engineers in the 1950s, the river used to be a fine amenity for the working class of downtown and East L.A. The river's bridges, from Hyperion to Olympic, include some of the most magnificent reinforced-concrete structures in the world, in a harmonic progression of styles from Gothic Revival to Moderne. Off Santa Fe at the junction of Sixth, you can turn down a ramp and onto the concrete bank of the river itself, comforted by a swirl of graffiti on the caissons and seized with the urban-pastoral melancholy of a distant fisherman casting his lure into the rills and eddies of sewage flowing down toward the harbor.

The question is whether the city will settle for a cosmetic façade to divert motorists or will actually wrench open the window of opportunity to restore the river as something people might care to visit and amuse themselves beside.

We headed for South Central, south down Santa Fe Avenue through the strange city of Vernon, as eloquent a tribute to business's sense of urban responsibility as you could hope to find. Vernon is a separately incorporated industrial enclave, the first of its kind in Southern California. By day some 45,000 men and women toil in the garment and furniture sweatshops of Vernon, and then they all go home to someplace else. By night the population of Vernon falls to 90. Meanwhile, the city fathers, democratically elected by their citizenry, supervise their city manager, at $165,804 a year the highest-paid city official in the state. He administers the five-square-mile empire, ensuring that sales and property taxes stay low, to the detriment of the tax base of Los Angeles County but to the great joy of Vernon's commercial residents, who enjoy all the appurtenances of civic pride but none of the actual costs.

Now we were running between Vernon and Huntington Park along Slauson, once the backbone of industrial Los Angeles. People tend to forget that Los Angeles has an industrial working class of over a million blue-collar workers. They toil and often live in the string of communities south of downtown and along the Los Angeles River. The good, high-wage jobs are gone. In the late 1970s the auto, steel, and rubber plants closed up, and 50,000 high-wage jobs dropped through the hole. The city tilted back toward the nineteenth century, for now in areas like Vernon there are 125,000 working in the garment industry, of whom 90 percent are women, 80 percent undocumented, and all on the minimum wage. This is the nineteenth century in brisk revival, just a few miles east of Redondo Beach and the LAX corridor, where resides the largest colony of scientists and engineers in the world.

Short of Watts we swung north again, along a historic stretch of Central Avenue, the former main street of black Los Angeles in the heyday of black immigration, during the 1940s and early 1950s. With scores of night spots, record stores, and prosperous churches, Central once rivaled Lenox Avenue in Harlem as the capital of black culture. Musically, it nurtured a distinctive West Coast jazz idiom and was the first major center of postwar rhythm-and-blues recording. It was also a bastion of black power in a hostile environment: here was the famed Dunbar Hotel, where Joe Louis and Ella Fitzgerald stayed in the years when the city was as rigidly segregated by restrictive covenants as any Jim Crow town in the South.

Today there is little obvious reminder of those vibrant times. Central Avenue bears too many of the brutal symptoms of South Central Los Angeles's political neglect and economic collapse. A turning point was in the mid-1950s, when LAPD chief Parker launched a war on race-mixing in the clubs. His men, prototypes of the fascist custodians of "Dragnet," harassed club owners, checking and rousting any white females. By the 1960s, moreover, the black community itself was moving westward, and the 1965 Watts rebellion left Central scorched for almost one hundred blocks.

All is not gone. Mike and I stopped to pay homage outside Babe and Ricky's, the last of Central's traditional blues clubs. On a recent Sunday night, old-timers in their churchgoing finery recalled the street's glory days and bemoaned the current generation's lack of interest in blues culture, as a tough-sounding band, led by Bobby Williams (saxophone) and Ray Brooks (lead guitar), backed the vocals by the great Delmar Evans.

We pushed farther north on Central, through burgeoning Central American neighborhoods, past the streamlined ocean liner of the Coca-Cola bottling plant, and then northwest on Third Street to the next explosion of supernova. The Temple-Beaudry neighborhood, tucked in the corner of the Harbor and Hollywood freeways, is the scene of a three-sided land war pitting outlaw speculators against local residents and the Central City Association.

First officially designated as a "blighted area" in the late 1940s, Temple-Beaudry has always been conceived as a potential service area and residential adjunct to skyscraper redevelopment across the freeway on Bunker Hill. Several generations of speculators, however, have calculated that they could harvest windfalls by hijacking development westward, undercutting the land prices and floor leases in the official growth corridor controlled by the Central City Association and the Community Redevelopment Agency. For years speculators have been consolidating parcels in

Temple-Beaudry, evicting residents and clearing sites. The dominant Downtown interests have always succeeded in preventing such speculators from getting planning clearance and building permits. Hence a brutal stalemate whose victims are the thousands of renters—principally immigrant garment workers—expelled from the district without compensation.

As whole hillsides have been razed, moreover, the neighborhood has acquired an almost apocalyptic visage—undoubtedly the reason why it has become a favorite location shot for Hollywood sci-fi films such as *Running Man, The Terminator*, and *They Live!* On top of Crown Hill we looked at the grassy site that was once occupied by the SDS office in which Mike worked in the mid-sixties, then drove down to the colorful frenzy of the entry to the Belmont tunnel.

Suddenly, in recent days, as some of the biggest developers in the Figueroa corridor have themselves begun to cross over to the West Bank, the stalemate is yielding to a fast-track attempt to develop a large swath known as the Central City West Specific Plan. Some of the proposed West Bank skyscrapers would tower immediately above the Belmont tunnel at First and Glendale. Here is the eerie graveyard of Los Angeles's first attempt, originally envisioned by E. H. Harriman, to build a subway in the 1920s; after titanic battles with the auto lobby, only a single mile of underground was actually constructed, from the intersection of First and Glendale to the Subway Terminal Building (still standing) at Fourth and Hill. The retaining wall which surrounds the wedge-shaped half-acre at the mouth of the tunnel has recently become the best museum of street art in the city: here affluent cyberpunkish kids from Palms can match "bombs" and compare techniques with the best of the street-gang graffiti painters from Temple-Beaudry and East Los Angeles. For those desiring a more occult experience, the derelict subway tunnel itself can easily be entered through a tear in the fence.

It is difficult to visualize that millions of people once used this tunnel to get to work. It has metamorphosed into something weirdly natural, like a lava tube. The floor is covered with delicate colonies of salt crystals, and there are pygmy stalagmites in the recesses of the old cable channels and manholes. There is also a sweet, sickening odor which grows stronger the deeper you proceed into the tunnel. Two-thirds of a mile from the mouth and fifty feet under the Harbor Freeway, the tunnel abruptly floods with water and ends in silent enigma.

Back aboveground, revived by the staccato bursts of Day-Glo colors on every wall and rock, Mike and I drove down Temple, past the northward-flowing lava of residential and commercial development from Chinatown. To our northwest, urban clearance was continuing that very evening, as arsonists did developers the favor of torching the great Moderne Pan Pacific Auditorium. Soon it lay in ashes. It was the end of the day, and we were retracing our steps to find "Dogtown." At the turn of the century this was the tough neighborhood of poor Italians near the Fremont Gate of Elysian Park, whose kids fought in the Los Angeles River bed with their Irish rivals from the original East Los Angeles (now Lincoln Heights). Since World War II, Dogtown has been the nickname for the William Mead Homes, the public housing project marooned between the industrial sites, the river, and the county jail, along North Main Street. Mike had suggested that we end our expedition in Dogtown for two reasons: first because it was as close as we would get to the site of Yang-na, the original native village and proto-city on the banks of the Rio Los Angeles, and second because the actual human community of the William Mead Homes is an eloquent summary of the qualities that may save Los Angeles in spite of itself. It is hardworking and integrated, owns great old cars, takes no shit from the police, and is proud of living in a well-defined human place which is not a testament to the dreams of the real-estate industry. Dogtown also has great murals along its eastern wall, displaying a dignity and repose that counterpoint the anguished paroxysms of the work of the gang "writers" on the walls outside the Belmont tunnel. DOGTOWN LIVES, says the defiant square logo on a twenty-foot mural of the Virgin and Savior, facing west toward the cruel frenzies of Downtown.

Postscript, July 30, 1991

Mike Davis and I took our tour of Downtown on May 24, 1989, when the real-estate boom was still cresting. Now the crash has come, even though, like hair growing on a corpse, there are office buildings in Downtown still going up. It is now calculated that in the commercial sector there has been overbuilding by anywhere from a quarter to a third and that office space will be in oversupply for at least a generation. Already in Downtown the vacancy rate is edging towards 20 percent. The Japanese who at one point owned close to 40 percent of all office buildings in Downtown and who were involved in most new development are in retreat.

Now imploding is the core equation of that Pacific Rim boom: Japanese capital, secured by the bubble of the Tokyo land boom, inflating the bubble of California commercial real estate. Los Angeles now faces a long twilight as aerospace declines, jobs migrate out of the region, and the "comparative advantages" of Southern California disappear. Speculative capital departs and harder times seize the small business folk in their minimalls—four thousand across Southern California. By the high summer of 1991 powerbrokers like Richard Riordan were canvassing long-term strategies to give some sense of hope to the city's entombed poor, while the banks and insurance companies, freighted with bad real-estate loans, gazed into the abyss of the S&Ls and prepared to follow.

Mike Davis

CHINATOWN, REVISITED?

The "Internationalization" of Downtown Los Angeles

JAKE GITTES: How much are you worth?

NOAH CROSS: I have no idea. How much do you want?

GITTES: I want to know what you're worth—over ten million?

CROSS: Oh, my, yes.

GITTES: Then why are you doing it? How much better can you eat? What can you buy that you can't already afford?

CROSS: The future, Mr. Gittes, the future . . .

Robert Towne, Chinatown script

The shortest route between Heaven and Hell in contemporary America is probably Fifth Street in Downtown L.A. West of the refurbished Biltmore Hotel, and spilling across the moat of the Harbor Freeway, a post-1970 glass and steel skyscape advertises the land rush of Pacific Rim capital to the central city. Here, Japanese megadevelopers, transnational bankers, and billionaire corporate raiders plot the restructuring of the California economy.[1] A few blocks east, across the no-man's-land of Pershing Square, Fifth Street metamorphoses into the "Nickel": the notorious half-mile strip of blood-and-vomit-spewn concrete where several thousand homeless people—

themselves trapped in the inner circle of Dante's inferno—
have become pawns in a vast local power struggle. Intersect-
ing these extremes of greed and immiseration is the axis of
a third reality: *el gran Broadway*, the reverberant commercial center of a burgeoning Spanish-speaking city-within-a-
city, whose barrios (interpenetrating the ghetto to the south)
now form a dense ring around the central business district.
A ten-minute walk down Fifth Street thus passes through
abrupt existential and class divides, a micro-tour of social
polarization in the Bush era. Moreover this landscape—
whether we recognize the location or not—has insinuated
itself into the contemporary imagination. Because the
Downtown skycity is so recent, and because of its proximity
to the media factories of Hollywood, it figures prominently
as a representation of the early twenty-first-century urbanism
that is now emerging. It has become de rigueur for passing
theorists and image-mongers, whether as critics or celebrants,
to stop and comment on the architectural order and
social topography that are coalescing out of the lava of
development around Fifth Street.

For Fredric Jameson, in a seminal essay, the built environment of Los Angeles, especially its "downtown renaissance,"
is a paradigm of the "postmodern" city where architecture
and electronic image have fused into a single hyperspace.[2]
For the well-known urban designer James Sanders, director
of the Bryant Park Project in Manhattan, the "intense—
even poetic—verticality" of Fifth and Grand is an expression
of Los Angeles imperialism: "The 'new' downtown Los Angeles is pulling away international banking and finance, es-
tablishing a center of great radiating lines of communication
and trade for the Pacific Rim. As on the East Coast, where
New York is grabbing the remaining marbles of the Atlantic
economy community, so Los Angeles is setting itself up as
the Pacific's economic capital. The two cities seem intent on
carving the world into two great economic entities, with
themselves as the centers."[3]

Hollywood, meanwhile, has reached for different hyperboles. Younger directors have relentlessly exploited the social extremes of Downtown as a nightmare stage, a ground zero, for such contemporary apocalypses as *Repo Man, The Terminator, To Live and Die in L.A.*, and so on. This dystopian figuration acquires a dark grandeur in Ridley Scott's *Blade Runner* with its images of mile-high towers, ruled by interplanetary genetic-engineering conglomerates, rising above the poisonous congealed smog that drips acid rain upon 30 million inhabitants. None of the theories or visions on offer (with the partial exception of the racist "yellow hordes" of *Blade Runner*), however, registers the presence, probably epochal, of an enlarged low-wage working class, living and working in the central city, and creating its own spatialized social world: networks of recreation, piety, reproduction, and, ultimately, struggle. They fail to capture the growing tension—relayed through various mediations to the traditional L.A. working and middle classes—between international capital and international labor migration in the contested terrain of the inner city. For if L.A.'s Downtown is in any sense paradigmatic, it is because it condenses the intended and unintended spatial consequences of the political economy of post-Fordism: that is to say, the rise of new, globalized circuits of finance and luxury consumption amid the decline of much of the old mass-consumption and high-wage industrial economy. But there is no single, master logic of restructuring, rather the complex intersection of two separate macro-processes: one based on the overaccumulation of bank and real-estate capital (most recently, from the recycling of the East Asian trade surplus to California); the other arising from the reflux of low-wage manufacturing and labor-intensive services in the wake of unprecedented mass immigration from Mexico and Central America.

Within the larger systems of metropolitan Los Angeles and Southern California (separately, the ninth largest economy in the world), Downtown has become the privileged crucible

where apparently infinite foreign capital and low-wage immigrant labor are first transformed into assets for the regional boom. But because Downtown is simultaneously a
portal for capital and for immigration, and because the two
functions remain concentrated in the same inner core of
land development and infrastructure, there are growing con-
tradictions. The yen-fueled momentum of high-rise development cuts into the crowded work and residential spaces of
the inner-city working poor: commercial overbuilding pro-
duces rampant underhousing. At the same time the uncoor-
dinated dynamics of redevelopment and immigration,
without investment in radically expanded welfare and physical infrastructures, are making powerful, if differential, im-
pacts upon the living standards and residential positions of
older working-class and middle-strata neighborhoods from
Boyle Heights to Venice and the San Fernando Valley. The
political consequence is a far-reaching electoral realignment, excluding the working poor, as the old pro-develop-
ment coalition under the figurehead of Mayor Bradley is
attacked by a populist homeowners' rebellion orchestrated
by his former Democratic allies on the white West Side. This
is a complicated scenario, with sweeping assertions. In the
meantime, let me sketch, in bold outlines, the major action.

What Jake Discovers About Downtown

The crisis of Downtown L.A. began in the same period in
which Polanski's brilliant historical *film noir* is set, immediately after the great high-rise building boom of 1923–24 that
constructed the skyline as it remained until the 1960s. Commercial life in the center began to wither as precocious au-
tomobilization (on a scale not achieved in Europe until the
1970s) gridlocked the Downtown traffic flow while the oil-

rubber-paving lobby sabotaged the recapitalization of the city's once superb electric rail systems. A middle-class exodus to the West Side was followed by relocation of the large department stores and retail trade outward along Wilshire Boulevard. Depression and war filled Downtown tenements with an increasingly impoverished and shifting population; once aristocratic Bunker Hill near the civic center became Raymond Chandler's notorious "lost town, shabby town, crook town" with "women with faces like stale beer . . . men with pulled-down hats."[4]

The New Deal hopes of local progressives and trade unionists that Downtown might be revivified with model public housing were vanquished in 1953 after a vicious, red-baiting mayoral campaign led by the *Los Angeles Times* and the traditional Downtown ruling circle. With a pliant city hall under Mayor Poulson, the *Times* and the Downtown Businessmen's Association, ventriloquizing their interests through the publicly unaccountable Community Redevelopment Agency (CRA), were able to ratify a master plan (first conceived in 1931) to evict the nine thousand residents of Bunker Hill to make way for the first phase of ambitious commercial renewal.[5] Redevelopment, however, was easier to fantasize about in the smoking rooms of the elite Jonathan Club than to implement in practice; it took almost a decade to clear Bunker Hill. Apart from the rearguard resistance of expropriated Downtown slumlords and the sporadic hostility of Valley taxpayers to costly improvements in the inner city (deftly exploited by the *poujadiste* demagoguery of Poulson's successor, Sam Yorty), the major obstacle to a vigorous recentralization of commercial development was the fragmentation of ruling-class interests in the L.A. Basin. Gone were the days when the Merchants and Manufacturers Association could mobilize the paramilitary unity of local business behind the Open Shop (invented in L.A. in the 1890s).

The first break in elite ranks had occurred in 1926 when

the Hollywood movie moguls seceded from the Open Shop to establish their own sweetheart-union labor-relations system (the famous Studio Basic Agreement). Repelled by the country-club anti-Semitism of L.A.'s WASP old money, and dealing with a different calculus of labor costs, the predominantly Jewish management of the entertainment industry evolved into a world apart. They endowed the state university system's UCLA, not the private University of Southern California (USC); generally contributed to the national Democrats not Republicans; and focused their speculative energies on the development of Beverly Hills and the greater West Side. Meanwhile, the crucial aerospace industry— closely integrated, like Hollywood, with Wall Street—was even less historically entangled with the old inner city; its regional interests were defined by the great airport-and-manufacturing complexes outside the city limits. Finally, at the turn of the sixties, the Downtown renewal strategy was frontally challenged by Alcoa's (i.e., the Mellon family's) announcement that it was building a huge high-rise center for the West Side on Twentieth Century-Fox's old back lot in what is now Century City.

Ironically the CRA's Downtown plan was saved by the explosion of the local black working class. The Watts rebellion was, among other things, a protest against the racist "Cotton Curtain" that excluded blacks from the higher-wage jobs in the industrial belt east of Alameda Street, as well as against rampant police brutality, rack-renting and petty usury. The crisis of 1965, which continued to resonate through waves of inner-city unrest and white backlash for almost a decade, was instrumentalized by redevelopment interests in two decisive ways. First and immediately, by raising the specter of Downtown and USC engulfed by a militant black population, the traditional corporate patrons of the CRA were able to galvanize broader ruling-class support for the renovation of Downtown, through the emergency Committee of 25 (later, the "Community Committee") and an expanded Central City Association.[6] The Community Committee, in particular, was the closest thing to an "executive committee of the bourgeoisie" that Southern California had seen since the class wars of the 1930s. It broke precedent by including Jewish entertainment sector leaders (like Lew Wasserman of MCA), the CEOs of major aerospace corporations (like Roy Anderson of Lockheed and Tom Jones of Northrup), and a visible quotient of prominent Democrats.[7] (USC and its alumni meanwhile used the crisis, with official city support, to evict poor households and impose a *cordon sanitaire*—parking lots, administrative buildings, shopping centers—between campus and the surrounding black-Latino community.)

The Growth Coalition

The second aftermath of the Watts uprising was the consolidation of a multiracial coalition, based on Jewish (10 percent of the electorate) and black votes under the dispensation of Downtown boosters led by Otis Chandler's "liberalized" *Los Angeles Times*. After six years of blistering warfare against Mayor Yorty's white backlash, the new coalition installed Thomas Bradley, a black ex-cop and city councilman, as mayor in 1973. Bradley's regime, which over the years has drawn support from such landed powers as BankAmerica, the Irvine Ranch, and ARCO, enlarged the CRA mandate to encompass all of Downtown, opening a real-estate bonanza to commercial developers. At the same time his fourteen-year reign has been little short of catastrophic for inner-city residents. As I will elaborate in a moment, black South Central Los Angeles has been reduced to a deindustrialized twilight zone, while East Side Chicano-Latino neighborhoods, unrepresented on the city council between 1963 and 1985, have been locked out of power.[8] The key Bradley constituencies, have been pacified with largely symbolic goods: for blacks, a few celebrity politicians; for Jews, City Hall's craven solicitation of Israel. The development interests, on the other hand, have received a plush welfare state all their own.

Because the city has avoided even the desultory levels of social service and patronage that have elsewhere been necessary supports of black-led crisis management, it has had still greater fiscal resources to subsidize urban renewal. The prime mechanism is "tax increment financing," which allows the CRA to function as an unelected, sovereign power, confiscating the tax increases from new development (the "increment") to subsidize further development. As black small businesses have been "red-lined" out of existence by discriminatory bank credit practices, and as East L.A. continues to pay more taxes than it receives in services,[9] Downtown redevelopers reap special low-interest loans, free infrastructural modernization, tax abatements, and, above all, discounted prime land.

This is where we pick up the plot of Polanski's *Chinatown*: for the last twenty years big developers could be confident that their subsidized parcels—made available by the CRA at half the cost of land in Century City or downtown San Francisco—would triple or quadruple in market value within a few years of construction; the resulting tax increment being sluiced off for the next stage of land development.[10] The CRA has quietly municipalized land speculation—just as in the early-twentieth-century aqueduct conspiracy upon which *Chinatown* was based, except on a vaster scale, with dirt and increments instead of dirt and water as the magic formula for superprofits.[11]

With the majority of the city council routinely approving every request of the developers' lobby (or abdicating power to the CRA and the City Planning Department), it was not surprising that almost $2.5 billion of new investment flowed into Downtown in the decade after Bradley's election. Where there were just five new high-rises above the old earthquake limit of thirteen floors in 1976, there are now forty-five. Increasingly, the CRA operated a casino as players moved in and out of speculative positions, nearly a third of Downtown exchanging hands between 1976 and 1982. Ironically, as the ante has inexorably risen, many of the original champions of Downtown renewal, including large regional banks and oil companies with troubled cashflows, have had to cash in their equity and withdraw to the sidelines. As Volckerism first created a superdollar and then weakened it, the volatile commercial real-estate markets around the country have favored highly liquid investors and foreign capital. In 1979 the *Los Angeles Times* reported that a quarter of Downtown's major properties were foreign-owned; six years later the figure was revised to 75 percent (one authority claims 90 percent).[12] The first wave of foreign investment in Downtown in the late 1970s, as in Manhattan, was led by Canadian real-estate capital, epitomized by Toronto-based Olympia and York. The Reichman clan who own Olympia and York collect skyscrapers like the mere rich collect rare stamps or Louis XIV furniture. Yet since 1984 they, along with the New York insurance companies and the British banks, have been swamped by a tsunami of East Asian finance and flight capital.

"Zaitech"

What the Japanese call *zaitech*, the strategy of using financial technologies to shift cashflow from production to speculation, radically restructured Downtown's investment portfolios and gave a new impetus to sagging office construction. The liquid resources of other investors were simply

dwarfed by the sheer mass of the Japanese trade surplus
which rapidly found its way from U.S. Treasury bonds to
prime real estate. The superyen of the late 1980s put the
skyscrapers along Figueroa's "Gold Coast" at a rummage-
sale discount: a virtually unknown condominium developer
from Tokyo, Shuwa Company Ltd., bought nearly $1 billion
of L.A.'s new skyscape, including the twin-towered ARCO
Plaza, in a single two-and-half-month shopping spree. Moreover, as local real-estate analysts complained, "the major
Japanese companies are borrowing at very cheap rates, usually 5 percent or less. They borrow in Japan [in Shuwa's case,
through ten L.A. branches of Japanese banks], deduct it
from their taxes in Japan and convert it to dollars, invest in
dollars in the United States."[13]

The Japanese surge into Downtown real estate was coor-
dinated with the wild stock market and property booms
within Japan itself that first raised alarm about the future of
the Pacific Rim economy.[14] As the superyen and foreign pro-
tectionism depressed industrial investment, most of the big
Japanese corporations and trading firms resorted to *zaitech*
to keep themselves in the black. At the same time, soaring
stock values and a 100 percent annual rate of property appreciation in central Tokyo inflated portfolios and pension
trusts which sought new outlets overseas. One result was the
impressive lineup of Mitsui Fudosan, Sumitomo, Dai-Ichi
Life, Mitsubishi, and a dozen other major Japanese players
in a race to grab new Downtown development sites. Together with more shadowy Kuomintang capital from Hong
Kong and the ASEAN region, they have positioned themselves to help push the frontiers of commercial speculation
into the Spanish-speaking neighborhoods west of the Harbor
Freeway, as well as lobbying for the redevelopment of skid
row as part of Little Tokyo. In 1990–91, however, the seemingly irresistible Gold Rush of Asian capital came to an
abrupt halt as hyperinflated property values in Japan—the

capital of firms like Shuwa—collapsed. The future of Downtown Los Angeles is now mortgaged to the fate of properties and financial markets thousands of miles across the Pacific.

THE DECLINE OF BLACK LOS ANGELES

At this point the forces of international capital encounter those of international labor migration. But before introducing the working classes into the plot, it is necessary to attempt a capsule characterization of the larger-scale restructuring of 1978–1990 of which the internationalization of Downtown redevelopment is only a particular instance.

- Since 1978 the branch-plant, metal-banging sector of the California economy, concentrated since the 1920s in the East Bay and East L.A. manufacturing belts, has been largely shut down. The economic linkages with the U.S. industrial heartland which these "Fordist" branch plants embodied have been supplanted by new dependencies upon East Asian consumer durables and fabricated metal. To give just two examples: half of the new car market in California is Japanese, while much of the structural steel for skyscraper construction is imported from Korea.
- This substitution of Asian imports for national integration has sponsored the rise of a vast Pacific trade and product services complex in the L.A. Harbor area which, along with Japanese direct investment, stimulates the movement of offshore bank and pension-fund capital to Southern California.
- The molecular action of the mass immigration of Korean and Chinese middle classes also contributes to the formation of capital in Southern California. The highly entrepreneurial enclave of "Koreatown" near Downtown L.A.

has absorbed 200,000 immigrants and formed 3,000 small businesses since the early 1970s. Immigrant small business and family self-exploitation have also been the foundation for piratical real-estate speculation: witness the 4,000 "minimalls" (street-corner shopping centers) which blight L.A. County.

· Income and demand in the white suburbs were sustained through the 1980s by the boom in military spending; a large net subsidy from the rest of the United States, especially the "rust belt," to Southern California. The Los Angeles area received about 17 percent of total defense spending, and the local association of prime contractors often boasted that the Southern California aerospace-electronics complex is a larger economy than India's.[15]

· The power structure of California, almost completely re-shaped by mergers and foreign trade, has shifted from San Francisco to Los Angeles, now the second largest financial center (and third corporate headquarters) in the United States. This has stimulated Downtown office development while also sharpening the rivalries with other Southern California "central places," "especially Century City and the Orange County "Golden Triangle."

· The continued expansion of the Southern California economy has become a major "pull" factor in the dis-articulation of the economies of Mexico and Central America. Most of the Salvadoran "foot people" whom President Duarte once begged Reagan to keep in the United States live within sight of L.A.'s City Hall. Paradox-ically, as high-productivity manufacturing in Los Angeles has collapsed, sweated and labor-intensive production has boomed.[16] This is explained by the emergence of a Third World sector within the regional economy, based on the minimum-wage labor of immigrants without citizen rights.

Black Los Angeles has been especially marginalized by this internationalization of the metropolitan economy. The

1978–1982 wave of deindustrialization, which shuttered ten
of the twelve largest nonaerospace plants in the region and
displaced more than 50,000 blue-collar workers, erased
ephemeral black (and Chicano) occupational gains won in
the late 1960s. An investigating committee of the California
legislature in 1982 confirmed a dismal pattern of benign neglect and economic devastation in South-Central neighborhoods. Unemployment has risen by nearly 50 percent since
the early 1970s while purchasing power in the community
has fallen by a third. Where local warehouses and factories
have not folded altogether, they have fled to the South Bay
or northern Orange County areas, leaving behind a waste-
land of derelict factories and abandoned industrial sites.[17]

Black retail business, meanwhile, has been driven into virtual extinction by discriminatory credit practices and the
competition of regional shopping malls. The CRA has
played a Mephistophelean role in fomenting disinvestment
in South Central L.A. Its sole project in the ghetto, a small
shopping complex near Watts's 1965 "Charcoal Alley," languished through fifteen years of "planning." More insidi-
ously, the CRA helped destroy the leading retail district in
the black community, the Crenshaw Shopping Center, by
providing redevelopment subsidies to the wealthy promoters
of the Fox Hills Plaza on the ghetto's periphery. As a critic
put it: "The CRA labeled one area blighted, which it wasn't,
in order to create a development that blighted existing
centers."[18]

Unlike some other large cities, Los Angeles makes no con-
tribution from the general city revenue for social programs
for the poor, and relies, at Mayor Bradley's insistence, entirely upon federal aid or county intervention. But as the
legislature found to its dismay, the sprawling South-Central
districts of the city, with the largest concentrations of poverty, have received merely twelve cents on the dollar of federal revenue sharing and block grants. The city council has
diverted most federal aid to Downtown–USC redevelop-

ment, or deployed it to win votes amongst middle-class homeowners.[19] With 78,000 unemployed youth in the Watts-Willowbrook area, it is not surprising that there are now 145 branches of the rival Crips and Bloods gangs in south L.A., or that the jobless resort to the opportunities of the burgeoning "crack" economy.[20]

At the same time, employed black workers, as well as many Chicanos, are beginning to feel the competitive pressures of the Third World sector in local services, construction, and manufacture. For example, Service Employees Local 399, which organized the primarily black custodial workers in the Downtown high-rises, has been smashed by contractors using undocumented, minimum-wage labor. Nearly 2,000 janitors have lost their jobs and wages have fallen from $13 to $3.50 per hour.[21] Similarly, blacks in Downtown hotels have been displaced by lower-wage workers.[22] Even where blacks, or Chicanos, are willing, in desperation, to enter the low-wage labor market, they are usually prevented (according to testimony to the legislature) by employer preferences for noncitizen labor—a discrimination redoubled by the racism that excludes most black males from retail or "public visibility" jobs outside the black community. Although redevelopment has been defended by Bradley and the building trades as a new source of compensatory high-wage employment, the job benefits have been overwhelmingly appropriated by white commuters. By concentrating public resources on the high-rise and financial-services boom, and by confiscating the tax increment, renewal has only accelerated the deterioration of socioeconomic conditions for citizen workers of color.

THIRD WORLD, SECOND CITY

Workers without citizen rights, on the other hand, have become the raw material for a major revival of absolute surplus extraction. Although their labor is essential to every locality and level of the Southern California economy, it is most visibly concentrated in the inner city. Mexican or Central American labor wipes the plates, mops the floors, empties the garbage, and, generally, performs every menial task in the Downtown service sector. At the same time, 200,000 immigrant workers, including many East Asians, have been conscripted into the low-wage manufactures that have replaced the "Fordist" auto, tire, and steel plants as the second largest sector of the local industrial economy. Much of the declining industrial belt east of Alameda Street has been recycled by new or "born-again" (deunionized) low-wage factories, including foundries, furniture and plastic plants, and some aerospace subcontracting. But the epicenter of low-wage industry remains L.A.'s apparel sector, the nation's second largest, with at least 120,000 workers, of whom only a few thousand are unionized despite a half-century of struggle. (In 1991 Los Angeles surpassed New York City as the leading garment center in the United States.)

By creating union-free, Third World conditions of labor within its specialty niche of women's sportswear production, the local garment industry has been able almost to double its work force during a decade when other U.S. apparel centers, like Manhattan, have been shrinking in the face of offshore competition. This "comparative advantage" in labor-intensive production explains part of the puzzle of how the L.A. metropolitan economy was capable of adding more net manufacturing jobs than any other region at the same time that its high-wage, nondefense industries were stricken.[23] (The military aerospace boom under Reagan obviously explains the other part.) The garment industry, depending on a propinquity of subcontracting and "homework" to final assembly and wholesale marketing, has been a powerful magnet concentrating immigration in the interstices and peripheries of Downtown. Other centralizing forces include Downtown's demand for menial service labor; its traditional function as an ethnic center for Hispanics, Filipinos, and Asians; centrality to the bus system; and, implacably, the racist and segmented rental markets which funnel the Spanish-speaking poor into the overcrowded districts of dilapidated housing that surround the redevelopment zones.

A million immigrants over the last decade have been crammed into older black and Chicano areas, forming a dense, continuous ring of slum housing around Downtown, with filaments and tentacles reaching out to Hollywood and the eastern San Fernando Valley in the north, the San Gabriel Valley as far as La Puente to the east, and Lynwood in the south. There has been no housing planning or social policy to accommodate this onrush of new low-wage residents. Since 1981 federal housing assistance has been slashed by 70 percent without compensatory support from state or city authorities. Los Angeles has not built a unit of public housing since the controversies of the McCarthy period, and the existing stock of older rental property is being systematically depleted by redevelopment and condominium conversion. In the near future rents in some 60,000 units will rise sharply as federal restrictions expire on subsidized housing, and as other private apartment owners pass on the costs of upgrading to earthquake safety standards. Simultaneously, the Department of Housing and Urban Development is crusading for the mass eviction of "illegal aliens" from publicly subsidized developments. The cheapest family units in the city, in the most dilapidated neighborhoods, now cost about 70 percent of the income of a minimum-wage worker.[24]

The result has been universal overcrowding as two or three, sometimes even four, immigrant families are forced to occupy a single-family dwelling or apartment. As this tenement strategy has reached its supersaturation point, families have spilled over into a burgeoning black market in housing. In a city where thousands of luxury condominiums stand unoccupied, at least 200,000 immigrants from Mexico and Central America are living in illegal garage conversions, typically without plumbing or heat.[25] Although many of the inner city's squalid apartment blocks are owned by Encino dentists and other caricaturable yuppie landlords, a large sector of rack-renting and housing exploitation is conducted by the citizen working class or *arriviste* immigrants. Amid such an acute crisis of affordable housing, the labor-market fragmentation of the L.A. working class between privileged and oppressed strata is redoubled by these relations of mass homelessness and mass landlordism. Some see the specter of a creeping "Brazilianization" of the city's social structure. "What kind of city will Los Angeles be in the year 2000 if we fail to provide needed housing? A city segregated into regions of affluence and poverty, like Rio de Janeiro? A city of gated communities and wandering groups of homeless, like the millions of street children in Brazil? Will we see children sleeping on street corners, forced to survive through panhandling and petty theft?"[26]

The Latino Urban Culture

Yet the immigrant working class does not simply submit to the city for the purposes of capital, it is not merely the collective victim of "urban crisis"; it also strives to transform and create the city, its praxis is a material force, however unrecognized or invisible in most accounts of contemporary Los Angeles. Though superficially the new ethnic mosaic of the inner city fits into the classical "Chicago School" model of the ghettoized North American city, the cultural thrust of immigration has changed. Like the enclave Asian boom-towns in the region (Koreatown, old Chinatown, "new Chinatown" in Alhambra–Monterey Park, and Westminster's Little Saigon), the Spanish-speaking neighborhoods of L.A. are more than melting pots for eventual assimilation to some hyphenated ethnicity. Together with their integral worlds of work and itineraries of movement, these residential environments comprise a virtually parallel urban structure—a second city.

Even in the face of strident nativism, exemplified by the recent success of the statewide "English as Official Language" initiative, Spanish-speaking Los Angeles—the second-largest Mexican, Guatemalan, and Salvadoran city in the hemisphere—has far in excess of the necessary critical mass of institutions and media to define its own distinctive urbanity: a different, more "classical" way of living in the city based on gregarious, communitarian uses of markets, boulevards, parks, and so on. The great Latino shopping streets—Broadway in Downtown and Brooklyn in Boyle Heights—have more in common with the early-twentieth-century city, with the culture of Ragtime, than they do with a death-wish "postmodernity." In contrast to the Yiddish East Side of 1920, however, the Spanish-speaking city has increasing, amplified connections with the mother culture(s): indeed, it is a direct, continuous extension of it, a vector of "Americanization" in the authentic sense of the term.

This second city collides with the movement of international capital in the arena of Downtown redevelopment, where the expanding high-rise frontier threatens to uproot poor neighborhoods. Originally the CRA had envisaged that redevelopment would be directed primarily southward towards USC, and therefore designated the Pico Union district, west of the Convention Center, as a "service area" for the planned office complexes and high-rise condominiums of the South Park development. Pico Union, however, is the oldest, most densely networked, Central American neighborhood in the city. Local resistance, supported by the city-wide Campaign for Economic Survival, forced the CRA to back down from its scheme of rezoning the area for light industry and parking. This has been virtually the only "popular" victory in thirty-eight years of urban renewal.[27]

Pico Union's success, moreover, was abetted by the developers' greater interest in expanding *westward* across the Harbor Freeway from Bunker Hill into the Temple-Beaudry district, and down Wilshire Boulevard toward MacArthur Park, the entire zone of prospective development now dubbed the "Central City West." This is also the poorest part of the city, the principal portal of entry for immigrants from Central America. Its population is severely overcrowded in an absentee-owned, nine-tenths dilapidated housing stock, with whole families compelled to "hot bed" sleep in shifts.[28] The big developers, with credit lines to limitless offshore capital, are already building on Crown Hill, the summit of Temple-Beaudry, and have assembled huge parcels along Wilshire for further development. Although the extent of their acquisitions is a $64,000 question, the threat to the communities is imminent. Dan Garcia, president of the Los Angeles Planning Commission, has warned that "we're not the relocation conscience of the city. Displacement is going to happen."[29] The ultimate human costs of Central City West redevelopment—unless it is vigorously contested by grass-roots mobilization with the support of local unions (most of whose headquarters are near MacArthur Park)—could be even greater than the original diaspora from Bunker Hill.

The other prime "soft spot" that international developers are probing is skid row, the "Nickel," whose blight blocks the expansion of Little Tokyo and a presumably massive inflow of Japanese capital. For a long time Councilman Gilbert Lindsay, the "Emperor of Downtown," who died last year, advocated a final solution, based on the deportation of the street people to a poor farm outside the city limits in Saugus or, most recently, the Santa Monica Mountains.[30] Two years ago Mayor Bradley and CRA chairman Jim Woods (*homo diabolus* from the L.A. building trades) set up a task force to explore the options for introducing commercial redevelopment into the area. In the winter of 1986–87, after a number of people froze to death on the streets, Bradley—at the urging of the Central City East Association of businessmen—ordered police sweeps to destroy the makeshift sidewalk camps that the homeless had erected as protection against hypothermia. In a Kafkaesque vein, Chairman Wood explained that only the shelters were illegal, not sleeping naked on the street in 0-degree Centigrade. "The camping aspect is what we are trying to get at, the jumble of furniture on the street, the open fires. But no one is telling people they can't sleep on the streets."[31]

But even this final, pathetic freedom was repealed in May 1987 as Police Chief Gates, again backed by the mayor and goaded by the developers, declared that the homeless had a week to clear the streets or face mass arrest. Despite protests from West Side liberals on the city council, the anxieties of Bradley's own advisers, and even the opposition of the district attorney—who tried to remind the police that homelessness was not actually a crime—Gates's men duly carted off street people, their advocates, and even a few sympathetic onlookers.[32] Although Bradley must have understood that such Rambo-like bullying of the helpless would damage his image in the forthcoming elections (as he stood for an unprecedented fifth term), the lobbying of the Little Tokyo real-estate interests was irresistible. Organizers among the homeless, like the radical-pacifist Catholic Workers, have conceded that defense of the neighborhood against a siege of international capital is probably a "losing battle." "The forces we're going up against are pretty monumental."[33]

The Limits of Redevelopment

Even more monumental are the diseconomies which the forces of Downtown development are generating for the rest of the metropolis. A hundred thousand new jobs have been added to Downtown in the last twenty years without corresponding new investment in rapid transit or freeway construction, apart from a jerry-built bus lane on the San Bernardino Freeway. Rush-hour traffic speed in the Downtown freeway interchanges—the choke points for hundreds of thousands of suburban commuters—has been reduced by 40 percent, while surface street flow has returned to the nightmare 1924 (!) peak of congestion that caused the decline of Downtown in the first place. In a typical incident, Mayor Bradley was unable to reach a topping-off ceremony for the new Citicorp Plaza less than a mile from City Hall (mayors, like other middle-glass Angelenos, do not walk). Caltrans has warned of imminent paralyzing gridlock on the freeways as morning and afternoon traffic jams coalesce in a twelve-hour continuum. Meanwhile, the city's expected schedule for meeting federal air-quality control standards had to be postponed from 1982 until 2020; ozone levels are currently triple the official (lenient) safety maximum.[34]

Thus the worse popular fears of a generation ago about the consequences of market-driven overdevelopment in the Los Angeles Basin are punctually coming true. Decades of systematic underinvestment in housing and urban infrastructure, combined with grotesque subsidies for speculators, permissive zoning for commercial development, the

absence of effective regional planning, and ludicrously low
property taxes for the wealthy have ensured an erosion of
the quality of life for the suburban middle classes as well as
for the inner-city poor. But the latter continue to bear the
brunt of the crisis. The transportation problems of Downtown, to take one instance, will only further increase pressures on inner-city housing, as a chorus of business interests
and politicians shouts for more peripheral parking, service
areas, and new transport corridors. A complex political
struggle, prefiguring the realignment of city politics as well
as additional evictions of low-income residents, envelops the
controversial $3.5 billion plan to build a Downtown fixed-rail
system.

Metro Rail was conceived initially, in the mid-1970s, less
as a coherent transport design than as a hurried response by
the Bradley regime to fears that the county supervisors were
preemptively dipping into the federal mass transit pork barrel.[35] Originally justified as a system to relieve congestion
along the Wilshire corridor (a separate "people mover" was
designated for Downtown itself), Metro Rail has metamorphosed, through various crisis and revisions, into yet another huge boondoggle for speculators (shades of the L.A.
aqueduct), primarily directed toward the redevelopment of
Hollywood. Planning for the original Wilshire route was re-
dolent with scandal, leading to the resignation of the city's
planning director after the revelation of his intimate business
ties with the key lobbyist for a more permissive zoning of the
route.[36] More important, Wilshire Metro Rail fell afoul of
the powerful West Side Valley political organization headed
by the Berman brothers and Henry Waxman—an omen, as
we shall see, of the breakup of the Bradley coalition.

Congressman Waxman, a major power in the Democratic
House, has won the appreciation of West Side homeowners
and small businessmen by his denunciations of Metro Rail
(and, by implication, more high-density development) as "an

absurd waste of money." For several years he held up construction by demanding safety checks of "hazardous gas pockets" in the mid-Wilshire and Fairfax areas. Then, in early 1987, he used his amanuensis, Congressman Julian Dixon ("I felt an obligation to Henry"), to veto altogether the Rapid Transit District's compromise proposal for a Wilshire branch. Planning for a westward route (now in the hands of a new transport superagency) has been adroitly deflected into a consideration of using other surface corridors—like Olympic or Washington—which run through the black and Asian communities.[37]

Whatever the ultimate fate of Metro Rail west of Western Avenue, construction of the initial Union Station–to–MacArthur Park leg of the country's most expensive transit system—ca. $200 million per mile—is in full progress. At this point, the priority for future construction, largely unopposed by the West Side forces, is a Hollywood branch comprising an elevated line along Sunset Boulevard, through the heart of Hollywood, and a subway tunnel through the hills to North Hollywood and the Valley. This will neatly link up CRA's Downtown empire with its new $1 billion, thirty-year redevelopment project in Hollywood, creating attractive nodes of speculation and high-rise development adjacent to the Metro Rail stations. As Hollywood becomes ripe for tourist and office-propelled revitalization (no doubt with offshore financing), many of its 40,000 immigrants and poor people will be pushed out.

As inner-city neighborhoods are broken up by redevelopment, how does the city propose to cope with displacement and homelessness? In the medium run, a strategic option is to set up a cheap commuting system to encourage dispersal of some of the low-income population to the south and southeast. City and county officials have been hurrying funding for a Light Rail line between Downtown and Long Beach, utilizing the old Pacific Electric right of way which runs down Alameda through Watts and Compton. At only one-sixth the per-mile cost of the baroque bamboozle of Metro Rail, Light Rail will not generate the same multi-billion-dollar real-estate fallout, but it could alleviate the critical overcrowding on buses serving black and Latino southside neighborhoods.

It is symptomatic of the historic fragmentation of L.A.'s power centers, and of the sheer scale of their endeavor, that elements of such a strategy—envisioning coordinate speculative potentials along a truly metropolitan axis—have only recently emerged, partly because of the stimulus of foreign capital. But it is unclear whether Downtown-sponsored transit planning, even under the auspices of big regional developers and offshore capital, can reconcile the interests of investors in the other, traditionally competitive, metropolitan office markets. Despite the official hoopla about Downtown's resurgence—toasted in champagne at Bradley's recent $90,000 groundbreaking party for Metro Rail—during the 1980s the West Side centers actually built more new office space (27 million square feet versus 24 million).[38] Indeed the rampant expansion of commercial complexes, residential high-rises, and supermalls in West L.A. during the 1980s, without any provision for extra traffic or other social costs, has fueled a powerful homeowners' revolt against high-density growth which threatens, as well, the Downtown developers' tenure in City Hall.

The Slow-Growth Rebellion

As previously indicated, the Bradley alliance of soul and lox has been the electoral underpinning of unrestrained urban development. The first major challenge to his coalition came from the unreconstructed right in 1978–1981, as former Yorty-ites, Jarvis tax protestors, and opponents of school busing regrouped in a coalition led by Bobbi Fiedler and Alan Robbins which succeeded in rolling back school desegregation and sabotaging the Downtown "people mover." The new right lacked the citywide electoral clout or business support to topple Bradley's multiracial coalition. However, in the wake of his unsuccessful bid for the California governorship in 1982 (disastrously repeated in 1986), the Berman-Waxman camp—which the *New Republic* has heralded as the "most powerful Democratic 'machine' in the country"— began to break away from the mayor, embracing the new gospel of "slow growth."[39]

As the local political establishment immediately recognized, the Berman-Waxman shift is a tactic in a larger maneuver. They are bidding not only for hegemony in City Hall, but above all to buttress their considerable influence in Sacramento and Washington. From their original base in the Jewish, liberal-Democratic districts of the West Side and the south San Fernando Valley, they have enlarged their influence over that neoliberal "dream constituency" of aerospace professionals, computer specialists, young entrepreneurs, and the like, in the surf-urban corridor that runs from the South Bay west of the San Diego Freeway, through Santa Monica, into the western San Fernando Valley, and, ultimately, up to trendy Ventura and Santa Barbara counties. In this coastal demi-paradise the preservation of community amenities underwrites soaring property values, and high-density developers are almost as resented as poor people of color. Moreover, as the Bermans and Waxman are intensely aware, yuppie political power is increasing, despite massive non-Anglo immigration. As a detailed socioelectoral analysis conducted by Caltech for the *Los Angeles Times* concluded:

In a city that thinks of itself as the nation's modern melting pot, the political controls rest securely in the middle class, with the number of white, affluent voters increasing at a greater rate than voters from the city's burgeoning non-white, immigrant population . . . the majority of the voters (59 percent) live in the city's whitest and wealthiest neighborhoods on the West Side and in the San Fernando Valley, areas that contain less than half (48 percent) of the city's population. These areas are 75 percent white and include 88 percent of the households in the city with incomes of $50,000 or more.[40]

This discrepancy between population and electoral power is a result partly of working-class abstentionism, but still more of diminishing citizen rights in the Latino working class. The once-pivotal black vote has also become less important to West Side politicos as they reach out to incorporate parts of the electoral base of the new right in their white-neighborhood-based revolt. Indeed, the Berman-Waxman camp and its followers of the moment are zealously promoting West Side separatism, emphasizing the divergent interests of the "beach and borsch" belt vis-à-vis Downtown and the smog belt. They have brilliantly appropriated the lessons of the late 1970s tax rebellion by capturing, for their own strategic purposes, the antipathy of homeowners to further high-density development, totally obscuring in the process such questions of equity as affordable housing, job creation, or the plight of the immigrant working poor.

The schism in the Bradley coalition emerged vividly during the November 1986 elections as a populist movement under the banner of "Not Yet New York," and with Waxman's avid support battled Bradley and the big developers. Recognizing the popularity of slow-growth Proposition U, which proposed to roll back commercial zoning in much of the West Side (although not, significantly, in Hollywood or Downtown) and to restrict high-rise construction in residential areas, Bradley's council majority—led by President Pat

Russell and urged on by Cadillac Fairview and other mega-developers—rushed through a questionable ordinance intended to exempt thirty pet projects. Galvanizing the slow-growth opposition was a key Berman-Waxman ally, Councilman Zev Yaroslavsky, an indigenous facsimile of Mayor Ed Koch who launched his career by making support of Ariel Sharon a "local" issue.

Proposition U passed by a landslide—"a watershed" and "the end of the boomtown mentality," according to a triumphant Yaroslavsky,[41] who promptly declared his official candidacy against Bradley as well as unveiling an even more drastic plan that would give the council veto power over any new development bigger than 50,000 square feet. Meanwhile, the mayor, clearly imitating Governor Jerry Brown's notorious volte-face over antiproperty-tax Proposition 13 in 1978, tried to recuperate slow-growth sentiment by pledging allegiance to Proposition U and offering the newly discovered panacea of community planning. But Bradley's sudden concern about minimall squalor and hillside despoliation (he predictably sidelined the fates of Central City West and Hollywood) came too late in the day to avoid the antidevelopment deluge in the June 1987 city council elections. The supposedly impregnable Russell, key strategist of the Bradley camp, was dramatically upset by Ruth Galanter, an urban planner from the Venice area with a New Left background and financial support from Henry Waxman. Galanter's victory, together with the loss of Bradley's nominee in his own old home district, has tilted the balance of power toward a realignment of the council majority.

It is significant, however, that the progressive Galanter, whom Russell tried to radical-bait because of her past association with Assemblyman Tom Hayden (another ardent Berman-Waxman supporter), won decisively in the traditionally conservative and white Westchester area while losing the liberal and black Crenshaw district. The point certainly has not been lost on the supporters of higher-density development, who have made hay out of the slow-growth movement's racial and class biases. As Planning Commission president Dan Garcia put it: "The old multi-racial coalition that Bradley presided over is breaking down. This slow-growth movement, or whatever you want to call it, is by any other name a movement of white, middle-class, affluent people who are out for themselves and their own neighborhoods."[42]

Despite the best efforts of some progressives, it is likely that the debate over the degradation of the urban environment in Los Angeles will stay focused on the needs of ascendant white homeowners, whose material interest is to maintain housing as "unaffordable" as the market will bear. Allies of juggernaut redevelopment will shed crocodile tears about the fate of the have-nots while preparing to evict them from their neighborhoods.

Meanwhile, the Los Angeles economy—that seemingly perpetual growth machine—entered a portentous period of restructuring and crisis in the 1990s. A new phase of deindustrialization began with the sudden downsizing of the region's crucial aerospace industry where one-third of jobs are estimated to be in imminent peril. At the same time, in anticipation of the free-trade agreement with Mexico, light manufacturing has accelerated its relocation to Tijuana and other border cities, while Los Angeles's ethnic small businesses have collapsed in unprecedented numbers. Humiliated regional planners and economic forecasters have had to scrap their optimistic predictions for the 1990s. Instead of endless growth, the Los Angeles region is now expected to experience a grim jobs/population scissors in the 1990s as the number of poor immigrants and their children grows much faster than originally predicted, while the supply of jobs expands much slower. Unfortunately, there is no public advocate of class consciousness, no Rainbow coalition, on the losing side of the current social polarization in Los Angeles. The Rodney King crisis of 1991, which exposed to the world the quotidian brutality of the LAPD, also revealed the dereliction of progressive politics in Los Angeles. The sounds of silence from the white, liberal West Side were echoed by the refusal of most Chicano leaders to make common cause with the outraged black community. Despite romantic invocations of the "new majority," it remains a dream deferred. The working classes of the inner city, for all their potential power, are still a sleeping dragon: blacks, declining in electoral influence and betrayed by City Hall; Chicanos, gerrymandered and divided between rival Democratic clans; new immigrants, disenfranchised and ignored. Whether this sleeper will awaken, or whether this remains "just Chinatown," is, as always, *the* question.

Notes

1. "Jeffries' trading room at Fifth and Figueroa streets in Downtown L.A. is just the kind of intense, fast-paced environment that attracts ambitious, wealth-driven kids. Spurred by a banner that reads 'Positive People with the Competitive Edge,' with buy-and-sell orders booming over a loudspeaker, young traders work night and day in plush purple chairs that rock and roll before Quotron terminals and keyboards. Phones crooked in their necks, they exploit their eighteen-hour edge on the N.Y. Stock Exchange to trade billion-dollar blocks of stock in Hong Kong, New York, London, or Amarillo for anonymous buyers identified only by numbers." (Moira Johnston, "The Takeover Wars," *California Magazine*, May 1987, p. 57.) Boyd Jeffries—"tanned, rich and handsome role model for the new crop of MBA's"—has pleaded guilty to a 1986 conspiracy to manipulate the price of a securities offering by American Express; he has also confessed to "parking stock" for Ivan Boesky.

2. Fredric Jameson, "The Cultural Logic of Late Capitalism," *New Left Review* 146 (July–August 1984).
3. "Look at Downtown, the New Los Angeles," *Los Angeles Times* (henceforth, *LAT*), February 16, 1986, V 2, p. 3.
4. Raymond Chandler, *The High Window*, (New York: Putnam, 1945), pp. 45–46.
5. Cf. Don Parsons, "LA's 'Headline-Happy' Public Housing Wars," *Southern California Quarterly* 45, no. 3 (Fall 1983); and Robert Gottlieb and Irene Wolt, *Thinking Big: The Story of the Los Angeles Times* (New York: Putnam, 1978), pp. 260–63. A 1953 amendment to the California constitution required voter approval for any further funding of public housing—a measure which effectively terminated construction.
6. The biggest Downtown-headquartered firms are ARCO, UNOCAL (Union Oil), Security Pacific Bank, First Interstate Bank, Carter Hawley Hale, Pacific Lighting, Transamerica, and Times Mirror.
7. *The Economist* (3 April 1982, 65–66) described the Community Committee as a "more significant" local power center than Reagan's L.A. "kitchen cabinet," but Robert Gottlieb and Peter Wiley (*Empires in the Sun* [New York: Putnam, 1981], pp. 116–17) point out that "despite its apparent clout . . . it never functioned as a policy-setting organization. Its members largely reacted to the events rather than initiated long-term and even international orientations." In recent years the committee has been closely bonded to the powerful California Business Roundtable through the overlapping chairmanships of Edward Carter, antidivestment University of California regent and head of the multinational department store chain, Carter Hawley Hale.
8. It required a lawsuit by Reagan's Justice Department invoking the 1965 Voting Rights Act to force a reapportionment of the city council to increase Latino representation. Los Angeles is currently about 30 percent Latino, 17 percent black, and almost 7 percent Asian. The impact of electoral gerrymandering has traditionally been reinforced by municipal fragmentation: an integral Chicano/Latino city-within-a-city of 2 million people is broken into more than a dozen jurisdictions between the city of Los Angeles, the county (East Los Angeles), and smaller incorporated cities.

9. For estimates of the deficit, see *LAT*, April 13, 1980, II, p. 6.

10. For example, the CRA bought sixteen rundown parcels at Fourth and Flower streets in the early 1960s for $3 million; in the early 1970s, despite the explosion in property values, it discounted the combined parcel to Security Pacific for a mere $5.4 million. By 1975 the land alone was worth over $100 million. In another instance, Richard Riordan, a prominent local speculator, bought property in 1969 at Ninth and Figueroa for $8 per square foot; within a decade it had soared to $225 per square foot. Cf. *LAT*, April 13, 1980, VI, p. 2; John Brohman, "Urban Restructuring in Downtown Los Angeles," MA thesis, School of Architecture and Urban Planning, UCLA, 1983, p. 111; and Joel Friedman, "The Political Economy of Urban Renewal: Changes in Land Ownership in Bunker Hill," MA thesis, School of Architecture and Urban Planning, UCLA, 1978, p. 261.

11. The CRA has been able to withdraw more than $1 billion in property taxes from the general revenue for these purposes: a massive redistribution from the city's underprivileged to transnational capital. Moreover, since the fiscal restrictions of Proposition 13 in 1978 (the famous Jarvis tax initiative), affluent suburban cities have rushed to form redevelopment agencies in order to hoard tax revenue. Wealthy Palm Springs, for example, subsidized a $9 million expansion of Saks Fifth Avenue through "redevelopment" transfers from county revenue.

12. Cf. Dick Turpin in *LAT*, September 21, 1986, pp. 1, 7—confirmed by *The National Real Estate Investor*, December 1986, p. 102; the higher estimate is from Howard Sadowski, *LAT*, June 17, 1984, VII, p. 2.

13. Stephen Weiner of Bear Stearns quoted in the *National Real Estate Investor*, December 1986, p. 132.

14. Dr. Gregory Clark, on the business faculty of Sophia University in Tokyo, has recently argued that the current out-of-control stock and land booms are taking Japan to the brink of its worst postwar recession. (See "Land and Stock Boom Take Up the Slack," *International Herald Tribune*, June 22, 1987, p. 13.)

15. Cf. *Golden State Report*, July 1986, p. 36; the survey of Julien Studley Co. in *LAT*, January 29, 1984, VII, p. 27; and the testimony of Maureen Frisch, chairperson of the California Aerospace

Alliance, to the California Assembly Economic Development and New Technologies Committee, December 4, 1984.

16. For a brilliant analysis of this phenomenon, see Edward Soja, "LA's the Place: Economic Restructuring and the Internationalization of the Los Angeles Region," Paper, Annual Meeting of the American Sociological Association, San Antonio, 1984; to appear as a chapter in *Postmodern Geographies: The Reassertion of Space in the Social Sciences* (London: Verso, forthcoming).

17. California, Joint Committee on the State's Economy and the Senate Committee on Government Organization, *Problems and Opportunities for Job Development in Urban Areas of Persistent High Unemployment* (Sacramento, 1982), pp. 29, 50, 58, 94, 108, 111, 115.

18. Conversation with Edward Soja, School of Architecture and Urban Planning, UCLA, 1986.

19. California, *Problems and Opportunities*, p. 108. Also see *LAT*, September 22, 1985, II, pp. 1, 6.

20. Los Angeles has surpassed Detroit to become the most dangerous city in the First World; its annual homicides have increased from 301 in 1964 to 1,372 in 1985. Martin Luther King, Jr. Hospital in the Watts area treats two thousand cases of gunshot trauma every year—the highest reported in the world and largely attributable to gang violence. See Robert Conot, "Watts: New Faces, Fresh Frustration," *LAT*, August 11, 1985, IV, pp. 1–2.

21. From testimony of labor expert Richard Mines, in California, Assembly Committee on Intergovernmental Relations, *Undocumented Mexican Immigration* (Sacramento, 1985), pp. 64–65. Union density has declined more rapidly in California than in the nation, and more sharply in L.A. than in the remainder of the state. According to the Los Angeles Labor Council ("Immigration and Jobs in Los Angeles County," June 1985) unionization since 1971 has fallen from nearly a third to less than a fifth of the labor force.

22. Example given in Judith Cummings, "Changing Demographics, and Politics, in Los Angeles," *New York Times*, August 24, 1986.

23. An Urban Institute study of the L.A. area attributes the dynamism of the area's low-wage manufactures to a widening wage gap between regions, and, within Southern California, between nonunion and union jobs. ". . . Relative average wages of unskilled

workers in the Los Angeles manufacturing sector have declined
dramatically—from 2 percent *above* the U.S. metropolitan average
in 1969 and 1970 to 12 percent *below* the average a decade later.
. . . In contrast, wages for skilled workers in Los Angeles in predominantly unionized industries . . . grew at about the national
average." See Thomas Muller et al., *The Fourth Wave: California's
Newest Immigrants* (Washington, D.C.: Urban Institute Press,
1985), p. 110.

24. See Neal Richman and Ruth Schwartz, "Housing Homeless Families: Why L.A. Lags Behind," *LAT*, May 24, 1987, Op Ed, pp. 1,
6.

25. See Stephanie Chavez and James Quinn, "Garages: Immigrants
In, Cars Out," *LAT*, May 24, 1987, I, pp. 1, 3, 19.

26. Richman and Schwartz, "Housing Homeless Families," Friedman
("Political Economy of Urban Renewal") calls Los Angeles "the
most highly ghettoized city in the country," a distinction which
probably could be contested only by Chicago. In a recent investigation, *Los Angeles Times* reporters encountered a 60 percent rate
of discrimination against nonwhite apartment seekers. (See Carol
McGraw, "Housing Bias Remains Rampant," May 3, 1984, p. 16).

27. "People United to Save Our Community" was formed as a grass-
roots alternative to the Pico Union Neighborhood Corporation,
which is one of the several "professionalized" community development corporations which the CRA has created as satellites for
its redevelopment programs. See Gilda Haas and Allen Heskin,
"Community Struggles in Los Angeles," Paper, School of Architecture and Urban Planning, DP147, UCLA, 1982.

28. Cf. Friedman, "Political Economy of Urban Renewal," pp. 135–
45; Brohman, "Urban Restructuring in Downtown Los Angeles,"
p. 154.

29. Interview in *LA Architect*, April 1987. The Planning Commission
is engaged in a power struggle to exclude the CRA from west-of-
the-freeway development. The Urban Design Committee of the
Los Angeles chapter of the American Institute of Architects has
raised concern about community displacement and inadequate
transport planning in the Central City West.

30. "That would be a beautiful place for them." Quoted in *LAT*, June
6, 1987, II, p. 6.

31. *LAT*, February 19, 1987, IV, p. 1.

32. "Gates said he did not have 'one ounce of concern' for the 'so-called homeless' . . . 'the vast majority want to be on the streets because of a range of indulgences. They are there because they want to be'." Quoted in the *Los Angeles Herald Examiner*, May 29, 1987, A, p. 12. It is estimated that there are at least 50,000 homeless people in Los Angeles county, 10,000 of them children. See editorial, "The Scandal of the Streets," *LAT*, August 20, 1984, I. p. 4.

33. *LAT*, August 5, 1985, II, p. 3; and articles May 29–30, 1987.

34. Cf. *LAT*, June 9, 1983, IV, p. 2; August 5, 1984, IX, p. 9; and series, April 19–21, 1987.

35. See Adriana Gianturco, "L.A. Has Lots of Weapons on Transit," *LAT*, April 1, 1986, II, p. 6. The five-person Los Angeles County Board of Supervisors ranks with New York's Board of Estimate as the most powerful, and least accountable, local governing body in the United States. The conservative L.A. County Supervisors, with their fabulous powers over land-use planning in the county's unincorporated 4,000 square miles, form a solid bloc with the twenty largest regional developers. According to an investigation by the *L.A. Weekly* (November 22–28, 1985), each of the supervisors had received at least $1 million in contributions from developers since 1980. Cf. Daryl Kelley, "Developer Donations Put Antonovich, Dana in the Driver's Seat," *LAT*, April 27, 1987, II, pp. 1, 3. Further environmental regulation of building within L.A. City will undoubtedly only push commercial development deeper into county areas.

36. Cf. *LAT*, February 19, 1984, VIII, pp. I *passim*; and January 29, 1984, p. 1.

37. Rich Connell, "Dixon's Objections May Block Wilshire Metro Rail Routing," *LAT*, April 28, 1987.

38. Grubb and Ellis figures from *The National Real Estate Investor*, December 1986, p. 112. Most significant of the new West Side developments will be the giant Howard Hughes Center with almost 3 million square feet of office space.

39. *New Republic* July 7, 1986, pp. 18–19. Slow-growth movements have also recently won victories in San Francisco and San Diego, heralds of a middle-class political revolution in California's coastal zone. As housing infill and increasing density become more polit-

ically difficult to achieve, home construction in California will shift even more radically to distant interior basins like the "Inland Empire" of western Riverside and San Bernardino counties (the most rapidly urbanizing area in the United States) and the Central Valley fringes of the Bay Area.

40. This study was conducted by Bruce Cain; see *LAT*, April 5, 1987, II., p. 1. The ethnic-cum-class spectrum of inequality in L.A. is indicated by the following comparison of per capita (household) income as a percentage of a "moderate standard of living" in 1981 (as computed from Census, BLS, and survey data in Thomas Muller, *The Fourth Wave*, pp. 46, 153):

Non-Hispanic Whites	180%
Asians	120%
Blacks	90%
Chicanos	80%
"New" Latinos	60%

41. *LAT*, June 4, 1987, I, p. 26.
42. Ibid.

THE EMPTY QUARTER

The descending sun is temporarily eclipsed by a huge water tower emblazoned THE CITY OF VERNON. Shadows play off the concrete embankments of the Los Angeles River and dance across the shallow trickle of sewage in its channel. A locomotive shunts a dozen hazardous-chemical cars into a siding. A trucker somewhere pulls hard at his air horn. A forklift scurries across a busy road. We are only about five miles from Downtown Los Angeles, but have entered a world invisible to its culture pundits, the "empty quarter" of its tourist guides. This is L.A.'s old industrial heartland—the Southeast.

It's 4:30 P.M. Two workers are standing behind an immense metal table, partially shaded by a ragged beach umbrella. A portable radio is blasting rock-'n'-roll *en español*, hot from Mexico City. Each man is armed with a Phillips screwdriver, a pliers, and a ball peen hammer. Eduardo, the taller, is from Guanajuato in north-central Mexico and he is wearing the camouflage-green "Border Patrol" baseball cap favored by so many of Los Angeles's illegal immigrants. Miguel, more slightly built and pensive, is from Honduras. They are unconsciously syncopating the beat as they alternate between hammering, prying, and unscrewing.

Towering in front of them is a twenty-foot-high mound of dead and discarded computer technology: obsolete word processors, damaged printers, virus-infected micros, last decade's state of the art. The Sisyphean task of Eduardo and Miguel is to smash up everything in order to salvage a few components that will be sent to England for the recovery of their gold content. Being a computer breaker is a monotonous $5.25-an-hour job in the black economy. There are no benefits, or taxes, just cash in a plain envelope every Friday.

Miguel is about to deliver a massive blow to the VDT of a Macintosh, when I ask him why he came to Los Angeles. His hammer hesitates for a second, then he smiles and answers, "Because I wanted to work in your high technology economy." I wince as the hammer falls. The Macintosh implodes.

L.A.'s RUSTBELT

The computer breakers have been in Los Angeles three years. Eduardo had a local network of contacts from his village; Miguel, who had none, lived feral on the streets for nearly two years. Now they share a tiny two-bedroom house in the nearby city of Maywood with four other immigrant workers (two of whom are also "illegal") for $1,100 per month. All are married, but no one has yet managed to save enough money to bring his wife or kids *al otro lado*. Like so many of the 400,000 new immigrants who work and live in southeast Los Angeles County, they feel trapped between low wages and high rents. "Just like peons," Miguel broods, "like slaves."

It wasn't always this way in the Southeast. Twenty-five years ago the archipelago of bungalow communities that surrounds the factories and warehouses was predominately Anglo. The Southeast area contained most of Southern California's nondefense factories, including three auto plants, four tire plants, and a huge complex of iron and steel fabrication. The plants were unionized and they paid the mortgages on bungalows and financed college educations. On weekends well-dressed couples swung to Jimmy Wright's band at the South Gate Women's Club or rocked with Eddie Cochran at Huntington Park's Lyric Theater. For sons of the Dustbowl like Cochran (from the nearby "Okie suburb" of Bell Gardens), the smokestacks of Bethlehem Steel and GM South Gate represented the happy ending to *The Grapes of Wrath*.

But this blue-collar version of the Southern California dream was reserved strictly for whites. Alameda Street, running from Downtown to the Harbor, and forming the western edge of the Southeast industrial district, was L.A.'s "Cotton Curtain" segregating immigrant black neighborhoods from the white-controlled job base. Blacks who crossed Alameda to shop in Huntington Park or South Gate risked beatings from redneck gangs with names like the "Spookhunters." In the early 1960s, as ghetto joblessness soared in an otherwise "full employment" economy, the situation became explosive. During the Watts rebellion in August 1965, black teenagers stoned the cars of white commuters, while Lynwood and South Gate police reciprocated with the beating and arrest of innocent black motorists. In the wake of rioting on its borders, the skilled white working class began to abandon the Southeast. Some entrenched themselves in the "white redoubt" of nearby Downey, but most moved to the rapidly industrializing northern tier of Orange County. Employers followed their labor force in a first wave of plant closings in the early 1970s.

This outward seepage of the Anglo population in the 1960s (−36,510) became an exodus in the 1970s (−123,812) and the 1980s (−43,734). Racial hysteria, abetted by "block-busting" in the city of Lynwood, was followed by a second wave of plant closings in the late 1970s. Much of the trucking industry, escaping gridlock and land inflation, migrated to new industrial zones in the Inland Empire, fifty miles east of L.A. And disastrously, within the short space of the "Volker recession," local heavy industry—including the entirety of the auto-tire-steel complex—collapsed in the face of relentless Japanese and Korean competition. In most cases, plant closure followed within a few years of watershed black and Chicano breakthroughs in shop-floor seniority and local union leadership. While white workers for the most part were able to retire or follow their jobs to the suburban periphery, nonwhites were stranded in an economy that was suddenly minus 50,000 high-wage manufacturing and trucking jobs.

Unlike Detroit or Youngstown, however, L.A.'s derelict industrial core was not simply abandoned. Almost as fast as *Fortune* 500 corporations shut down their L.A. branch plants, local capitalists rushed in to take advantage of the Southeast's cheap leases, tax incentives, and burgeoning supply of immigrant Mexican labor. Minimum-wage apparel and furniture makers, fleeing land inflation in Downtown L.A., were in the vanguard of the movement. Within the dead shell of heavy manufacturing, a new sweatshop economy emerged.

The old Firestone Rubber and American Can plants, for

instance, have been converted into nonunion furniture factories, while the great Bethlehem Steel Works on Slauson
Avenue has been replaced by a hot-dog distributor, a
Chinese food-products company, and a maker of rattan
patio furniture. Chrysler Maywood is now a bank "back office," while U.S. Steel has metamorphosed into a warehouse
complex and the "Assyrian" wall of Uniroyal Tire has become a façade for a designer-label outlet center. (On the
other hand, the area's former largest employer, GM South
Gate, remains a ninety-acre vacant lot.)

A FAMILY DICTATORSHIP

Although on a site-by-site average, two high-wage heavy
manufacturing jobs have been replaced by only one low-
wage sweatshop or warehouse job, the aggregate employment level in the Southeast has been sustained at 80 to 85
percent of its 1970s peak by the infiltration of hundreds of
small employers. The secret formula of this new, low-wage
"reindustrialization" has been the combination of a seemingly infinite supply of immigrant labor from Mexico and
Central America with the entrepreneurial energy of East
Asia. Chinese diaspora capital (whose second language in
Los Angeles is as likely to be Spanish as English) has been
particularly vigorous in such sectors as food processing,
apparel, novelties, and furniture, which employ large
minimum-wage work forces of Latino immigrants. As a result, much of southeast L.A. County has come to resemble
a free-trade zone or manufacturing platform of ambiguous
nationality. Along Telegraph Road in the aptly named City
of Commerce, for instance, the yellow sun of the Republic
of China (Taiwan) flies side by side with the stars and stripes,
while billboards advertise beer and cigarettes in Spanish.

The nation-state, moreover, yields real sovereignty to the city-states, which contain most of L.A. County's industrial assets. Exploiting the prerogatives of California's promiscuous constitution, a half-dozen industrial districts have incorporated themselves, almost without residential populations, as independent cities, selfishly enabled to monopolize land use and tax resources. The oldest, and strangest, of these "phantom cities" is the City of Vernon—the industrial *hacienda* to which Eduardo, Miguel, and thousands of their *compañeros* commute each morning for work.

The two most important facts about Vernon are: first, that it has a permanent residential population of only 90 adult citizens (70 of them municipal employees and their families living in city-owned housing) but a work force of more than 48,000—that is to say, a resident-to-commuter ratio of 600:1. Second, the city has been controlled by a single family, the Basque-origin Leonis dynasty, since its formation in 1905.

Originally established to provide a safe haven for "sporting" activities (e.g., boxing, gambling, drinking, etcetera) under attack by Los Angeles's early municipal reformers, Vernon evolved during the 1920s into an "exclusively industrial" (official city motto) base for eastern corporate branch plants. Under the iron heel of John Leonis, city founder, existing housing was condemned or bought out in order to reduce the residential population to a handful of loyal retainers living in the literal shadow of the Hitler-bunker-like City Hall. Elections in Vernon thereby became a biennial farce where the Leonis slate (now headed by grandson Leonis Malburg) is *unanimously* reelected by a micro-citizenry of Leonis employees. (Although civic officials are required to live in the city of their election, Mayor Malburg has for decades brazenly flouted state law by residing in a family mansion in Los Angeles.)

This family dictatorship has been routinely accepted by Vernon industrialists in exchange for exceedingly low tax rates and high standards of municipal police and fire services. Conversely, Vernon cityhood has been a disaster for the city of Los Angeles, which has lost perhaps 20 percent of its potential industrial property-tax base. Now Vernon is angling to establish a "community redevelopment" project that will authorize it to withhold $873 million in tax revenues from the county general fund (i.e., schools, welfare, and hospitals) over the next generation. The primary beneficiaries of this raid on the county treasury—to be used to "modernize" the city's older plant and warehouse sites—will be Vernon's major landowners: a list headed by the Santa Fe Railroad Land Company (now Catellus Development—forty-one parcels) and hizzoner Leonis Malburg (nineteen parcels).

The thousand-odd pages of documents used to argue Vernon's case for redevelopment inadvertently unmask an economy capitalized on poverty and pollution. A detailed survey of local wages, for example, reveals that 96 percent of Vernon's 48,000 workers earn incomes so low that they would qualify for public housing assistance. At least 58 percent of this largely unorganized work force fall into the official "very low income" category, making less than half the county median—a dramatic downturn from the area's union-wage norms twenty years before.

Moreover, this low-wage army is working under conditions of increasing toxicity. Vernon has long been the worst air polluter in the county; but public health officials in nearby communities are most worried by the 365 hazardous material use or storage sites within the city. A recent investigation by the California Public Interest Research Group revealed that Vernon annually emits, processes, or stores 27 million pounds of toxics—more than three times as much as the entire city of Los Angeles. As part of its early 1980s "replacement" industry—especially apparel and furniture—has begun to relocate to Mexico or East Asia, Vernon is becom-

ing increasingly dependent on an odd couple of growth industries: ethnic-food processing and toxic waste disposal. In
Vernon there is nothing unusual about a Chinese frozen-
shrimp processor being located on the same block with a
company recycling battery acids or treating industrial sol-
vents. Vernon's neighbors have been especially alarmed by
the city's plans to build an incinerator for infectious hospital
debris, as well as by a proposal to locate a plant processing
up to 60,000 gallons per day of deadly cyanide on the city
border, less than a thousand feet from overcrowded Huntington Park High School. Local activists nervously wonder
if hypertoxic Vernon might not become the Bhopal of Los
Angeles County.

RENT PLANTATIONS

Like Gaul, the Southeast is divided into three parts: 1) the
industrial incorporations, Vernon and City of Commerce,
containing nearly 100,000 jobs; 2) three "normal" suburbs,
Huntington Park, South Gate, and Lynwood, that retain
some semblance of downtowns as well as significant industrial land use; and 3) the more or less exclusively residential
and very poor cities of Bell Gardens, Cudahy, Maywood,
and Bell that have almost no industry and lack recognizable
business centers.

Jim McIntyre is city planner for Bell Gardens, the third
poorest suburb in the United States (nearby Cudahy is the
second). He is denouncing the slumlords "who turn up at
meetings in torn T-shirts pleading poverty but actually own
scores of units." He is particularly incensed that the worst
offenders include such sanctimonious types as the head of a
local realty board, the pastor of a prominent church, and the
president of the Korean-American Chamber of Commerce.

Once the "workingman's paradise," where a dust-bowl immigrant could buy a home and garden $20 down and $10 per month, Bell Gardens has become a "rent plantation," controlled by absentee landlords, where Mexican immigrants (88 percent of the population) are forced to squeeze sometimes fifteen people per unit to afford housing. McIntyre explains that local landlords can charge much higher rents than their counterparts in nearby white middle-class Downey because Bell Gardens is a "totally cash economy," catering to Mexican blue-collar workers, many of them "illegal," without bank balances or credit lines. In exchange for not requiring credit checks or deposits, landlords routinely demand extortionate rents for units that they fail to maintain or repair. Tenants adapt to the high cost of housing by overcrowding.

As a result, population densities in Bell Gardens as well as Huntington Park, Cudahy, and Maywood are beginning to approach the threshold of New York (26,000 people per square mile). Since officially, by the 1990 census, the population in eight residential Southeast cities has grown by 85,145, while the housing stock has declined by 1,120 units, the person-per-dwelling ratio has had to increase by nearly a third. In effect, this has been accomplished by a variety of strategies. In tiny Maywood, where the computer breakers live, "hotbedding" (rotating occupancy of the same bed) is common. In South Gate, once the richest of Southeast communities, every other garage has been illegally converted into a rental unit. In Cudahy, the poorest and densest of all, "victory garden" lots, 60 feet wide and as much as 390 feet deep, which were designed for a bungalow, a chicken house, and an orchard, now accommodate "six-pack" stucco tenements three or four deep—in effect, continuous barracks housing as many as 125 people on a former single-family site.

Southeast local governments have reacted to this overcrowding crisis by trying to restrict the supply of illegal or tenement housing. Rather than seeking assistance to meet the demand for low-income housing, they have torn down cheap housing in order to build strip malls or up-scale town houses. The explicit aim has been to reduce (or "stabilize") the number of poor renters, while importing new tax resources in the form of retail businesses and middle-class residents. Thus Bell Gardens destroyed a poor neighborhood on its west side in order to build a shopping center and poker casino, while Huntington Park, the area's most ardent "gentrifier," has actually reduced its housing stock by 3 percent. Even the apparently laudable local effort to enforce building codes against slumlords and the owners of illegal garage conversions is fundamentally a stratagem to limit the growth of the renter population, not a serious crusade to improve housing conditions.

Meanwhile, a sea of children has simply overwhelmed the aging physical plant of the Southeast schools (Region B of Los Angeles Unified). Over the last quarter-century, as 204,000 aging Anglos have been replaced by 328,000 young Latinos, the median age in the Southeast has fallen from thirty to thirty-two to eighteen to twenty. There are 125,000 children in the area, almost double the number in 1960. Although local secondary schools are among the largest in the country and have long operated on staggered year-round schedules, they have failed to absorb the burgeoning teenage population. New students in the Southeast are now immediately bused across Los Angeles, as far as the San Fernando Valley. The shortfall in school capacity was aggravated in 1988–89 by the closures of elementary schools in Cudahy and South Gate after the discovery of dangerous chemical contamination in their playgrounds. (In the case of Park Avenue Elementary, kindergarteners found toxic tars and methane gas bubbling under their swings.)

Nor has the school district been able to adequately address the needs of students who, in nine out of ten cases, now come from Spanish-speaking households. There have been numerous battles between majority-Anglo teaching staffs and Latino parents incensed over low test scores and 50 percent high school dropout rates. Despite the Southeast's population, there is no nearby community college, and per capita recreational space is a tiny fraction of the county average. It is not surprising, therefore, that many local kids—betrayed by bad schools and predestined for sweatshop jobs—choose, instead, to join the flourishing gang subculture. Although the Southeast is not yet a full-fledged war zone like South Central L.A., it offers a broad array of *las vidas locas*, from traditional local gangs like Florentia and Clara (Street), to newer affiliations like the all-around-town 18th Street supergang.

"Law and order" in the Southeast long meant keeping blacks out of the area. Now, more than anything, it has become carte blanche to terrorize Latino youngsters, especially suspected gang members. A few sensational cases hint at widespread practices. Several years ago two Huntington Park policemen were prosecuted for "torturing" a gang member with an electric cattle prod. In 1990, twenty-two sheriffs based at the Lynwood station were accused of illegal beatings and shootings in a federal class-action lawsuit filed by eighty-one local victims, most of them Latino or black. In spring 1991, while the world was watching the LAPD club Rodney King on video, a superior court jury convicted three officers for a savage beating of a Latino suspect in the Maywood jail the previous year.

ROTTEN BOROUGHS

Unfortunately, police brutality, like sweatshop wages and overcrowded housing, has become routine fare in the communities of the Southeast. The Latino majority (mainly immigrants from west-central Mexico, especially Jalisco) is as effectively disfranchised as were blacks in Mississippi a generation ago. Although the population of the Southeast has increased by 174,000 since the 1960s, the active electorate has *shrunk* by 40,000 votes (from one-half of the population to less than one-sixth). A geriatric Anglo residue, only 6 percent of the total population, remains an electoral majority, dominating politics in a region that is now 90 percent Latino. In Bell Gardens (population 42,000), for example, 600 aged Anglos outpolled 300 Latinos in April 1990 to re-elect an all-white city council. Indeed, until the April elections, only three out of thirty councilpeople in a bloc of six Southeast cities had Spanish surnames (the number has now increased, by election and appointment, to seven).

Latino powerlessness in the Southeast is a collusion of demography, citizen status, and benign neglect by the Democratic party. The restrictive electoral mathematics work as follows: first, deducting the large number of children on the Latino side of the ledger reduces the population ratio from 9:1 to 5:1 (adults). Second, a large percentage of adult Latino residents are noncitizens. Accepting the high-range figure ventured by Jim McIntyre in Bell Gardens of 60 percent, the overwhelming Latino majority is further whittled down to a ratio of 2.5:1 or even 2:1 (potential electorates). At this point, the actual balance of power is a function of electoral mobilization, which, in turn, depends on issue salience and political resources. Given the partisan propensities of blue-collar Latinos, it seems logical to assume that Democrats would make major efforts to activate this electorate.

To date, however, they have failed to make a significant investment in voter registration. To understand why not, it is necessary to evoke the peculiar geopolitical evolution of the region. Until reapportionment in the early 1970s, the Southeast had a strongly reinforced political identity from overlapping state and federal legislative boundaries, making it a key prize in long struggles between liberal and conservative Democrats, and infusing local councilmanic politics with the larger passions of assembly or congressional rivalries. In the 1940s and 1950s, for example, the Southeast's Twenty-third Congressional District was the crucible of repeated attempts by large CIO locals to create a liberal-labor political majority. By the 1960s, however, racial hysteria eclipsed class consciousness, and the region became the bedrock of the statewide anti–school integration and anti–fair housing campaigns led by reactionary assemblyman Floyd Wakefield of South Gate. Partially to punish Wakefield and to break up his political base, the Democratic state legislature redrew electoral boundaries to distribute fragments of the old Twenty-third C.D. among districts anchored by black majority votes in South Central L.A. The legislature's nullification of the Southeast as a distinctive political entity, together with the reliability of the black vote, vastly diminished Democratic attention to the fate of nonpartisan local politics. At the same time, Latino civil rights and community-power movements in Los Angeles County have almost totally concentrated on mobilizing neighborhoods with high percentages of Chicano (second-through-fourth-generation Mexican-American) homeowners and middle-income earners. Only desultory resources have been made available to such port-of-entry areas for Mexican and Central American immigrants as the Southeast, Boyle Heights (east of Downtown), or the Westlake District (west of Downtown). Although the recent election of Gloria Molina as the first Spanish-surname L.A. County supervisor in the twentieth century has rekindled rhetoric about the "Latino decade," grass-roots activists in the Southeast have yet to see even Chicano Democrats focus adequately on the problems of their rotten borough.

Indeed, to the extent that power sharing—which, of

course, is different from empowerment—is occurring in the Southeast, it is being instigated from the right. The two Latinos, for example, elected last year to the Huntington Park city council were both Republicans, and there is evidence that the county Republican campaign fund operated by ex-supervisor Peter Schabarum is playing a significant role in encouraging conservative Latino businessmen to run for office. In Bell Gardens, community activists criticized the appointment of businesswoman and police advocate Rosa Maria Hernandez, to fill a council vacancy, as a crude attempt by the Anglo leadership to placate the community symbolically without surrendering any real power. Others worry that as elderly white voters die off, the old Anglo business elite will simply be replaced by a look-alike clique of conservative Latino realtors and shopkeepers elected by an attenuated and unrepresentative electorate.

Poker Faces

In the meantime, the still-dominant Anglo establishment has enjoyed a generation of untrammeled control over municipal affairs. The shrinkage of the electorate in the early seventies and the disappearance of the big union locals as political actors, combined with Anglo solidarity and paranoia, consolidated the power of local chamber of commerce types, ruling from smoke-filled rooms in relaxed unaccountability. In Huntington Park, for example, the same five Anglo businessmen (with one substitution) composed the city council from 1970 to 1990 (three still remain). In Bell Gardens, Claude Booker, the city manager who has also been councilman, represents a continuity of power from the 1960s. In other cities, power has alternated between conservative cliques with only the rare reformist candidate (like

UAW leader Henry Gonzales in South Gate) to brighten the picture.

The chief interest of these "good ole boys" has been to manipulate the lucrative pork barrel of redevelopment. California law allows municipalities to fight "blight" with urban renewal financed by tax increments withheld from the general fund. In smaller cities, the city council acts as the executive of the redevelopment agency, which typically means that the same local realtors and businessmen who will benefit directly from renewal are also its administrators. "Blight," moreover, has become a conveniently elastic category, encompassing everything from too many railroad spurs in Vernon to too many poor renters in Bell Gardens or Huntington Park.

In the Balkanized landscape of the Southeast, redevelopment has devolved into a crazy zero-sum competition between impoverished municipalities. While the Lilliputian towns of Maywood, Bell, and Cudahy wager scarce tax resources in a "war of supermarkets" along Atlantic Boulevard, the larger cities—Huntington Park, South Gate, and Lynwood—struggle to resurrect central shopping districts wiped out by the competition of regional malls in Downey and Carson. The result is excessive strip development, a redundancy of franchises, and profligate sales-tax abatement. Never having recovered from the twin blows of plant closure and Proposition 13 in the late 1970s, most Southeast communities have only exacerbated their fiscal distress with overly ambitious and poorly targeted redevelopment projects. Huntington Park, for example, has almost ruined itself in the course of revitalizing its Pacific Avenue shopping corridor, while South Gate lost a quarter of its sales-tax income when one heavily subsidized car dealership suddenly went bankrupt.

In the face of the unforeseen costs of retail modernization, gambling on redevelopment has literally become redevelopment by gambling. For decades, Southeast citizens' groups, led by the Methodist Church, had successfully resisted attempts by outside gambling interests to establish poker parlors (a constitutional local option in California). But with the attrition of the electorate in the late 1970s, pro-gambling forces managed to legalize card casinos in Bell, Commerce, Bell Gardens, Huntington Park, and Cudahy. Using their redevelopment powers to discount land to casino developers, these five cities have attempted to utilize gambling as a tax generator to keep housing and retail development alive.

The record is mixed. Bell Gardens' Bicycle Club, the largest card casino in the country (and perhaps the world), turns over $100 million of gross profits each year, $10 to $12 million of which become local tax revenue—most of it immediately loaned to the city's aggressive redevelopment program. The giant 120-table Commerce Casino generates almost as much cashflow as the Bicycle Club and has long been the city's chief source of revenue. In Bell, Cudahy, and Huntington Park, on the other hand, smaller-scale casinos have collapsed in bankruptcy (although a new Bell casino has emerged). Whether solvent or not, however, each card club has offered seductive opportunities to councilmen and their cronies.

In the Bell case, Mayor Pete Werrlein, a council member for sixteen years and archtypical "good ole boy," convinced anxious Anglo voters that without the additional revenue from poker, the police would be unable to protect them from an influx of "dangerous Mexican gangs." Shortly after the opening of the California Bell Club in 1980, however, the county grand jury revealed that Werrlein, together with his city administrator and the former police chief of Huntington Park, had been engaged in "sex orgies" in a Cudahy warehouse with eighteen-year-old prostitutes supplied by Kenneth Bianchi—a.k.a. the Hillside Strangler, L.A.'s most notorious serial murderer. Two years later, in 1984, Werrlein and the city administrator were indicted for bribery, fraud, and racketeering when their secret ownership of the Bell Club was exposed.

Hard on the heels of the Bell scandal, the ex-mayor of Commerce and two councilmen were arrested in a similar hidden shareholding conspiracy, this time in partnership with Vegas mobsters. Perennial rumors that the casinos are laundries for drug money were partially confirmed in 1990 when the Feds seized the almighty Bicycle Club after evidence emerged that the casino had been financed with coke-tainted dollars. Finally, throughout the spring of 1991, the old-guard three-Anglo majority on the Huntington Park council has waited nervously for the district attorney to issue possible indictments in an ongoing investigation that links them to a profit-skimming operation at the city's now bankrupt card club.

SUPER-PAN NINE

As the sun plunges into the ocean off Venice Beach the yellow-brown smog over Southeast L.A. suddenly turns pastel in a cheap imitation of an Ed Ruscha painting. The two square-block parking lots of the Bicycle Club are already full, and several thousand Friday paychecks have been converted into poker chips. Around the seven-card stud and Texas hold-'em tables, the professional card cheats are sizing up an excited mob of bikers, housewives, truck drivers, hippies, and senior citizens—all of them wearing their best poker face. They are sweet meat to the cheats, who are usually tolerated by the management as long as they keep the tables busy.

But the real action is happening at the other half of the casino devoted to Asian card games. On the super-pan nine tables there is no bluff or bluster, just silence and intense concentration as the dealers fire cards from 432-card stacks and players respond with volleys of $100 bills. Over half of the club's income now comes from the high-speed, high-stake play of the Asian games. For the intrigued but uninitiated player, there are convenient instruction sheets in English, Chinese, Korean, Spanish, Vietnamese, and Cambodian. In the exclusive inner sanctum of the Asian Room, off-limits to ordinary punters, wealthy Chinese and Korean businessmen, some of whom own nearby factories and warehouses, venture a year's sweatshop wages in a single hand. They accept their losses with icy composure.

Meanwhile, a few miles away, a man is standing in the twilight on the curb of Alameda Street selling oranges. Behind him is the vast empty lot, overgrown with jimsonweed and salt grass, that used to be General Motor's South Gate assembly plant. He has been standing on Alameda, gagging on smog and carbon monoxide, since seven in the morning. A bag of plump but second-rate navel oranges costs $1. He has sold twenty-five bags and will be allowed to keep half his earnings by the boss who drops him off in the morning and picks up in the evening. He is anxious because he still has three bags left to sell.

There are at least a thousand other men—most of them destitute recent arrivals from Central America—selling oranges on freeway ramps and busy street corners in L.A. I ask him in broken Spanish if he is Salvadoran or Guatemalan. He replies in abrupt English that he was born in San Antonio and until 1982 was a machinist making $12 per hour in nearby Lynwood. When his shop went out of business, he was certain that he could easily find another job. He hasn't, and at age fifty-two he is selling oranges for $12 a day. So that's his story, and if my curiosity is satisfied, how about buying three bags of oranges? I pay him, he shuffles off, and when I get home I discover that the oranges have a strangely bitter taste.

SEX

MELTING

H e was driving by school to pick me up and take me home. Outside John Marshall High at 3:15 P.M. everyone was always getting rides from everyone. That and smoking over by the side wall. If it was a Tuesday, those boys who had given their chosen girls their Y club jackets to wear (satin Eisenhower jobs, the kind that dedicated Dodger fans wear now) might sidle up and ask for them back. If it was Wednesday, the same thing went on with letterman sweaters. These were delicious encounters, taking those garments, still warm from their bodies, giving them back seven hours later, still warm from yours . . . .

But this afternoon wasn't a Tuesday or a Wednesday, and

I wasn't in some sweet boy's favor. An older man had come into our drama class the week before; he went to UCLA, he said. He'd written a play. Would we like to put it on? (Even the dumbest of us recognized this as a transparent ploy to meet girls.) And I don't remember how it happened but he lived close enough to me to take me home, so I waited as little deuce coupes sped up and down the ribbon street in the heart of white L.A., each rear-view mirror decorated—if there were good boys driving—with stuffed pairs of hand-knit argyle socks, no more than three inches long, the designs done in angora, the heels turned perfectly. If they were bad boys, they couldn't drive their low-riders without hanging their left arms out of the car with cigarettes dangling negligently from their grimy, lock-picking fingers.

So I waited. Black flats, circle skirt, borrowed blouse—since I was poor—curled hair, books pressed to my chest. Then there was a steaming and a grinding and a jangling and a puffing and wheezing, and a huge brown Chrysler, with its axle all screwed up so that it dragged along sideways like a wounded roach, shuddered to a stop in front of me. Walter Wong, as I shall call him, beautiful and slightly almond-eyed, motioned for me to get in. Though every cell in my practical, poor, virginal, unloved Irish body told me that this was not the way to keep my nose clean and move *up*, I got in.

My memory tells me that before we had even left the brick façade of Marshall High behind us, we began a conversation that changed our lives, and made us authorities on melting. Walter allowed as how he was a quarter Chinese, and I said, clutching my books, that I loved Anna May Wong—she had been my favorite movie star when I was little. He said, driving with one hand in this newspaper-strewn, crappy monument of a motorcar, that he had played poker with Anna May Wong the week before, that Anna May was a friend of the family.

I'm not sure how to go on from here. My own unhappy adolescence is not the way to go. The three years between the time Walter and I took that drive and the hot February day we got married in the Unitarian Church on Eighth and Vermont. No. The church was having its own troubles then, with FBI men taking snapshots of every living human who postulated the possibility that there might be a Progressive God, a Liberal Higher Power, and that He/She might be best found in the same church where they insisted on holding Paul Robeson concerts, but that's not the way to go—except to say that there were couches in the upstairs room of that church on either side of the fireplace to accommodate the prostrate mothers whose sons and daughters were embarking on mixed or otherwise unsuitable marriages.

And not the way, either, to say that after I graduated from high school I moved immediately into the home of my best friend. Her single mother, a nice woman, had some pretty permissive moral habits, but she drew the line at Walter Wong. When Walter came to call, he brought three or four full-blooded Chinese uncles and cousins, and they would stand around outside on her lawn. That's where she drew the line, because no matter that she had a hundred chinchillas dying from neglect in her garage, no matter that she often slept in her dress and went to work without changing her stockings from the day before, a flock of Chinese out on the lawn was another thing entirely.

I suppose the thing to write is that once in that three years, my girlfriend and I went on a double date with two nice boys; angora socks hung from the rear-view mirror, and my friend had already rapped out smartly to the driver, "Get your hand off my knee!" We had gone to a movie, eaten hamburgers at Bob's Big Boy, and were on our way home along Riverside Drive, when one of the three of them said, "Look at that!" Chugging alongside us in a big, brown, lopsided bug of a car was a guy who looked like Fu Manchu, screaming to himself and making faces. It's a mark of friendship's endurance that when my friend turned around and said, "Carolyn's gone *out* with that guy," and they all laughed, I forgave her even then—but I didn't invite her to the wedding.

During those three years, when Walter Wong and I sometimes went out (driving, never on a date, never anywhere in public), he would tell me about his life. Other times, when he didn't like me, I'd slink around in search of his life. Ten o'clock at night, in genuine Chinatown, with real fog, upstairs from a splendid art store, behind shrouded windows in soft yellow light, the full-blooded half of his family lived. Again, how do you trace it or tell it? From the top: Walter's grandfather, a ten-year-old orphan, came over in the 1880s from Canton. According to stories of the Wong family, that boy went up and down central California selling crotchless underwear to prostitutes; also selling tickets to a "mermaid" that he pushed around in a wheelbarrow. ("Where *is* that mermaid?" my ex–mother-in-law muttered a few years back. "I've got it around here somewhere.") In due time, Wong hooked up with a penniless Irish girl, known to me, in story only, as "Ma." With "Ma" he built up a business in L.A. Oriental art, instant antiques, brass items left out all night in dung to age. But these were only stories. When I saw them, Mr. Wong's art objects were precious beyond words, and beautiful, and once when Frank Lloyd Wright questioned their quality, he was whipped summarily out of the store by Mr. Wong's cane.

Wong lived with Ma and had five Eurasian children. He was Cantonese, but he was melting, melting into L.A. Yet, when he got some money together, he went back to his home village and brought back a Chinese girl. Finally, after the disgrace of the railroads, the American government was letting a few Oriental females in: had the government been afraid, in its bureaucratic, freckled, loutish way, of the sexuality of these slim, wicked, prideful, grudge-holding China-*men*?

In Los Angeles, in the teens and twenties, the two families lived on the same street: Eurasian Wongs and Chinese Wongs. The scared Chinese wife never spoke to the penniless Irish girl who could never marry her husband—although that girl bore him five beautiful children—because miscegenation was not allowed.

I never was too crazy about my Eurasian father-in-law, who worked in the *other* family business, the Eurasian-owned Oriental art store, certainly the best in town and maybe the best in America. To my mind, he was high-strung and humorless, tyrannical and tiresome. I never, while he was alive, heard his wife utter a verb. She'd start off with the subject of a sentence, pause, and he'd finish: verb and direct object. Surely how they spoke as a couple was their business, but that man disliked me intensely: he made me a wedding ring of hammered 24-carat gold, then took it back for "repairs" after a couple of weeks, and I never saw it again. I took it personally then, in the fifties, but I see now that his anger was generational, racial. His father had reached for an Irish girl; melting. He had done the same thing. His quiet, one-syllable wife was an exquisite woman with red-gold hair, a girl from the inland badlands of Southern California; a girl who was a functional orphan when he found her; a plucky, lonely girl who, when she was seventeen, had suffered diphtheria and been "put in the pest house, across the Los Angeles River."

I believe now that my Eurasian father-in-law had already had enough of melting. In a family whose men could only pick up their wives at a metaphysical K mart, he wanted something better for his son, and what did he get? Another penniless Irish girl, in love with camelback bridges and statues of Kwan Yin and the double-exposed cinematic image of Anna May Wong standing up to the Japs even after she'd been shot down, enumerating the virtues of Free China. An Irish girl in love with rice patterns in teacups and embroidered sleeve pieces done in blind stitch which had to have "room to breathe," even when they were framed. In love with ivory "medicine ladies" (those ivory figurines female patients gave their doctors to fondle, since their own bodies were not allowed to be seen) and jade bracelets and dark-wood, bright-lit Chinese restaurants where Walter would take me late at night—a teenager, having adventures—to eat jook, rice gruel with dried fish in it; Walter gazing at me sardonically as I messed inefficiently with chopsticks: a hazing process, part of the daughter-in-law routine I was to go through for five married years, as the Wong family would get on my case for reaching for the food first, or whatever.

Because—and I believe this must be true for the Chinese, the Japanese, the Koreans, the Vietnamese, the Sikhs, the Indonesians who have come in such lovely sparkling waves across the Pacific, or the Mexicans who have bravely trudged up through the abominable and almost impassable Sonoran desert—there is a bridge, a tension bridge, between fantasy and reality that closely parallels a dazzling romance and then an interminable and irritating marriage. There was and is a world of difference between the gold-burnished cavern of the Wong art store in old Chinatown with the circular door and the stone lions in front (or the gold brick from Macao that a Wong uncle showed me once, pressed into the palm of my hand then, laughing, snatched back, wrapped up, and put in his pocket), and one of the Chinese houses we'd go to on Thanksgiving, where forty lonesome Chinese bachelors in their undershirts would eat turkey and stuffing, then crowd into the kitchen, doing hundreds and hundreds of dirty dishes, while the few women would repair to a back bedroom to make conversation about diapers, sickness, bargains; no jokes, no beauty. Sure, Anna May came to our wedding, but I saw her only a few times after that, hanging out with Eurasians, perhaps, because her own folks, her extended family, took her money but didn't want her company: they had to draw the line somewhere.

I'm talking about melting. Not about the East Coast melting *pot*, where the poor and the wretched came over to push carts on the Lower East Side and bash rats in stifling tenements. I'm talking about a whole other thing. About love and money; blue skies, pink roses, air like babies' breath, abundance beyond belief—what the Chinese called, from across the peaceful ocean, the Mountain of Gold (and for once they weren't just talking gold coin). I don't think numbers are the way to figure it, or economics either. I think love is the first way to get a handle on it, that kind of love that the novelist Alison Lurie once postulated as she ate a shrimp salad on top of a Pacific palisade that looked out over Marion Davies's old mansion and the venerable merry-go-round on the Santa Monica pier: "Certain kinds of love," she said, "are like this: you see someone who is everything you're *not*. Everything you want to be, everything you can't be. You and Walter were like that." (Because by this time Walter and I were divorced.) "People see each other, and they run to each other as fast as they can, *and then they run right past each other.* So, now, you're wearing a black turtleneck and writing, and he's off somewhere married to a white Protestant." It was true. By this time Walter had married an awfully nice woman who wore pink button-down oxford shirts and Bermuda shorts; they had a house at the beach and played tennis and rode bikes on the weekends. So there's that kind of melting, that rush toward your opposite; that displacement of the ego, the rush to lose yourself in exotic love. And underneath that there is, in L.A., the wish perhaps to make love to the earth itself, disappear in it, because it's so inutterably seductive, sulky, nourishing, beautiful.

"In 1821," writes Jacqueline Higuera McMahan, "the last Spanish governor of Alta California, Pablo Vicente de Sola, granted to my great-great-great grandfather, Don José Loreto Higuera, 4,394 acres . . . a lush plain covered with noble

oaks and blue lupine, golden poppies and mustard in the
springtime. Wild oats grew so high horsemen could tie the
grasses together above their horses' saddles. . . . In this idyllic land, where few silver coins passed from hand to hand,
business affairs were bound by gentlemen's agreements, a
glass of wine and an abrazo. . . . A bowl of silver coins was
customarily left in the room of a guest, to take from as was
needed for the journey ahead. When too many visiting
Americans took the whole bowl, the old custom could no
longer be observed."

Forty years before this halcyon time, Los Angeles-the-
Town counted as its population "Europeans, 1; Spaniards,
72; Indians, 7; Mulattos, 22; and Mestizos, 30." That was
1781. Flash forward a hundred years, during which time dirt
roads got paved and the central plaza built and eucalyptus
came over here from Australia, and people dug in and grew
oranges. As in some Bible for Realtors, men in business suits
took a look at all that mustard and lupine and yucca, all
those green hills and golden plains and the Pacific just a
streetcar ride away, and they said, for better or worse, let
there be development! And anybody who could stay awake
during their California history classes knows about the great
railroad giveaways, when a ride across the United States (in
a wooden seat, no food included) could cost as little as $11.
This California dream, this immigration fever, was fueled by
travel posters of oranges as big as basketballs, mimicking the
sun, mimicking gold itself.

Immigration came in definable waves, something like the
last part of Ravel's *Bolero*. The first immigrants (and the most
consistent ones) were white folks, sick of the East, sick of the
Midwest, sick of being dealt just one not-very-good hand in
the cosmic poker game. They didn't like the farm, or the
apartment; sometimes they didn't even want to be rich—in
the same old way. They wanted a new deal, and if sometimes
it didn't work out (Nathanael West ranted about L.A., even

as he fell in love here, got happy here), well, there was no better place to fail than this temperate, laid-back Paradise.

That accounts for the whites. I don't know how the Mexicans got here except that it was their land to begin with. The whole world knows by now that after you cross an invisible boundary just east of Union Station (very close to the old boardinghouse on Clara Street where a short, scary bubonic plague epidemic started and stopped in the early part of this century), well, then, you're in *East Los*, a city that is home to more Mexicans than any other metropolis besides Mexico City. More than Mazatlán. More than Morelos. More than Guadalajara. Think of it.

War, not love, brought the next set of waves. With World War II came more: poor whites from the South and Midwest, and blacks—who found poverty in Watts, but at least a poverty that included backyards and bougainvillaea.

Then the Korean War, which certain militaristic nitwits insisted we had to fight "or else the Chinese Communists will simply invade—I mean, they'll be coming across the Pacific in a fleet of rowboats if they have to—you won't even be able to *see* the ocean!" That war, which started in 1950, was really just a savage way of saying "hi there" to our ferocious neighbors. Its ultimate result was a wave of Korean immigrants, scrupulous, cleanly, ambitious, and inordinately fond of minimalls. Somewhere behind them (but not in rowboats), a new passel of Chinese bounced off their mainland on to Taiwan or Hong Kong and then took another salubrious, really big bounce over here, to happenin' L.A. "You don't *know* these people!" one of my ex–Chinese-uncles-by-marriage told me in the early eighties (because we were all friends, or at least "speaking"; that's the point of melting). "Some of these Chinese have money. Not like our money. *New* money. You know what I mean?" But I was raised a penniless Irish girl. I didn't know what he meant, except that because of the Koreans and the Chinese, you could get barbecued beef and exquisite kimchi (that soul-food-cabbage Korean soldiers ate daily during the war so that they could cut down our boys with glee and dispatch), and that over in Alhambra and Monterey Park where the "new" Chinese money was, you could buy seafood so fresh it swam in your mouth, in a last-ditch attempt to get away.

And everyone knows the Vietnam War brought us the Vietnamese. Drugs and more war brought us Thai restaurants. If I mention these noble peoples only in terms of food, I defend myself by saying, *sure*, some financier could quote you immigration numbers or list their banks, but that doesn't tell you much. Love says something, war says something— even if it's disagreeable—sickness, death say something.

In 1980, my mother got very sick. It seemed she was dying. My mother lives in Victorville, in some senses the very farthest suburb of L.A.: east and north past Pasadena, Arcadia, Pomona, Claremont, Azusa, West Covina, Covina, San Bernardino. Past that town, there's the Low Desert (Palm Springs) or the mountains (the Cajon Pass). Over Cajon there's the High Desert, going on for hundreds of miles, across several states. On its edge, Victorville, a town some might call a godforsaken hole, but World War II and the prospect of a Great Big III have been good to it. The Space Shuttle lands nearby in sand flats; Rafer Johnson was raised there in an abandoned railroad boxcar, and that's all you used to be able to say for Victorville. In the forty years I'd known the place it possessed cowboys, an annual fiesta (Tyrone Power used to come), average temperatures of 110 degrees, scorpions in the houses and sidewinders in the street, a dude ranch or two, and a preponderance of rednecks who drank hard, had sex with people they weren't married to, and made sure the Negroes and the Mexicans stayed in their place across the tracks. "Across the tracks" was not a figure of speech.

Imagine our surprise, then, when my daughters and I

strolled the hospital halls, wondering if and when my mother
would come out of her coma, to see, moseying just in front
of us in a doctor's coat, a seven-foot Indian, an *Indian* Indian with a giant turban. Yes, this was High Desert Victorville, where as far as I know the recreation of choice, still, is
to get drunk at the Greentree Inn or the Hilton, and throw
up in the driveway in broad daylight, but shut my mouth
and turn off my lights if that guy wasn't a *Sikh*.

And during the blinding sorrow of my mother's illness,
didn't I open my eyes one day when a surgeon and an internist were having a big fight about my mother's fate (the
surgeon shouting, "Whattya you wan'? You wan' her to die
inna bed?" And the internist, equally irate, answering back,
"Whattya *you* wan'? You wan' her to die onna *table?*"), I
noticed that the people who held my mother's fate in their
delicate little hands were both Filipinos, that they both came
no higher than my shoulder, that I weighed more than both
of them put together. My mother survived because the internist won the argument. There wasn't an operation. But then
the almond-eyed physician nearly gave my mother a whole
separate heart attack by assuring her repeatedly, "Don'
worry, Kate. You *arn'* going to have a colostomy!" And, yes,
my mother's favorite nurse was Indonesian. If you were to
ask me why these diminutive Orientals chose this scorching
outpost of the wild West, L.A.'s own last eastern frontier, to
build lives and purchase piano lessons for their children, I
would answer only, Orientals really *are* inscrutable. I learned
that from my marriage to Walter. (Maybe they have their
own melting fantasies that have to do with sweating to death,
who knows?) Maybe they were only happy minnows in a
great big wave.

Why not admit it? After my marriage to Walter, I married a
Slovak. Our relationship, though respectably long, was a

stormy one. I won't say what *he* did, but I went to the trouble of looking up a book put out by the United Nations that said Slovaks were the very last "civilized people" to worship fire —they worshiped fire up until 1926. I reminded that Slovak of this fire worship quite often.

So I was divorced again, and you'd think I'd learn, but out here we all have another think coming. Some time during the eight years after my second divorce, when, as my father might have said, I went out with "some fairly miscellaneous people," there came a night in the little house up in Topanga Canyon where I lived with my two daughters, Lisa and Clara, when some dingbat single-mother friend of mine brought up, as a member of her own ongoing, scruffy entourage, a stocky, bearded, chubby-handed Mexican. An artist, a victim of divorce himself, he had a kid with him, a cute little girl about three, named Coco. He was looking to melt, pronto. He needed heavy domestic help.

No, I don't mean this to become the demented memoirs of some sex-crazed Casanovette. I mean only to illustrate how divorce, as much as love or war or economic need, becomes a factor in melting, allowing folks to meet who might never have socialized in any way. In Los Angeles in the early 1970s, the large racial, geographical configurations were still simple and straightforward. Whites to the west, blacks to the south, Mexicans in *East Los*, Asians a dot in the middle. The north taken up by scrubby hills, or the desert, or up along the coast, Santa Barbara, or missiles in their missile bases. Blacks and Mexicans might venture west to commit crimes or work in dead-end, demeaning jobs, but the whites who went east and south were few and far between. That may be one of twenty reasons why Los Angeles Man invented freeways: there had to be some means of driving south to Disneyland without going through Watts; some way to hit Palm Springs without driving through a Mexican city bigger than Guadalajara.

Divorce, when it hit L.A. in the sixties and seventies, was a bigger quake than the Big Quake, if you follow me. Suddenly things were not what they seemed. A friend of mine, living in a then-safe white bedroom community in the San Fernando Valley, found herself—around 1971—no longer part of a nice family with three children and a patio in back but an overworked, economically terrified single mother with three children. She had the choice of going to work or going on welfare. In those days the job of choice for a woman who had a liberal arts B.A. and a driver's license and was otherwise unemployable was to become a social worker, helping other women who did not have a liberal arts B.A. or a driver's license, or even a car. Every day my friend saw her three kids off to school and drove down into Watts, where she weathered postriot disdain, had a few rocks thrown at her car, and learned about another kind of life—not, it turned out, terribly different from our own. She took me with her a few times, and what I liked was that though these large, beautiful black women had, in all cases, been abandoned, they were not suffering from it. They had slipped out of the configuration: they played records, read magazines, did each other's hair, and once in a while went out to talk to the flocks of swains who lingered outside on their dying lawns.

So things were not what they had seemed. "I was driving home from Watts one night, dead tired," my friend told me, "and they said on the news that the San Fernando Valley was a hotbed of sex crime. And I thought, *Swell!* And they said that Van Nuys was especially bad. And I thought, *Great!* And they said that one square block, bounded by this street and that street and this street and that street had twenty-one registered sex offenders! And I got really bitter because I realized that square block was the square block I lived on. Then, of course, I remembered that my ex-husband was one of the offenders."

In the new scheme of things, as a decade or two rolled by, this white, well-brought-up woman friend began to teach at a community college and found a beautiful black guy twenty years her junior. They lived together very happily under a different set of rules, for about a dozen years.

If it hadn't been for divorce and this new scheme of things, I would never have met Frank Romero. A chubby Mexican would never have found his way up into the woods of Topanga. If I had not been desperate to get away, to get out from under responsibilities I couldn't handle, if I hadn't felt that I wasn't sure what I wanted, but I certainly knew what I *didn't* want and that was the hand I was currently holding, I wouldn't have had the world's shortest romance with a Chicano artist. "Geez," Frank once remarked mildly to me, "do you always have to introduce me to your friends as "Frank, the Chicano artist? Couldn't you just say, like, *Frank?*"

What I knew, then, of Mexican life in L.A. (that's almost one-half of this city, remember, and I've lived here all my life) was only the food and the music that everybody who had any style knew about—and the life of Frank Romero. He had bought a big house, at a bargain price, on the east side of Echo Park, the south side of Sunset, near Downtown, up on a hill with a nice smoggy view. He'd begun to take apart the kitchen, one side of it painted cinnamon red and bright sky blue, another wall totally caved in, a mountain of mustard-colored stucco rubble. "I haven't decided what to do with that yet," he said cheerfully. His mother must have taken care of Coco; someone did, some older woman to whom he was continually saying on the phone, "I'm very *upset* about this," but in the mildest possible voice.

I'd scored a junket for some magazine having to do with night life in Mazatlán—ten days in the just-opened Camino Real Hotel. I invited Frank to go down with me, thinking, from a practical point of view, what better escort than a Mexican? It was not a successful trip. At the border it turned out that we needed birth certificates (or we could walk down the street, pay somebody $3, swear to some clerk that we were who we were, come back, and *then* cross the border). Frank Romero became expressionless and gained twenty pounds on the spot. "I can't understand what he's saying." I translated. "I don't have a birth certificate." I explained what was needed. But it took a couple of hours to persuade Frank Romero that the $3 would be well spent, that he didn't have to stand there like a big furry buffalo looking dense. Well, you can see that I was in a divorced harridan phase. But also, Frank had melted. He was Mexican enough to remember how to take being bullied and oppressed, to know enough not to mess with the government, *any* government, but he had forgotten his own language, never been south of his own border before this trip, and didn't even know the concept of the *mordita*, those government-sanctioned bribes that keep the roofs over Mexican bureaucrats' heads.

Frank told me lots of stories on that journey. I've forgotten them all, knowing, even then, that our acquaintance would be short. But he was a nice person and he owes something to our family. On a day trip to the beach, back here in L.A., he was spacing out, as usual, letting the sand into his sandals, wearing street clothes right down to the water. That is *Mexican*, remember; in Mazatlán and Manzanillo, whole families approach the beach with all their clothes on and refrain from swimming; they recline, rather, in laughing or serious groups, just at that three-foot margin where the ocean meets land, and let sand and foam swarm over them. But Coco, third generation, walked into that water and got carried out by a wave. Frank and I stood paralyzed. Surely, I thought, he's going to save his daughter! He can't be that much of a space case! My own younger daughter, Clara, daughter of the fiery, athletic Slovak, gave us both the scathing glance we deserved, dove into the Pacific herself, and dragged out the waterlogged Coco, dropping the toddler at her father's feet.

Frank owes us his daughter. I hope he reads this and remembers the familial debt, and here's why. Frank really *was* a "Chicano artist." Several years after we'd stopped seeing each other, he became part of a group called "Los Four," a lovely name designed to show that they had feet in each camp, in each country. Los Four consisted of Carlos Almaraz, who went on to become very rich and famous; Gilbert Lujan, who hated the social-climbing part of the art world and took his work back to East L.A.; Frank; and a man I don't remember. When I was seeing Frank, they were all the kind of guys who might hang out on your lawn or get out in the driveway with a six-pack, looking serious and inept as they tried to fix their cars.

For a long time, Frank had experimented with a series called "Elephants and Stars." They really didn't work very well. He gave my oldest daughter, Lisa, a watercolor of a train, with the handwritten caption, "Your Good Girl Is Going Bad." It was a toy train, because Frank was a sweet guy; he liked toys, he liked to play. While Carlos and Gilbert were "protesting," composing great, serious murals, Frank kept working on little dorky cars. There was a stubbornness in that: you could see the little kid in him, hunched over. "Leave me alone! I want to play with my *car!*" He drew me a little watercolor of the old Topanga house, with him as a suitor, in a little toy car at the bottom of a chaparral-covered cliff.

Time passed. Driving the freeways you'd see Gilbert's work. Carlos got himself an unlisted number with a garbled message on his machine because he needed so much privacy. One day, downtown, stuck near the Civic Center in a traffic jam, I looked over at a freeway wall, and there, catching the afternoon sun, was a vivid mural, a fleet of great big toy cars? Way to go, Frank! A year or so after that there was Frank's work in a gallery. Those little wooden cars he used to carve were going for eight thousand dollars and the paintings were selling for fifteen. I thought, just a little sourly,

way to go, Frank! And the last straw came from *Time* magazine, which never gave *me* anything but a snippy review, but
here's what they said about Frank: "The 'obsessive urbanism'
of Los Angeles Barrio painter Frank Romero, for whom the
recurrent image of the car, that chariot of the ego, turns up
even in toy form in a passionately brushed still life." Way
to go.

So, Frank, if you're reading, I just want to say this. Remember our two weeks in Mexico and how I only got a little
upset when it turned out you'd "forgotten" to get gas in
Caborca, either because you were too shy or because you
couldn't remember that "*Lleno, por favor*" was how you said
"fill 'er up"? And there we were, running on empty through
the Sonora Desert and you kept *smiling* about it? Remember
the sea-drenched breezes that whiffled the blinds of the
Camino Real? Remember the thunder and lightning at
breakfast and the iguana on the windowsill? Remember sitting in that swimming pool on a barstool drinking margaritas
with parasols in them? Remember everything I told you
about Mexican music? Remember *Coco* and what a cute
little kid she used to be?

Here's the way it was, Frank. My oldest daughter, Lisa,
got married, and she took "Your Good Girl Is Going Bad"
with her. It hangs over her upstairs fireplace and every time
I see it I get a twinge. I'm just wondering now if you could
spare one of those toy cars, Frank, one of those "chariots
of the ego" you must have around the house. Because
my watercolor is very small and it isn't even signed, because
who *knew*, then, in the Los Angeles scheme of things, that
even *Time* magazine would melt before the vision of your
spacey cosmos? Old time's sake, Frank. Running at each
other and past each other. I'm still up in Topanga, *amigo
mio*. Yearning for a cute little car that never runs out of
gas.

Here I begin to speak from an old family story, one of those tales that get spun this way and that with no expectation that the slightest detail will ever be got right, because the dozenth time around, everybody has some kind of axe to grind, some kind of point to prove about whether somebody is a good person or a bad person, so don't take *my* word for it. This is only a story about Melting. Sometime around seven years into his second marriage, and here I speak speculatively, Walter Wong must have begun to feel that he had *had* it.

He'd had these disturbing thoughts before: "You don't know what it means to be a marginal *man!*" he'd declaim, waving his arms like Alexandra Danilova in her last days at the Ballet Russe de Monte Carlo. But one of the sorrows of humankind is that they aren't that hot at tuning in to each others' dramas; they're listening too intently to their own. I'd be sitting on the couch, during our marriage, in our poor-but-pure graduate-student bungalow, trying to change my status from penniless Irish girl to learned woman of letters, always reading (it seemed for years) Susanne K. Langer's *Philosophy in a New Key*. It took me forever to get through it because here was this semi-Eurasian shouting around the living room, "I'm a marginal *man*, and I'll never get over it!" I had a hard time getting past page twenty-seven.

Other days, when Walter told stories of his youth and childhood, I'd listen raptly. Those stories were what I craved and loved, and saw in my mind as he drew pictures: a basement apartment just west of Clara Street, downstairs from a sidewalk in old Chinatown, *real* Chinatown, where, during World War II, Union Station reigned supreme. In that old, real Chinatown—destroyed even by then, forever—his beautiful red-headed mom swept the floor and chased rats with the same broom. There, in an incredible mixture of the squalid and the spotless, she raised her son and her little brother. No couch—in my memory that family never had a couch—but great stone lions on either side of their tenement front door. Inside, there must have been that intoxicating mixture of the scents of furniture polish, fresh oranges, and sandalwood, that fresh, smart, sassy aroma my mother-in-law created around her always.

What had I grown up with, I thought on my bad days, except the ability to turn a square corner on a bed and an in-depth knowledge of chipped beef on toast? Didn't Walter know he was lucky, *lucky*?

No, he didn't know. He was a "marginal man," he wore shirts of Afghan cotton and he'd go with that. (When his Chinese uncles bought American ski gear and we all went skiing, Walter came flapping down the mountain like Saint Joseph in some sixth-grade nativity play.) Then, after a while, Walter would get sick of bemoaning his marginality and start up a war game with water pistols, careening through the house with his Chinese buddies and relatives. I'd think dark thoughts, and I was only the *first* wife who didn't understand him.

Time for a digression. One of those uncles, a handsome full-blooded Chinese, once went on a buying trip to Japan and spent one fateful night at the home of a wealthy Japanese merchant, whose daughter came slinking in, snatched Walter's uncle's socks, and washed and ironed them in the shape of a butterfly. That uncle went back to Japan and married her, because he could certainly see, from the state of Walter's socks, that there wasn't a whole lot to be expected in the laundry department from an American wife.

Though they didn't speak each other's language or share each other's culture, they got married. He was in love with an ironed butterfly and, *my* guess, she might have had some California dreamin' in her mind. This isn't her story but I just want to say that she hated those ski trips more than I did. Her husband got his socks the normal way after they were married. That girl wouldn't allow a water pistol in the house. I remember, one night, Walter's uncle asked us over,

but then he came to the door and said we couldn't come in.
His Japanese wife was exercising the prerogative of being a
Japanese wife. In China a husband might order his spouse
around inside her four walls, but in Japan it didn't work that
way. *Out*side, maybe, just to keep the peace. But once a
Japanese wife was inside her home (an upstairs apartment,
in this case, very new, clean, and Californian), it was hers.
So that night we couldn't come in. We scuffed and shuffled
out on the narrow balcony waiting for the Japanese wife to
change her mind. I got to experience standing around on
the lawn, while inside there's someone at the end of his or
her rope, announcing "You've got to draw the line somewhere, and I'm drawing it right now, with them!"

The stone lions were majestic and Anna May Wong dazzling; those woolen butterflies, the very cat's meow. But over
the years this exoticism took a human toll. Everyone I knew
had attempted the culturally impossible, marrying up, down,
and sideways. Walter Wong, though he had biked for untold
miles with his decent, straightforward second wife, decided
one fateful day to fly out of the problem.

"Did you hear about Walter's altar?" one of our mutual
friends asked me one night. "Worked pretty well, don't you
think?"

One Sunday afternoon, they said, down in a southern Los
Angeles suburb, as his wife read or napped and his second
daughter played innocently with her friends, Walter went
out into the backyard and built an altar. He'd never been a
God-fearing man. For him, that White, Protestant, Lady
Clairol Christ who'd just come out of the beauty parlor with
His blond finger wave was a pathetic figure of fun. But this
was the seventies, remember, and hordes of other people
were coming into L.A. with more powerful visions of the
Mind That Ran Things in the Universe. Anyone who'd ever
melted a tab of acid on his or her tongue knew Somebody
Was Paying Attention. Walter, burnt out and at the very end

of his tether from the demands of the dominant culture, built—as I've been trying to get around to saying—an altar for a Beautiful Black Woman. He sincerely—even though some of us in his extended family still feel that he might have spent the time better mowing the lawn—asked Whoever Ran Things to send him a Beautiful Black Woman. No more Suzanne K. Langer, okay? No more bike rides. He'd *had* it.

That was on a Sunday. Walter shared an office at his university: it held an empty desk; someone had died or gone away or gotten sick of the whole damn thing. When Walter came to work the following Monday he found the desk next to him occupied by the new professor in town, and it wasn't a short guy with a moustache from Iran. Walter's life changed, probably forever.

Just as suddenly, it was as if all of us had temporarily *had* it with this hands-across-the-border stuff. Walter, not because of his new girl friend, but because of his *nyah-nyah* attitude about everything ("Top *this*, you turkeys! See my beautiful black woman? There's no way you can find someone to top my beautiful *black* woman!") finally succeeded in pressing some Irish, Chinese, midwestern buttons. A family that had prided itself on tolerance and civility found itself just a little bit at odds. After an accumulated twenty years in my memory and a hundred years in their memory, lifetimes and generations of sickness and health and quarrels and reconciliations and Thanksgivings and Christmases and Rose Parades and bouts of measles and exceeding civility on every side, they now found themselves in what could only be called a very small squabble.

I will say, the Beautiful Black Woman was tactless, is tactless, in one respect. She will never clear a dish. I guess she figures that her ancestors cleared enough dishes, but at some grandchild's birthday or when some kid is graduating, and every last wife, ex-wife, mother, ex-mother, stepmother, sister-in-law, and lady whose name you didn't catch is clearing dishes out of the living room, there the Beautiful Black Woman sits, like Odetta or Ella or Lady Day herself.

Some bad things came down. "You're a racist," my first husband told his daughter, *my* daughter, and nothing, nothing on earth could have infuriated her more, since she was an expert in Mexican dance and (naturally) Oriental art, especially Korean roof tile, and had a good working knowledge of demotic Greek. "You're a racist, and so's your mother!" Well, for crying out loud, I'd married *him*, hadn't I, and listened to a thousand stories about the general stupidity of "round-eyes." Hadn't his family insisted that I eat the cheesy middle of the steamed crabs they ordered, while they chomped down on the succulent legs? Hadn't I been made to wait respectfully until the men filled their bowls? Wasn't this, so to say, the pot calling the kettle *white?* "You're a racist, and your mother's a racist, and so is the man she's living with!" The man I lived with, and it was going to be forever, may have had white Protestant skin, but he'd been born and raised in Shanghai and spoke the Wu dialect fluently, while that Fu Manchu first husband of mine thought "Wu" was something owls said, and the only Chinese words he knew was *cha* for tea, as in "Can I have some more *cha?*" Only he was too shy to ever say it, so get off my back, Walter!

But by then Walter and his beautiful woman were off in Egypt, Ethiopia, Zaire.

All this I'm-a-racist-you're-a-racist material soon became demoralizing. The ghost of Walter began to hover over our every conversation. For instance: one of our friends took a lot of harmless pleasure in mimicking an Indian-Indian accent. He liked it. It sounded funny to him. But the ghost of Walter, hovering sadly up around the corners of rooms in our houses in Topanga, the Palisades, and so on, queried us silently: "Why is that so funny? It's just things like that, you know, that ruined my eighth birthday party. Remember, I told you about that house we had in the middle of town on the Micheltorena Hill, and my parents put up a fish kite like they do for Boy's Day in China, only the neighbors called the cops because they thought our family was Japanese and —even though the ocean was thirty miles away—we were signaling to Jap submarines in the harbor?" I remembered, sure, and it was a damn shame to spoil a kid's birthday, but did that mean we never got to listen to a fake Indian accent again, or mix up our l's and r's if we were playing "Chinese"? When I had first been infatuated with Walter—so endearing then, so puritanical now—I had once called his house; my intention had been just to hear him say hello and then hang up—something mature like that. A Chinese guy had answered and, desperately emboldened, I asked for Walter. "Wahrtal, A*h*my, foo-day," the gentleman told me. After that, since Walter had joined the army, he got lonesome and we married. But hadn't we both repeated, more than once, in jest, "Wahrtal, A*h*my, foo-day?" What about that, Walter, huh? Huh? A*nd*, who taught me the immortal phrase, "Fifty million Chinamen can't be Wong"?

"You don't know how lonely I was," his ghost told me mournfully. "You are totally *clueless* about the Chinese who come to The Mountain Of Gold. You still think being a Chicano artist is some kind of a joke. You don't even respect those Filipino doctors who saved your mother's life. And you think that just because every other crumbling downtown tenement has some purple bougainvillaea drooping over it, that L.A. is fucking Paradise. You're wrong."

Ah, shut *up*, I told him, just go back to your Beautiful Black Woman. White isn't good enough for you? His prim and ghostly lips told me I was right on the money.

In dark nights when I couldn't sleep after the eleven o'clock news, when blacks and Hispanics had fallen from drive-by shootings in the street, my ex-husband's new super-ego tried to convince me that racism was a cause of the gang

wars in beautiful L.A. But I insisted (because I am sexist),
"Don't talk to *me* about race, creed, or color! Those guys are
just doing *guy* things: those drive-by shootings, that's just
war and greed: blacks against blacks (although defining
themselves, I admit it, by color: blue and red). You tell *me*,
buster," I said to my new semi-Eurasian conscience, "how
are those guys different from our boys taking potshots at the
Germans or the Russians or"—here my inner voice faltered
—"the Japanese, Koreans, uh, Vietnamese?" Walter rested
his case. "Please, Walt! Let *up*," said I. "I know: some of the
time, in some places, some of us are racist. But this is Los
Angeles. It really is, like, the home of the angels. Couldn't
we think of this problem as something like troubles in an
extended family? It's *hard*, these days, with all the extra millions of people and all the extra cars, and L.A. doesn't even
look like it used to. Still, these are family problems. We're
going to work it out. Because if there's any one place where
people can live together in beauty and harmony, isn't it
here?"

But Walter—made of air, up in the corner of the room—
turned his head away. He had the moral high ground this
time, and he wasn't letting go. "*Okay* then!" I raged. "Call
your daughters sometimes. From *either* marriage, *I'm* not
particular!" "Phone?" he answered dimly. "My ancestors
were not hampered by your materialistic gadgetry. This must
be some debased Western notion. . . . I'm getting back to
my altar to get in tune with the larger universe, and you're
not invited."

It's hard in the early nineties in L.A., not to be a racist. Hard
to know the correct response to all the waves that have come
sloshing into this basin in the last 110 years.

I sit with my head back, getting my hair washed, in a fairly
flossy Brentwood beauty salon. The lady who washes my hair

is black, my age. I've known her about eight years now, but
only in this weird relationship: I sit in the chair and lean
my head back, while she washes my hair. I'm quite familiar
with her right breast, actually. Her name is Jackie, and for
the past six months she's been on a fierce diet. At 130, she
looks great. "I don't eat no mo'," she says. (Is that racist? I
guess.)

Jackie leans over, washing my hair. I always feel sorry
about this. I'm capable of washing my own hair, but stuck
with the fact that hair grows, has to be cut, but first washed.

Jackie speaks. "You heah 'bout dem seeks?" I answer
"uhuh," or "yes," not paying real attention, because sometimes I can't understand her.

"A girl I wash, she goin' out with a seek."

"Uhuh?"

"You know, a tall man, with a *turban?* He wear white? He
come in here once?"

A Sikh! I got it now.

"She a Jewish girl."

"Some girls will do anything to shock their parents," I say
thoughtlessly, and then would bang my forehead in shame
and exasperation were not Jackie's soft and fragrant breast
resting on my nose. "*You incredible lame shit,*" the ghost of
my almost-Eurasian ex-husband remarks, resignedly. But
Jackie is still speaking.

"She a heavy girl, of course. She must be, oh, a hundred
and eighty-five."

What's happening here? I'm getting my hair washed by a
weightist? I begin to feel oppressed and harassed. I could
lose thirty pounds myself. But I begin to think about the
marketplace of love: a penniless Irish girl, an extended
Chinese-Eurasian family. A Mexican toddler rolling head
over heels in one of those mythic waves that come sailing
across from the other side of the Pacific Rim. In the sixties,
in L.A., people really did melt together for "love": you could

go up to a place like Sandstone in Topanga and see spongy naked ladies and gents rolling around on each other like some kind of scrimmage in a high school football game. Let's get together! Let's figure it out! *Let's fall in love!*

Now that fantasy has happened. We've gotten together. And now we've got to figure it out. A month ago I went to speak at a writers' conference in what used to be the far western boundary of my own world in L.A.—Barnsdall Park, created by Mrs. Barnsdall, who, sometime in the twenties, hired Frank Lloyd Wright to create a "compound for the arts," a combination of public arenas and private residences that would enhance the city's cultural life, the several square blocks bumped up out of L.A.'s central flatlands. In the grassy woods around Barnsdall, we parked, to neck, in high school. My girlfriend lost her virginity there, and Caryl Chessman so scandalized some lady with his lust for "oral copulation" that the authorities sent him to the electric chair. The phrase "old days" seems to pertain here, but what I mean to say is in the old L.A. pie cut into three pieces (black, brown, white, with a cluster of Asians stuck right in the center like a purple pansy in the middle of a caviar tart), Barnsdall was squarely in the middle of the "white" part, the safe part, where poverty meant Kraft Dinners, not breaking and entering.

So listen to this. I get to Barnsdall and I'm literally afraid to park my car, because there are hordes of Mexican guys *malamming** about with all the hoods of all their cars up, and be sure the adult part of my mind is saying *steady* on! You lived in Mexico, this is a hot day, they can't stay in their houses, they've got a right to socialize like everybody else, but I have just seen the movie *Colors* and the hysteria in me is literally keeping my head down to avoid bullets. I get a grip, park the car, give my talk, walk back, exhilarated,

* Indonesian for either standing in line or milling around and hitting each other.

through Hispanic winos both prone and supine. Now my frame of mind is: Why, they're just taking a *nap!* And those boys huddled over their cars—they're just fixing their *cars.* Is that a crime? And the ever-present ghost of Walter remains dormant (though he was a person who could take Mexico or leave it alone, as I remember).

So I think, why, instead of taking the Santa Monica Freeway out to the coast, then north along the highway to Topanga Canyon where I live, don't I drive Santa Monica Boulevard itself west to the coast? I've done my work for the day, I could use a treat, and part of Santa Monica Boulevard is my old home, since I went to City College for two years. I turn south on Vermont and see the shabby old hotels and nightclubs with belly dancers and turn right (west) on Santa Monica Boulevard, and pass the old College Grill where every day we ate a regular balanced meal, so interested were we in trying to stay alive: brown, white, and green, every day.

After a few minutes I notice that everyone on Santa Monica Boulevard is Mexican. Every person in every car is a Mexican. Every sign on every store is Mexican (and every store is open). Saturday in Mexico is shopping day and so it is on Santa Monica Boulevard. I reach into the glove compartment and pull out some Mexican cassettes: I'm singing along—*Los barandales del puente!* The *spokes* on the bridge? *Escaleras! de la cárcel!* The *steps* of the jail! *Ay Ay Ay Ay Ay! Las olas de la laguna!* The *waves* on the lake? How can they sing so exquisitely about so little? What strength! What beauty! And "they" walk their babies in perambulators and lean their elbows on cars stalled in traffic and haul their string bags around, and two hours later I'm still on Santa Monica Boulevard having gone a quarter of a mile, but my temper's a little shorter now, because I'm thinking, they're great, but couldn't they just hurry *up?*

Then, still on SMB, I'm in a section of town where, again,

there's not an English sign to be found. Here, all is neon
signs and minimalls and businessmen and women in high
heels and shirtwaist dresses, and I'm wondering, why, when
the U.N. supposedly fought the Korean War, did the U.S.
end up with all the Koreans? Because, outside of kimchi, I
just don't like Koreans. They seem to me to be the white
Protestants of the Orient: all their Korean Airlines ads are
just big lies—when you fly coach on that airline it's somewhere down below a zoo and into the prison-camp category.
They are bad business as far as I'm concerned, but at least
I'm making good time driving this stretch because if you
caused or participated in a traffic jam in Korea-Town they'd
haul you out of your car, take you into a freshly swept and
whitewashed alley, put you into a tear gas canister, and sell
your car for a tidy profit, but not before they detailed it
carefully, and I don't like their roof tiles either!

Then my car slows to a total stop again, because the people along this stretch of the boulevard are putting up bleach-
ers for a parade. If you know L.A., you know that by now,
before I hit Beverly Hills, I'm in West Hollywood. A place
once rowdy, now somber. Here, the sun shines brightly, and
all the cafés are open, and the boutiques, and the designer-
cake bakeries, some bars—but bright and airy-seeming in
this afternoon light—and the art galleries. Some guys (white
and black, old and young) are getting ready for the parade.
They string thick strands of colorful balloons, then, carefully, holding on tight to either end, raise them, anchor
them, so that they arch cheerfully across the boulevard.
Some boys and men carry those waist-high poles with heavy
metal plate brass that, when strung together with rope, can
hold back a crowd, keeping the crowd on the sidewalk, the
parade in the street. Here are youngsters in shorts and tank
tops, muscled and carefully groomed. Well, most of them
are young but sometimes, two to three in a block, there are
men in their fifties or sixties, some of them looking shy, but

with their khaki shorts spotlessly neat, rigorously pleated. And couples taking the air, hand in hand.

This has never been the Castro, never will be. Politics, the "militant" commitment to some strong point or other, never really gets going here. Los Angeles is about living together nicely, striking it rich—if you get around to it—and taking the afternoon sun. But in all these preparations here, all the gesturing, binding, tying, braiding, hammering of those last finishing touches, I don't see a single smile or hear a single laugh. This Annual Gay Rights Parade has become—who am I to even say or comment?—a statement of mourning, of courage, and a certain doleful, prideful stubbornness: We made these choices. We made them for pleasure, for love, for integrity. We changed from what our parents might have wanted us to be. We melted into what it was *we* wanted to be. We live here now. And only death will take us away.

Now I drive through easygoing Beverly Hills, with a lot of shoppers it's easy to hate, and then past the Mormon Temple and UCLA and farther west. I'm into the safe white margin now—what Vermont Avenue used to be. Then it's the bright blue familiar Pacific—*our* Pacific, the Bellevue Restaurant on top of the Santa Monica Palisades. The drive has taken more than three hours, and, and—God, L.A. has changed. When you take the freeways, you tend not to notice.

This week, my older daughter, Walter's daughter, Lisa, and I drive to Orange County. That's seventy miles south of L.A., more or less equidistant between home and San Diego. The dire prophesies of geographic pundits twenty, thirty years ago have come to pass: it's really one big city now, from Santa Barbara to the Mexican border. If you say you're in Torrance or Lakewood, that's part of L.A. (Brea or Orange, that's part of Orange County, but they'd have to take your word for it.) Where we drive is all light industry, medium-sized business buildings with glass for outside walls, and streets where something is going on but you're not sure what.

We're doing low-grade publicity at a small cable TV station in the middle of nowhere. It doesn't matter. It's a nice drive.

We get there early, and sit on a loveseat in the waiting room by the cashier's window. Over on one wall six different monitors with six different programs flicker, in color. One after another, young women with small children come in to pay their bills to the cashier at the very, very, very last minute. The kids, all towheaded and pink-faced, with prodigiously running noses, do their best, in the short time allotted to them, to destroy the one or more monitors within their grasp. The mothers pay up, receive a ritual chiding from the career woman in the cashier's window, furiously whap their two or three toddlers, and exit in chagrin and dudgeon, only to make room for another set of poor wives, another sick set of tots. Lisa sighs. I sigh. *Life.* Don't these wives deserve a little better than to be stuck down here in *Orange County*, fighting like tigers just to keep their cable television running? (Isn't that why the "rest of us" go to school, read books, exercise, learn to dance, marry Eurasians, pray for black lovers, run off—even if only for two weeks—with a Chicano artist? Go to France? Study Sanskrit? Do anything at all to escape our fate?)

Fairly recently, my mother sent me the wedding certificate of her maternal grandparents. It was a huge, faded, old document. You could barely read the names, although the idealized sepia-tinted outlines of an 1890s bride and groom could plainly be seen. I had little idea of my mother's family —except for what she told me of her tea-and-toast, poverty-stricken, TB-ridden, penniless Irish-Catholic childhood, so I was looking for names—so faint now—on the brittle document. My longtime friend, white Protestant, born in Shanghai, picked up on something else. "Your great-grandparents weren't married by 'Father' anyone," he told me gravely. "They were married by a 'Reverend Mr.' Someone. This certificate—everything in it—points to the fact that, I'm sorry to have to tell you this, your family was white Protestant."

Indeed, under close questioning, my mother very grudgingly admitted that, yes, her grandparents had been Protestant, her grandfather a hunting guide in the Maine woods. Only her mother, in a foolish act of headstrong rebellion, had run off with a handsome Irishman, the most exotic thing she could get her hands on, at that time, up in Maine. My own mother, though she represented herself as Kate Sullivan, penniless Irish girl, had been born stainless-white Protestant.

After our little publicity errand, Lisa and I were hungry. Should we drive back to the city and eat someplace nice? No, we were *hungry*. Let's just find someplace here, quick. After a line of buildings with tin walls and businesses that didn't mean anything, we rolled under the freeway and hit a minimall.

"Chinese, Japanese, Mexican, or Indonesian?" my daughter asked.

Indonesian, of course.

There is no way to say, no set of words to document, how, in one tiny storefront, the owners had perfectly replicated a second-class restaurant in a side street of Djakarta. One wall was stacked, floor to ceiling, unneatly, with greasy and dented cardboard boxes. Another wall featured pills and unguents, liniments and lotions, sometimes marked in Indonesian alone, sometimes in both languages; remedies for "weak heart," "fever," "female problems," "love troubles." Where outside it had been a dry 75 degrees, in here it was a humid 90 or above. Four or five tables, plastic-topped, squeezed together. You ordered at a counter, from a menu in Indonesian, helped out by illustrations so murky that, outside of satay, everything *did* look alike. The man behind the counter urged us to take the combination plate.

Lisa, for the past months, had been in a bad mood about her dad. No one can say for sure what goes on between two people, but she had taken his "racist" sermons to mean that he didn't love her, or didn't love her enough. She'd reacted in an "Irish"—that is to say, feisty—way about it, with an "I don't care *what* he thinks" as an oft-murmured refrain. But next week he had a birthday coming up, and Lisa began to browse along the third wall of this jam-packed restaurant, as a Dutch husband having lunch browbeat his tired Indonesian wife and absentminded half-caste kid.

"I think I'll get him some of this," Lisa said, taking down a cake of dried gado-gado, "and I think he'd probably like some of *that*," daintily picking up a jar of pickled garlic. And a bag of colored shrimp chips. And some of that good Vietnamese chili sauce. And a jar of onions braised into a brown mush. And fish paste. And some dried fish for the top of his rice. Finally, a small fortune in exotic groceries. These, along with an exquisitely wrapped Bruce Lee skateboard, would be his birthday present. Lisa drew the line, however, at the clumsily wrapped transparent packages of two-toned bright green and white tapioca. Neither one of us could figure out what to do with it, how it could possibly be used.

Self-consciously we returned to our small table, with our mountain of groceries, to our waiting meal. It was unbearably authentic, heavy on tubers and plantains. A couple of Javanese youths snickered at us, but not unkindly—plainly taken with Lisa's halo of Irish red-gold hair.

Across the asphalt of the minimall, two middle-aged couples approached. The men wore business suits, the women silk print dresses. Their hair was "done." They walked carefully in three-inch high heels. They came in, sat down. No combination plates for them. They ordered carefully and expensively. Their husbands drank several rounds of iced coffee with two-inch layers of green and white tapioca swirling and thickening across the top.

That foursome began to talk to another couple close to them. After their initial *Sallamatt pagi*, they used English. How long had all of them been here in Southern California? Did they come here often? Wasn't this a nice place? And a final question to one of the ladies in the silk dresses, who answered demurely. No, she didn't *ever* plan to go back to Djakarta. It was so hot and messy there! No, she loved it here. This was her home now.

Up at the counter, my daughter decided to get some last-minute things for her dad. Plus, she had a headache; she needed a remedy. They tried to sell her a colorful jar of Oriental ointment, but she dismissed it. "That's just Tiger Balm!" They found her something else made out of lizards; very nice. For a last few delicious minutes her fingers flicked among the counter items, finally settling on a package of green pills, unlabeled. "What are these?"

"Very bitter. Very good for you. Cleans the blood." The son translated this, after consulting with his father.

Lisa bought two packages. One for her father. One for herself.

And there we were again, outside on the asphalt of a no-'count minimall, smack dab in the middle of melting, loving Los Angeles. I could leave it at that. I could say that this city is like nowhere else, blah blah blah, but my still-loved ghost in the corner compels me to say that both of us, Lisa and I, were so self-conscious and stressed out in the middle of all that fish paste, and what with those snickering adolescents, and those quintessentially foreign guys from the last-known Pacific wave drinking that two-toned tapioca, we got rattled and stiffed the waiter.

Walter, Dear Heart, I'm sorry.

Swear to God.

We're doing the best we can.

BODIES AND SOULS

I t has always seemed to me, ever since I was little, that sex (i.e., inspiring lust) was what L.A. was about. And that the thing to do was inspire lust so mighty that it would overcome those who might inspire lust in you.

I would read books like *The Loved One* or *Day of the Locust* or *Ape and Essence* by Aldous Huxley. The point of these books as far as I, a bleached blond teenager growing up in Hollywood, was concerned was that though the authors thought they were so smart—being from England or the East Coast and so well educated and everything—they were suckers for trashy cute girls who looked like goddesses and just wanted to have fun. These men could say what they liked about how stupid and shabby and ridiculous L.A. was, but the minute they stepped off the train, they were lost. All their belief in the morals and tenets of Western civilization was just a handful of dust.

Growing up reading these books, I decided it was a good idea to get a head start on these men, so in case any more of them came traipsing by, I could beat them at their own game by having read more than they did—and also be totally devastating when it came to pulchritude, blond-haired and smoldering.

So I read Jane Austen, Dickens, Camus, Tolstoi, Colette, Trollope, Dostoevski, Zola, and Dreiser while I looked like Suzanne Somers. It was my plan and ambition to look like that (even before she actually showed up in *American Graffiti*) the whole time I was growing up. And the really terrible thing is that I haven't found a better ambition even now, when I'm so old that to inspire lust, I actually have to skip lunch.

Or eat only half a tuna sandwich.

("If God wanted me thinner," this man I knew once said, "he would have made me younger.")

If you don't have a flat stomach, it's hard to inspire lust in L.A. unless you have a father who's a producer of a hit TV series or you're an artistic giant like Francis Coppola used to be, who could do it while living in San Francisco and eating anything he wanted.

Actually living in L.A. and knowing just how boring sex can be here—and how impossible to scrounge up most of the time—I tend to think that sex must be in Brazil with all those bathing suits. Rio must be where all the sex is.

But if you live in New York or anywhere else in this particular country other than Hawaii, L.A. looks like Brazil does to me—especially to my friend Annie, who comes here every few months from the East Coast. The first thing she always says when she drives in from the airport is, "All anyone thinks about here is sex."

"That's all *you* think about, you mean," I point out ruthlessly.

"But look at all those arms and legs," she insists, especially if we're on the Venice boardwalk where we often go on mornings when it's sunny and we're both on diets (which we always are) so we can walk.

(When people don't think I'm Suzanne Somers, they think I'm Sally Kellerman.)

"Look at the way people look at each other here," she complains. "It's just disgusting."

Of course, if you ask me, New York is disgusting. For almost six months out of the year, from October to March, it doesn't matter if you've got a flat stomach and do Nautilus for your thighs because no one can see. All you have to show for yourself in the game of seduction, exchanging sly glances on the street, is your little multicolored face peeping out from a lot of black and navy blue that's keeping you warm. You can spend all the money you want on clothes in New York but the sad truth is, you have to *wear* them, whereas in L.A.—at least on the Venice boardwalk where I take all my East Coast friends—you have to have a flat stomach or you'll be subjected to liposuction ads mailed to you anonymously.

"Why don't you take off your clothes?" my . . . well, this guy I know, Rodney, wonders once or twice a day, now that he's been calling me for the last three weeks. "Come over wearing nothing but a fur coat."

"No earrings?"

"No, Marilyn Monroe never wore earrings," he explains, "unless they made her."

"What about shoes?" I inquire.

"Whatever you like," he magnanimously declares.

"Well," I sigh, "I'll think about it."

Rodney is about as East Coast a guy as you're ever likely to find stuck here in Beverly Hills, with his Rolls-Royce and his list of art clients who take his screaming word for it when he tells them what art to like. To buy. To sell. To loan. And where to loan it.

He is very good-looking in a tough New York kind of way, which he's overlaid with fine Italian clothes and shoes. He has as many shoes in his closet as Juan Perón. I couldn't resist photographing them one day, out of sheer documentary zeal.

If Rodney wanted to, he could have dozens of cute little L.A. ducklettes, but for some reason he's bored with ducklettes and wants someone more able to resist him.

Me.

Unlike my poor friend Ty, Rodney knows ducklettes aren't as dumb as they look.

Ty is another friend of mine who dealt in art. After he'd made so much money in oil down in Texas that he could afford to indulge himself in dilettantism, he decided to become an art collector and fill his house in Pacific Palisades with serious choices.

The only trouble was Darlene. Darlene was not a serious choice.

She was a nineteen-year-old "little honey bee," as he called her, from Orange County. She worked in the gallery he visited most frequently, mainly to see her.

Darlene had real short hair except for her bangs, which hung over her hazelly eyes and her freckled nose. She had an hourglass waistline, sweet breasts and hips, white-white skin, and a lisp.

Ty was a forty-seven-year-old man, with five ex-wives, nine children (including a son who was thirty), alimony in three states, and he also supported his mother back in St. Martinsville, Louisiana, where he was born.

Darlene wanted to be an actress and was working at the

gallery to pay for her apartment and acting lessons. She drove an old VW bug painted yellow.

She was not a high school graduate. But then, neither was Ty.

One day, before Darlene appeared on the scene, Ty was taking me out for dinner at Il Giardino and telling me about this Rothko he was trying to acquire and about how in the mornings he runs five miles, swims a mile, and then does an hour of Ashtanga yoga. (That's the kind people are warned to stay away from by other yoga teachers who say, "Only people under twenty-five should do Ashtanga.")

Ty positively glowed. He radiated health. He didn't eat meat or cheese, drink, or take pills. He had cheekbones like a saint in a religious painting. When he wasn't talking about art, what he preferred to discuss were mangoes—whether they're better in Maui after you've done three hours of Ashtanga and are totally dehydrated or better in Bogotá after you've been fasting for a week.

The reason we were at Il Giardino is that he loved gnocchi. He thought they were divine in plain ordinary Italian restaurants. He had never had them any place special. Being from Louisiana, he had no idea these gnocchi were made with cheese. The Italians in the restaurants he went to persuaded him they were made only from semolina or potatoes. I wasn't about to disillusion him by mentioning that these were stuffed with cheese. He had few enough pleasures in his rigorously spartan life.

Other men his age are proud if they can quit smoking or stop eating cheeseburgers. Ty had renounced almost everything mankind knows is fun. But not quite.

"I'm getting a Ferrari next week," he said.

"Oh, really," I replied, "what color?"

"They only come in one color."

"They do?"

"Red," he said.

I had visions of us driving up to Big Sur, staying in some divine lover's hideaway and eating mangoes. All I had to do was to figure out some way to seduce him, even though he didn't get my jokes and his last devotion was to an aerobics instructor who looked like Farrah Fawcett.

Anyway, we kissed good-bye after Il Giardino. And the next thing I knew it was a year later and I ran into him on Rodeo Drive in Beverly Hills.

Unbelievably, he was fat.

Well, not *fat* exactly, but he had gained twenty pounds and no longer had that incandescent translucent look of people who do yoga and eat mangoes.

"What happened?" I asked him.

"I got married," he said.

"You *what?*"

"To Darlene," he replied. "You remember Darlene, don't you?"

"That girl who worked in the gallery, right?"

I flashed back to a vision of her lifting her arms to hang some picture, her supple geisha posture really adorable, with this "I'll do anything you ask" kind of shyness about her.

"Yeah," he said, "I married that little honey bee."

"Oh," I said, stalling for time. "Let's go get a smoothie."

So we both went into this muffin store where they made smoothies, these fruit drinks thickened with bananas instead of anything worse. Poor Ty looked like he'd been eating . . . well, meat, his skin tone was so degenerated.

The first time I met Ty was in I Love Juicy, this purist health-food place on Melrose where nothing was contaminated by salt, sugar, wheat, or honey. I mean, everything was angelically pure. And there was Ty, wearing all white, his cheekbones jutting out like the Fonda family (Peter, mainly), this watch on his wrist which looked like it had been sprayed, on the face and the band, with diamonds from an Uzi.

"Where on earth did you get that watch?" I wondered.

"I had Salvador Dali design it for me last year when I was down in Spain," he said, sending bolts of pure blue energy from his eyes to my plain brown ones.

With that, he unclasped his watch and said, "Would you like to try it on?"

"Oh, I couldn't," I said. "How much did it cost?"

"A hundred and sixty . . ." he said.

"What? Not dollars. Thousand?"

"Try it on, honey," he drawled. "It won't bite you. I might, but not my watch."

He slid the watch over my paltry wrist, which was worth a lot less than what was on it, and I got to look down at this flash force of white gold and diamonds on the face of time itself.

"Oh, this is . . . wonderful," I said. I had never liked jewelry before, but I suddenly changed my mind.

Our smoothies arrived as he was comparing the mangoes in Maui, which you picked off the trees yourself, to the mangoes in northern South America on down to Brazil, which were smaller but better.

"Well," I said, "what I really like are dates. Medjool."

"You like them, do you?" He smiled, sort of caressing me with this Pure State he was in. "I just got back from the desert. I have a crate of them in my trunk."

"You have a crate of Medjool dates in the trunk of your car?"

"Sure. I know a guy who grows them."

It was lucky for me that at that time I was in the midst of a crazed bunch of people called "yoga jocks" by their not-quite peers, people who did Ashtanga yoga every day. When they weren't doing it in Santa Monica, they were off in Encinitas doing it or up in Santa Barbara or taking a six-week course in Hawaii, on the big island. The truly driven had gotten themselves all the way to India to Patabi Jois himself, the inventor and great master of Ashtanga, whose classes started at 5:00 A.M. and were populated by skiers, surfers, yoga devotees, and even Marcel Marceau's son. These people lived on the edge of physical insanity. These people who had their choice, from all the world, of which regimen to fling themselves into and who had known from early on just what pinnacles bodily obsession could reach had chosen this Fire Yoga or Gorilla Yoga or this strange brand of nonstop moving yoga some called Jumping Yoga. When real experts did it, it looked as though they were swimming under water, indifferent to the laws of gravity. Rays of slow-motion heat seemed to emanate from their bodies. From standing straight, they could bend forward to touch their palms flat on the ground, raise their torsos and legs up into handstands, and then seem to breathe through their upside-down air into all sorts of impossible postures.

The people who did this all looked like they'd just Seen the Light in the Desert and had returned to the corruption of civilization to make others See the Light too. Like Mad Max.

Since you could actually see the light shining from the way they moved, their eyes, and everything about them, they were the physical embodiment of the fact that Ashtanga was unlike anything yet known to the mind—or at least the bodies—of mankind.

If I hadn't known at least a dozen of these people, I might have mistaken Ty for the Messiah. But once I found out that he was an Ashtanga devotee, I knew that was all that was the matter with him. He wasn't really God Incarnate here at I Love Juicy's talking mangoes and Medjool dates.

For at that time, I myself had begun taking Ashtanga seriously, even though I was too weak, graceless, and unbalanced ever to do more than wish I could do it. But try and try I did.

One thing I'll tell you about doing Ashtanga. Your sex life

takes on an entirely different character. Your caliber of physical ecstasy goes markedly into an entirely new gear. Ashtanga is such a total bitch to do for even five minutes, *not* doing it seems such a respite by comparison that it makes the entire rest of your day just great. But sex—using your body simply for pleasure instead of trying to drive it into the Land of Impossibilities—is really cosmic.

People told me about one young man in his twenties who had a twenty-three-year-old girlfriend who also did Ashtanga. When they went home from class, their breathing together became positively psychedelic in orgasms, their heartbeats became one, physical reality became entirely transcended into another dimension. But it was sex, nevertheless.

(Every time I run into that young man I feel sorry for him. He wanted to marry that girl but she came from a family of Scientologists who didn't want her marrying outside the religion, so she married someone else.)

When it comes to physical things, Los Angeles is like a marriage. It gives you the baseline security to try putting your body into something like Ashtanga and not to worry about coming down. I mean, if a marriage is a union that gives you the freedom to stop thinking about who you're going out with on Saturday night, then Los Angeles and the weather here is a union with the human body that gives you the freedom not to worry about what you're going to do when winter comes.

Yoga means yoke or union too, in case you miss the point and think it's just about sitting in the lotus position.

Anyway, when Ty was in this extraordinary state, the day I first met him, he had just been to Maui and then gone off to the desert for dates. When he took me half a block from I Love Juicy to his car, what I saw was a Rolls-Royce Corniche, painted an opalescent shade of white that seemed to be blue as well. In the trunk was a wooden crate of Medjool dates. He filled the paper bag I'd gotten at the restaurant and handed it to me.

"I'd like to get together with you," he said.

"Give me your card," I said.

So he handed me this card which said he was president of this oil exploration company in Beverly Hills and we said good-bye.

I never called him because he was simply too divine and I was simply too much of an earthling. And besides, I was too much of a reader; Ty only read spiritual books from India.

But I ran into him a month later and, as I said, took him to Il Giardino with plans—finally—to seduce him, mostly because he told me he thought I was twenty-eight (which I hadn't been in over a decade). That was the night he told me he was getting a Ferrari. And then I didn't see him again until a year later, when he was fat and had gotten hopelessly entangled with the nineteen-year-old Darlene of the "honey bee" description.

The thing about poor Ty was that he was really miserable.

"What happened?" I asked. "So you got married, right?"

"Yes," he said, "that was six months ago. And I moved her into my house in Brentwood. And all she had to do, really, was be my wife. Stay at home. I was devoted."

"So?"

"So she told me she wants to continue her acting career," he said, "and I said, what does that mean? And she said she wants to get an agent and needs pictures."

"So?" I said. This all sounded totally logical to me.

"So I told her it was okay to get pictures but I didn't want her ex-boyfriend taking them."

"Oh," I said.

"And one day she wasn't home. I called her. She was out. And when I got home she told me she went and got pictures and *he* shot them."

"Oh," I said.

"So I made her move out, gave her the Ferrari, and now she's out driving around, my little honey bee, in my Ferrari."

"Oh," I said. "So she made a mistake."

"That's right," he said.

"Was that her first mistake?" I asked.

"That was her first," he said.

"And you just left after one mistake?" I asked.

"That's right," he said. "She still says she loves me."

I didn't say, "How can you leave a poor nineteen-year-old girl for one mistake?" But I didn't have to. It was beginning to dawn on him without my saying it that perhaps he, at forty-eight, ought to be generous enough to allow her more than one mistake, especially when he was still pining and lusting after her in the worst way. Plus she had the red Ferrari.

(Of course he still had the Corniche.)

"What have you been eating?" I wondered. "Hot dogs?"

"Yeah," he said. "Ain't it awful?"

"Why don't you call her?" I said.

"Maybe I'd better," he said. And he went to the phone and did and when he came back he was beaming and glowing and looking a lot better and he said, "She says she misses me. She wants to come home."

"Great, Ty," I said, wishing I weren't so nice since if I weren't he might land on me on the rebound. Except I could never be with anyone who would eventually think it was a swell idea to head out for the Big Island for a six-week blaze of Ashtanga. Sex or no, I'm not ready. I've never been strong enough. For me, the kind of flat stomach you get with Nautilus and having only a smoothie and half a tuna sandwich for lunch is enough of a penance. I'll settle for sex that's not quite psychedelic if only I can have the rest of my life away from those yoga jocks with their mythological muscles and outback zealous grace.

Of course I know that in L.A. my yoga friends win hands

down when it comes to inspiring lust, but then once you do
—and you get someone like Darlene—*then* what do you do?

Recently I met this young man in his mid-twenties who told
me he was taking yoga and how much he loved it.

"I did that," I said, "for three years."

"How often?"

"Did I go to class?" I asked. "Well, at the place I went,
there were a lot of fanatics. I went to class six times a week.
But there was one girl who went twice a day."

"Twice a day?" he exclaimed. "Those people must be
maniacs."

"*I* was a maniac," I replied.

"Why did you quit?" he asked.

"Because I couldn't do that Ashtanga. I couldn't do handstands and I couldn't even do push-ups. After I tried and
tried and tried for three years, I still couldn't do them."

"What kind of yoga was *that?*" he wondered. "We don't do
push-ups."

"You're just taking normal yoga," I explained. "This was a
kind . . . well, it involved . . . jumps."

"*You* were taking Gorilla yoga," he cried. "*We* don't do
that. That's for the advanced. The *really* advanced. My
teacher says, don't even think about that for five years."

"But it's . . ." I sighed, remembering my beautiful yoga-
jock friends, "it's so beautiful. I just *had* to do it."

"You fool," he said.

And he's right. I am a fool for beauty.

Anyway, once I found out that, after all is said and done,
yoga doesn't give you a flat stomach—doesn't even care if
you have one, in fact—and that the Nautilus machine at the
gym *does*, I made the choice any true daughter of the City
of Angels would have to make under the circumstances. I
joined the Hollywood YMCA. And it was there that I ran

into my old friend Max, who had been a member of the YMCA since before I was born, when he was five and the maid took him and his twin sister swimming there.

Max and Betty, his twin, were born in this old house in Hollywood and into old, old California money. They were the kind of WASPs who owned all the land between Ventura and Santa Barbara, the kind who sent their children to schools in Ojai to ride horses and pray, to learn Latin and Greek, philosophy, math, history, and how to drink.

Looking at Max in the Y with this lavender headband on, you just knew he was gay. He had that kind of arrogant bearing that gay men with all the money in the world have.

Of course, the Hollywood YMCA was once infamously gay and sort of a joke, but for the last ten years the people who go there are mainly basketball jocks, body builders, and studio executives who know how cheap the racquetball courts are. The gay men, in fact, have all opted for the Sports Connection and more elegant *tableaux* for them to be *vivant* in. But Max, who wore his hair in a blond streaky ponytail down to his shoulders and who threw his sweatshirt over his shoulders like Oscar Wilde's cape, really didn't notice because really he only came to the gym to take ballet and go to the steam room. He was, in fact, on his way to ballet when I saw him one day.

"I hear you're a writer now," he said.

"Sort of," I agreed. By then I had five books published.

"I'd love to read one," he said, "but I'm dyslexic, I'm afraid. Money was all that got us out of high school and I have no idea how we got through USC. But in those days it was easy to buy them off."

Being the fool for beauty that I am, I had half-decided that maybe Max wasn't *that* gay. Maybe now, with AIDS, he had decided to give women a tumble.

Max's sister Betty had been one of the first in our crowd actually to die of alcoholism. She was found in her bed at home, totally dehydrated, with a liver the size of a football. According to his astrology chart, Max should have died too, but instead he "sought help" and had been totally among the living for the last five years, able to take care of his family business, which was real estate, transportation, and import-export from Asia.

I had known Max and Betty back in the psychedelic days of the late 1960s and early 1970s, when Max traipsed around in these embroidered satin Chinese robes that were worth a king's ransom or had belonged to a king or both. They were from the San Francisco side of the family. His mother's fortune had come from shipping that traveled the Pacific Rim.

Max was the wild one. His sister Betty married young, into Republican real-estate money in Orange County, where she lived a straight life, with bottles hidden under embroidered satin pillows and pills from her doctor lining the medicine cabinet. Betty purported to despise all of Max's flamboyance and dissolute decadence and reckless, rich, hippy attitudes —which was funny when you realize that it was Betty who died and not Max. Not funny, exactly, but not what she predicted.

Of course, by the time I ran into Max at the Y, he and I had both resigned ourselves to lives of health instead of going downhill in a barrel. Neither of us drank, took pills, or so much as ate chocolate anymore. For us, nothing was left but the pleasures of Perrier and romantic friendships.

What I loved about Max was that just because he was sober didn't mean he turned into that Grant Wood painting —which was what I was afraid would happen to me and why I didn't do it sooner.

That day when I ran into him, he invited me to his house for dinner. "Wear clothes," he said. "It ain't casual."

That night when I went to his incredible house for dinner and saw him once more layered in Chinese silks, I realized that for Max being sober meant having a supremely fabulous time from dawn till dusk till bedtime and then beginning again the next dawn and that his natural impulse to be Wildly Divine had simply been channeled into sanity and laughter.

When he greeted me at the door, his blond hair was braided and tied with a golden rope, his neck was draped with satin twine hung with carved jade medallions, his fingers were heavy with gold and ruby rings, and his feet were enclosed in gold brocade slippers which made it easier for him to do the waltz soundlessly.

Which he did.

"Oh," he said, "I'm so *glad* you could come!"

"My God, Max," I said, "it's so beautiful here."

The house he lived in, the one his parents built before he was born, was this huge Greene and Greene–style hacienda with polished wooden floors, gardens in the back, Chinese tapestries on the walls, and a dining-room table laden with Victorian silver.

"Darling," he said, "you know I've always loved you. We just missed each other. Until now. I'm so happy you were at the Y today."

On the piano in the living room was a Ming vase filled with birds of paradise and bougainvillaea. Over the mantle I saw a painting of the twins when they were ten or so—both with blond hair, both with hazel eyes, both intense and well dressed and wary—sitting on either side of their mother, a dark-haired beauty looking listlessly out into the horizon, with their father standing beside them, leaning against her chair, looking like a king. Now Max looked like a king himself.

I wanted nothing more than to be inside this family and never come out—having been raised, myself, in a casual style from which the only portraits that survive are either Brownie snapshots or else the ones my father took with his

Leica during the years he decided to become Cartier-Bresson for a while.

Of course, I too was raised in Hollywood, not too far from Max's house, in fact, but the Hollywood I was from and the Hollywood he was from were two entirely different kettles of fish.

My sister and I, for example, never once went to the Y. My father didn't believe in anything with the word Christian associated with it and, besides, there was no reason for us to go since we never had to be gotten rid of. We were perfectly willing, my sister and I, to be let out after breakfast and not come back till lunch, play all morning in the Hollywood hills among the lupine and poison oak, flee after lunch into the neighborhood and, hours later, have to be wrested from games on the street by bribes of tacos, or else we might never have come home.

In fact, we were such pagans that the lady across the street, who loathed me all my life, once grabbed my mother and said, "You let Eve do whatever she wants. No wonder she's too creative."

Max came from a family—the kind I've since met and been amazed by—for whom the concept of a day without Activities was unthinkable. So Max had gone to the Y and I hadn't, until just then.

That night Max's guests, maybe twelve people in all, were artists from New York and women friends of his who looked like goddesses. The food was simple but great and there was too much of it. I couldn't get over the fresh tomatoes which he had grown himself and which, when I see them, I always refuse to stop eating in case I get hit by a bus.

"So what are you doing these days, Max?" someone asked him.

And he said, "Well, Eve and I are driving up to Santa Barbara tomorrow."

We were?

"Yes," he went on, "we're just going to have a fabulous day, maybe a picnic in Ojai, and then, who knows. . . ."

He looked at me, squeezed my hand under the table, and laughed.

"You can, can't you?" he murmured to me so that only I could hear. "Come to Santa Barbara?"

"What's tomorrow?" I asked, having lost track of days and my agenda.

"Sunday," he said.

"Sunday," I replied.

"That is," he said, "unless you've something more pressing."

So the next morning his Lincoln Continental (white) pulled up and Max, wearing jeans and a normal plaid shirt (except it was by some Italian designer and not *quite* normal) and these yellow Reeboks, came to the door to get me and said, "My, you look wonderful. I hate to say who you remind me of."

"Who?" I wondered.

"I hate to say."

Of course, I did have the same blond hair he did (only mine was heavily reconcocted), I was nearly his height, I did have the same color eyes and the same nose. I didn't have a moustache, but if you didn't look closely, you might have thought I looked just like Max himself. Or at least like Betty.

I mean, if there's any truth in the rumors about narcissism, we were a sad footnote to it. Of course, I myself have always thought what Gore Vidal said about narcissists is true —a narcissist is anyone better looking than you are—which is why I think psychiatrists are always thinking other people are and they aren't.

I'd love to say that in Santa Barbara Max and I went to a motel and things were just ducky because that's my idea, really, of how things should turn out. But instead he took me to a Dominican monastery and we heard this incredible monk choir doing Palestrina and I tried not to sulk, surrounded by this transcendent beauty.

But after that, every Sunday for an entire summer we drove up to hear the monks and pretty soon my idea that things should eventually end in bodies twisting away on sweaty sheets was lifted and I began to relax and stopped trying to picture things being better than they were. After all, what I knew about myself was that if there were champagne cocktails, there were never *enough*. If there was a hot fudge sundae one innocent afternoon at lunch at 72 Market Street, I would end up craving chocolate so badly I'd be hanging around Baskin-Robbins on Thursday mornings at 9:00 A.M. waiting for them to open so I could have doubles. And if there were orgasms, I instantly conceived that the kinds I was having weren't enough or with the right person.

But Max already knew that, since even with Palestrina, you could never get over it.

What I learned from Max was kindness or some kind of compassionate state that, at least when I was with him, seemed to descend on me like a mantle of flowers. Since this is supposed to be about sex in L.A., I don't know why I mention him, but for me this episode in my life was the most elegantly sexy I've ever had, and to be treated the way Max treated me that summer—before he fell in love with Richard and got all tangled up in mashing his head against the brick wall of how you never get your way once True Love beckons with its irresistible talons and dashes all compassion into a thousand pieces—was a prize above rubies.

"Oh, Eve," he said, the day he met Richard. "I thought I was too old."

"Humph," I said.

"When Betty died," he said, "I thought I died too."

"Humph," I said.

But nothing I could say would dissuade him. And to make me see how completely he was in the hands of fate, he told me that he and Betty had been lovers since they were eight, stayed lovers all the time Betty was married and living as a straight wife, and had, in fact, been together the entire time everyone in the family thought they were estranged.

"You actually were in love with your own twin," I replied, mystified. If I'd had a twin I think I would have gotten mad at myself too often to sneak into my own room at night—if that's what being in love with a twin is like, which is all that I, with my limited experience, can imagine.

Of course, I only know what love is from the way Max treated me—the tenderness, the compassion, the elegant playfulness.

Anyway, when I saw Richard, I knew. Richard was a dark-haired beauty who stared listlessly out into the horizon, just like Max's mother in the portrait.

Though everyone said, when seeing them together, that Max was old enough to be Richard's father, it was of course something else altogether.

What it was for Richard, I never knew.

All I knew about Richard was that he only listened to rock 'n' roll. And all they did at the Y was fight.

Fortunately, by then Tango Argentino came to town and changed all our lives. Or mine, anyway.

I'm afraid that although I come from a Trotskyite family —at least on my father's two cents' worth side—I'm finding myself more and more drawn, these days, to downright fascist decadence. I mean, every time I discover a writer I like, like Paul Johnson, the English historian, or V. S. Naipaul, someone will tell me he is a fascist or worse, just when I think I've hit on someone with flair.

And the tango, according to legend, was directly indebted to Evita Perón (I first heard of her in grammar school and was later tortured by my friends at school for having the

same name as hers) for taking it out of disrepute and bringing it back into society.

Not that a fascist like Evita knew what society *was*, mind
you, but apparently she was the one responsible for deciding
what the world needed was more tango dancing and bringing
it into fashion in Buenos Aires, the home of *los porteños*,
people of the port, who are supposed to be the only real
tangueros.

Of course, according to Paul Johnson, who everyone says
is a fascist, Juan Perón totally destroyed Argentina's economy by promising everyone everything and delivering. But
according to my friend Raul, who was in Buenos Aires at the
time, Juan Perón couldn't have been nicer and everyone
loved getting everything and didn't mind the economy being
destroyed until it was too late.

At least everyone who was like Raul—a *porteño*, who
wanted nothing more than to tango.

Of course, once the economy fell to pieces, people like
Raul and my tango teacher Orlando had to leave Argentina
and get real jobs in America and could only do tango for
their immediate peers in the Argentine community in L.A.
They went almost unnoticed until, suddenly, Tango Argentino came to Paris, then to New York, and then to Los Angeles, where it was held over and held over and held over
and where the dancers in the show went every night afterward to Norah's, this Bolivian nightclub in North Hollywood
where they installed a dance floor and hired a tango band
and, for a long time, people addicted to doing tango just
plunged in wholesale.

Suddenly Raul who was a masseur in Inglewood, became
totally irresistible to rich dilettante tango dancers who
weren't from any port whatsoever but merely had a lust to
dance the way they'd seen women dance in the show. Orlando, who was a machinist in El Monte, began teaching,
and the way he moved so startled and thrilled and inspired

his students and people in the show and anyone who saw him that suddenly he was teaching tango full-time and was no longer a machinist at all.

Orlando moved the way Frank Sinatra's voice sounded in the 1950s. (Of course, I know Frank Sinatra's a Republican, but still . . .)

Orlando moved like warm honey carressing your torso.

Orlando held you the way every woman I've ever known who has been held by Orlando ever dreamed of in her fantasies.

"Oh, to be in Orlando's arms," one woman put it, and I have nothing to add.

Orlando's style was like the Eiffel Tower. There were four legs at the bottom, but along toward the middle the figures melded together, and at the top both heads, facing one direction and leaning against each other, were as one. The trick in Orlando's tango was to keep your balance while leaning, no matter what you did, and though it looked like the easiest and sweetest thing a man and woman could possibly get themselves into trouble doing, actually doing it was impossible.

Or impossible if you understood the tango to be anything less than an obsession.

People went to three or four classes a week and took private lessons with Orlando on the side to augment their footwork. For a while, two hundred people were taking lessons in Hollywood with Orlando and an incredible woman choreographer named Teresa, and people tell me that to see Orlando and Teresa dancing together was unlike anything else in the world.

Apparently Teresa began not as a dancer but as a trapeze artist and tightrope walker, so to her balance was the name of staying alive. One man, Jim, told me that it was as though she was trying to stay on the floor and keep from flying— completely unlike us, just trying to do the steps and not to look like jerks.

"To see them together, it was like angels," he said. "They just seemed to float."

So if you can imagine people leaning against each other and seeming to float, that was the tango we were trying to do here. And the people who saw us—who actually *came* from Buenos Aires and were there in the days when the tango was all anyone did—were amazed.

"But how did you learn this tango?" one man, astonished and dazzled and nearly but not quite speechless, cried. "*We* never did tango like that. *Never.*"

"It's Orlando," someone exclaimed. "He's from Rosario."

So this man left Norah's that night, in North Hollywood, confused by the explanation that people in Rosario did tango even more gorgeously than people in Buenos Aires— whereas the truth was that Orlando invented this style and just happened to live and teach in Rosario in the days when tango was all anyone craved out of life.

Of course, Los Angeles has incredible dancers, and the ones who came to do tango from a background in ballet found it much more interesting than ballroom dancing. This was mainly because Orlando put no emphasis at all on boring concepts like the beat. He followed the melodic line, and so he could slow down the way he did tango until it looked like a moving still life.

At first, when I began, I thought the tango was chiefly about wearing high heels. The women's feet looked so breathtaking I thought about nothing else. But after I tried, I realized the dance was about incredibly strong feet and— once I danced with Orlando—about being so attuned to the man's body that you did anything he decided to do.

For someone like me, who'd been fleeing from intimacy all my life, being drawn to the tango because it was *about* intimacy—the art of it—drove me nuts. It was a lot worse than yoga because I knew I'd never ever be any good, but it was also a lot more fun because it was a dance, at night, with men.

With yoga, when you can't do it, you're all alone and in pain. When you can't do tango, there's a man to get mad at you and make you try again.

What I got out of all this is that whenever I hear Latin music, I can sort of fake the latest Latin dance craze that everyone is doing now. People who know nothing about dancing see me begin to move in slow motion and say, "Oh, you can mambo!"

"That's not the mambo," I say. "It's cumbia."

"Oh, that's right. You did tango, didn't you?"

"Yes," I say.

"Are you still doing it?"

"No. My tango teacher went back to Rosario."

"Where's that?"

"In Argentina," I sigh.

"Maybe he'll come back," they say.

"He won't come back."

"He won't?"

"No," I say, "he wants *us* to come *there.*"

Which, if you want to do tango badly enough, is something to consider. And I'm still considering it.

After all, I drove so many nights to so many strange places to tango and be with my friends who did it too. What's five thousand miles to be in Orlando's arms once more?

I'm really considering it.

Even though, God knows, the tango is not kosher for a girl who grew up in a house where fascism was worse than what Oedipus did to his mother (which at least Freud had an excuse for). I can't believe I'm thinking of going to the country of Evita Perón to do her dance.

Of course, with politics nobody can predict how things will turn out until it's much too late. With tango, for me anyway, it was too late before I even began. If there is one thing I learned from Orlando, it's that I'm not a dancer.

But there's more to love than doing the tango. Even

though I could barely do it and then only by mistake, it almost seems, I would travel the world to be in Orlando's arms again, to feel that feeling I got when Norah's was empty at 6:00 P.M. and only the waiters were witness to my private lessons, when, in the heat of North Hollywood, in Orlando's arms, I would be sailing across the floor, feeling like a swan, hearing him say, "*Lean* me."

There's more to life than politics.

But then, I wouldn't live in Hollywood if I didn't know that.

And there's more to tango than sex.

Even in L.A., where my friend Annie thinks that's all we care about.

And there's more to sex in L.A. than just sex.

What was so great about the tango craze was that it brought sex back to where it should have been all along— men making women do things they're not about to do unless they're overwhelmed with minute attention, patience, and reverence.

Not fascism, exactly. More like benevolent dictatorship.

At least one hopes.

But then, good men are hard to find.

You always get . . .

You always get the Other Kind.

Some of them run around with other women, others don't. Both kinds, at least in my experience, are perfectly faithful except for a little too much heroism when you're not looking.

I used to think that any man who ran around with other women was just the scum of the earth. Totally impossible. How on earth could he say he loved his wife when look what he was doing with every woman in the Western Hemisphere. Here's his wife sitting at home with the baby eating TV dinners and thinking, gee, maybe he's impotent or something or just doesn't like sex any more, and there he is, up to his ears in models' kneecaps. And then one day the wife finally notices.

Maybe, like my friend Bonnie, she only notices that they hadn't done anything in ages, hadn't gone anywhere or so much as had dinner in maybe eight months. The thing is, she didn't like to complain—she wasn't the complaining type, which was why he married her—but really. What she really thought she might relish was a date.

They had been married about six years and, as far as she could tell, a nice date was just what she wanted.

She spoke to a number of women friends about her idea. This was just at the time, in the early seventies, when feminism was sprouting up shoots, and a lot of her friends thought that if she wanted to go on a date, she might as well do it.

"I think I'd like to go on a date," she told her husband.

"*What?*" he screamed. And with that he exploded.

Of course, dates had been the mainstay of his existence since about two weeks after their honeymoon, when he was over at my house laughing me backwards onto my couch, just like the olden days. He'd had huge affairs with rather public women, taking them places and just barely remembering to bring along a few men friends as beards. His career as an actor was taking off, and the women who slept with him didn't care if he was married or anything really. He was so cute and adorable and so sweet—not to mention his stamina and his willingness to do *anything* to please. No matter how often.

He was generous. He bought women suede coats and jewelry and sexy Charles Jourdan shoes. Really, except for his wife, none of his women had anything to complain about.

But when he found out that Bonnie had this idea of going out on a date, he just unraveled. It was as if someone had knocked him against a brick wall and every tooth in his head had come loose. It wasn't long until he was telling his wife about five of the main women he'd gone out with since they were married. These were the ones he could remember off-hand. Luckily he didn't tell her about the endless stream of three-or-four-a-day others.

She was awestruck.

She burst into tears and cried for two months.

He got deathly ill and moved to his brother's, where he was too sick to do anything except complain and make people bring him passion fruit juice.

Of course, Bonnie was the only woman he ever loved, but he noticed it too late. She was up on her own two feet, determined to rustle up dates. And since she was so oddly beautiful, with straight honey-colored hair and an unusually interested face, she had no trouble pulling it off. The thing about Bonnie that made so many men her slaves was that she would listen to each one as if he were the most intelligent man on the face of the earth and she was honored and grateful just to hear him speak. Soon there were so many men in her kitchen (she would make them dinner) that they all realized she was that way to everyone, including her girl friends, her mother, and her child. But still . . .

Meanwhile Alex, the husband, began a full-blown tornado of an affair with this gorgeous singer who looked sort of like Bonnie but ten times more beautiful. She only lacked two things—she wasn't Bonnie and she never listened.

Alex tortured the singer. She was used to it. Unless she was in pain, she didn't notice a man was there. She was willing to wait until his divorce came through—which took most of the 1970s. By the time Bonnie and Alex managed to sign the papers, they were both so used to spending weekends, vacations, dinners, and holidays together, they hardly noticed they were divorced at all.

"Are they divorced or what?" people would ask.

Finally one day Alex proposed again and they got married again and are now living happily ever after—again. And, you know, I have never been quite sure if he was a good man or if my original premise, that a man can't love you if he's sleeping with five people a day, is true. Of course, what with AIDS and everything, the sexual revolution has calmed down and a lot of women suddenly realized that maybe actors weren't who you should be sleeping with if you didn't want to catch things. But I don't know. Maybe Alex, in spite of everything, just grew up.

Anyway, in the end he turned out to be a good man even if he does have children on four continents.

But my favorite kind of men are the same ones my friend Rene is drawn to. Just yesterday, she left me this message on my machine:

"Evie, listen to this. I know you'll appreciate it. Today I was driving along in Van Nuys on my way to the post office when I saw this really depraved-looking guy in a white Cadillac convertible with the top down. You know how I'm never attracted to anyone and haven't thought anyone is cute enough since Jack died? Well, this man, I mean, my gut nearly wrenched out of my body, he was so beautiful. And you know what I did? I followed him.

"And you know where he parked?

"In front of the parole office.

"I thought you'd love it. Talk to you later."

"How did you know it was the parole office?" I asked her later.

"Because," she laughed, "I used to have to take Jack there."

When you meet Rene for the first time, if the word "lady-like" doesn't occur to you, you don't know what a lady is. Even when she was growing up in Oakland because her Trotskyite mother married this guy who insisted on living with the masses—and working in a factory—you would see Rene and think to yourself, surely this child is the daughter of royalty captured by gypsies, no longer in her rightful land. She looked like Elizabeth Taylor, only more aristocratic and skinnier—a mere slip of a princess, like Audrey Hepburn.

When the drunken (but cute) Irish madman walked out on Rene's mother, she and Rene moved to Hollywood. I met Rene one horrible summer when my parents sent me to this socialist summer camp. She and I vowed that when we grew up we were going to be capitalists and amass all the decadence we could get, starting with Christian Diors and jazz musicians.

And this almost happened to Rene. At the age of sixteen, when she was supposed to be going to Hollywood High, she was really across the street at the Westlake School of Music, this hangout for jazz musicians, where she befriended a piano player named Maxie. Maxie was extremely concerned about her welfare, as well he might have been, seeing as how she was plunging headlong toward disaster with another jazz musician—who couldn't even play, according to Maxie.

In those days, any girl with an eye for the degenerate music scene was keeping her eyes on people like Chet Baker and Art Pepper, both of whom had incredible cheekbones and famous habits.

But we never met these guys. We were too young, and they already had old ladies.

When Rene managed to graduate from high school, her mother and her new stepfather (also a Trotskyite, only this one had money) decided to send her to Berkeley, to get her out of L.A. and to get her horrible boyfriends out of the house. This was really for the best. Rene had a lot of horrible boyfriends.

But at Cal (as U.C. Berkeley was called in those days) she met a young intellectual East Coast radical who studied architecture and temporarily captured her imagination by knowing how to do city planning. They got married, had a

child, and were more or less thriving—at least outwardly—
when the late sixties came along. Then Rene's husband took
LSD and wanted to move back East. They divorced.

By this time she had come back to L.A., where she was
taking speed, downers, and vodka, and chasing dangerous
rock stars. Somehow she wound up, at twenty-nine, in one
of those drug rehab places, where she was forced to work in
the bookkeeping department and where, one bright day, she
met Jack, a totally wiped-out jazz musician with the world's
most foxlike cheekbones. By then, Rene had long curly black
hair down to her shoulders and she was so radiant and tan
from sunning on the beach that no one in his right—or even
wrong—mind could resist her, especially when she was
wearing her lavender shorts and T-shirt, as she was the day
Jack first saw her.

I used to visit her at the rehab place and feel sorry for all
the people there. At that time I couldn't imagine taking my
clothes off without at least half a Quaalude and a bottle of
wine, but people there told me that sex was better without
drugs—because it was *all* they thought about after they were
no longer on drugs. Before, all they ever thought about was
scoring, which was something else entirely.

"They're all a bunch of animals," Rene explained, "but
they know I'm a lady and they leave me alone."

Except for Jack, who thought that was what ladies were
for—scoring. He pursued her and pursued her until finally
she agreed to go for a walk with him, and the next thing she
knew they were married.

Jack hated the rehab place generally, but after the person
running it decided everyone there had to quit smoking, he
decided they had to leave. Or at least *he* did. Quitting heroin
was one thing, but smoking was quite another.

So one night Jack left, begging Rene to join him. Finally,
a couple of week later she did, after he wrote her a letter
promising never to do drugs again and always to love her.

Of course, he was already doing drugs when he wrote the letter, and when she found him he was such a wreck it was all she could do to get him on a methadone program which enabled him to have a life, playing clarinet at bar mitzvahs and weddings.

Now everyone knows that alcohol can remove your self-respect.

And drugs like heroin remove your mind.

But cocaine erases your soul, and this was what Jack found out about once the seventies got into full swing and everyone realized cocaine was what was missing in their daily lives. Jack loved it, and he was a cult hero. When he began performing in little jazz clubs, people who came to see him play brought him handfuls of drugs. Samples, stashes, little bottles, promises of more.

One woman, an Italian countess, had an endless supply of pure Peruvian which she tried to use to seduce him away from Rene. This, of course, was impossible because cocaine made him impotent and not in the least in the mood for love.

The countess would keep him away from home for days and days, but he would never so much as kiss her—and one kiss was all she wanted from him in the end.

"Just one kiss, just one," she would rant.

But no, he wouldn't do it. He was in love with Rene.

Rene, meanwhile, was tearing around her apartment like a raving lunatic, which was what she had become. It was hard to imagine this incredibly ladylike vessel being reduced to snarling rage, but she was—a tempest in a size six Chanel suit, with short dark hair, perfect shoes, perfect lipstick.

But everyone was doing cocaine—even Rene, when she could get her hands on Jack's. Because once you had it, you wanted nothing but more, more, more.

Fortunately or unfortunately, Rene had grown up with her mother suffering like a martyr for "love" (i.e., hope of sex), so Rene hung in there up to the final moment when crack entered their lives and Jack landed on it with all fours. Crack and shooting coke were his ideas of a nice afternoon. One moment he was fine, having a nice afternoon, and the next he was on his way to the hospital in an ambulance, telling Rene he loved her. And then he was dead. A stroke, they called it.

So many of my friends had died around that time, when I went to parties the survivors would stand around looking embarrassed for having lasted so long. The only people who seemed to be having any fun at all were the ones who had forsaken even the minutest particle of anything chemical, even grass. And because I've always preferred fun to dying, I allowed myself to be sweet-talked into quitting everything too and only hanging around with the spanking clean, the tan, and the lovely. I fell in love right away with a guy who looked like an Arrow shirt ad from the twenties even though he was an actor. But when I heard that Jack had died—Jack, whom only months before I'd hidden in bathrooms and taken drugs with myself—I felt as though too much had happened too fast for me to see it coming.

At Jack's funeral in the Hollywood Cemetery—our favorite cemetery because it looks like a Jean Cocteau dream—Rene and I watched sadly as all his friends came and his fans and even his ex-wives. Even though that was five years ago, Rene is such a lady that she still dreams of him at night and never allows any other man in her life to violate her condition of widowhood.

Whether a man like Jack, who swears eternal love and then is swept away by death, is better than the kind who loves you and can't resist other women, I don't know. I just know that for people like me and Rene, death seems a lot more loyal and devoted.

"The only reason he was monogamous," Rene once told

me, "was because he thought women were all tramps who carried diseases. But he thought that I was such a lady. . . ."

"Well," I reminded her, "you are."

So naturally a guy in a Cadillac on his way to the parole board would be just our cup of tea, and that's why she called, laughing, to tell me all about it.

Rene and I were addicted to guys like Chet Baker before we knew what being a junkie meant. We were born that way, and all the behavioral sciences in Atlantis aren't gonna cure us.

And, you know, neither of us spent one moment wondering if perhaps this guy was parked outside the parole board because he *worked* there.

At least we both know better than that by now.

I remember the first time I saw Tess. It must have been ten years ago or so. She was twenty-four but looked about eleven, with these sad brown braids looped around her head and these little glasses stuck on her shiny scrubbed face.

She had gone to Vassar and married some Ivy League teacher who had just gotten his first book published and optioned by some producer. They were moving to L.A., and her husband Ralph called me because he and I had the same magazine editor, a guy named Brad, in New York. Brad was a man so unspontaneous and crabby that he would never do anything like introduce you to someone unless there was some hidden agenda in it. (I know this from personal experience. Once when I went into his office another one of his authors was there, someone I wanted to meet, and Brad simply pretended he was invisible.)

Anyway, Brad called me up and told me to go to lunch with Ralph. When Ralph called, I suggested he meet me at West Beach in Venice, where I went whether I was meeting someone or not. Ralph was easy to spot. He had a blond beard, a jacket with patches on the elbows, and a scholarly slouch. But Tess—well, she was wearing these overalls and her hair in braids and of course they asked for her I.D. when she ordered a mimosa.

She too wanted to be a writer, she told me. She wanted to write movies.

"Oh?" I said. "What movies do you like?"

"My two favorites are *National Velvet* and *Eraserhead*," she said. And I began to think a lot more of her potential.

In fact, then and there I fell in love with both of them, but especially her, sitting there like an eleven-year-old, smoking Camels and ordering a brandy for dessert.

When I got home there was a message on my machine to call Brad in New York. He was never there, but this time he was right by the phone.

"So?" he said.

"So? What?" I replied.

"How do you like her?" he asked.

"Oh," I said. "Brad, you cradle robber."

(So that's the kind of girl he likes, I thought to myself. Here all this time I've been trying to vamp him with my femme fatale charms when what he really likes are baby weirdos.)

After that, every Sunday Tess and Ralph and I went out with Tess's poor old dog Roux for arthritic walks on the beach and then put the dog in the car while we went to the West Beach and had smoked salmon eggs Benedict with orange caviar on top.

"I used to want a horse," Tess said, regarding the caviar, "just this color."

When a friend of mine's apartment became vacant in Santa Monica, just north of Venice—two bedrooms, a view of the ocean to Catalina, and it actually allowed pets (which Tess had in abundance)—they got it for only $650 a month. A miracle of rent control, it was perfect for them.

For a couple of years everything was sublime, until the summer Ralph got a job in Oslo for two months. There, he ran into their (Santa Monica) next-door neighbor, a girl named Gittle, and fell madly in love with her. When he came home, and Gittle came back home next door, he asked Tess for a divorce.

"I don't know what he sees in her," Tess would cry. "She has this laugh just like a little baby. And she *looks* just like some kind of freak ten-year-old."

I didn't feel it was my duty to point out that Ralph definitely went for babyhood when it came to wives, since by this time Tess had toughened up her act, gotten a haircut, and looked as adult and mature as Audrey Hepburn in *Charade*. She was wearing little skirts and was altogether the cutest thing you ever saw—if you liked innocent convent girls who smoked and talked dirty, as opposed to smoldering odalisques, which was my own specialty. In fact, it was great going around with Tess because men who liked her would never like me and vice versa.

Ralph moved next door and Tess was left with the great apartment and Roux, who had begun to die during the divorce. Physically, the poor dog was going through exactly what Tess was suffering inside—bleeding on the walls, the floors, the doors.

"Tess," I said, "there's blood all over everything."

"I know," she wept.

"You've got to put poor Roux to sleep," I said. "I'll call the vet."

But in a final moment of gallantry, Ralph came and took Tess and Roux to the vet, where the dog and their love were put to sleep one bleak smoggy afternoon.

"I've started riding," she told me later.

"Great," I said, since I knew that women who had horses were a lot happier than normal people. "You mean riding horses, right?"

I remembered her loyalty to *National Velvet* and the horse the color of orange caviar that she used to dream of, and I was relieved when she told me she had found a riding school out in Glendale where she was going three times a week.

Actually, she began by going once a week, then it was three times a week, then every day, rain or shine.

"I'm learning to jump," she said, "and I'm keeping an eye out for a horse I can buy myself. Cheap."

"Oh," I said, thinking this was going too far.

But once she got a rewrite job on a sort of psycho teen movie (not *Nightmare on Elm Street* but close), money was no problem.

Meanwhile, with Ralph gone, she began hitting the bars down at the beach, populated with the hip art crowd, movie people, and even rock musicians, and she had the usual string of lovers, who were glad she lived nearby since they were too drunk to drive far.

"All I want to do," she said, "is go riding."

It was about this time that she met Clove Furnace, a horse that had been abandoned and left to atrophy in a stall somewhere in Burbank. He was for sale for $300.

"That's it," she said. "I'm buying him. I feel so sorry for him, this big horse with no one to ride him."

"But where will he live?" I wondered.

"You can rent stalls," she said.

Well, once Clove Furnace got out of the stall and had Tess to ride him, he turned into this monster who only wanted to jump higher and higher—as high as five feet. He would fume if he didn't get out to run every day, and he would blame Tess if it was raining. Clove Furnace was a horse of many moods, none of them good.

"Clove is more of a man than Ralph ever was," she said.

"Where do the two of you go?"

"Oh," she said. "there are mountains out in Burbank. Lots of people ride there."

It was hard for me to imagine this little ninety-seven-pound weakling with flapper hair on top of a monster pounding his hoofbeats over the Hollywood Hills. But stranger things have happened, I suppose, especially to people I know.

All of it sounded like too much trouble to me—buying a horse, renting a stable, feeding the damn thing, taking lessons, jumping. And Clove Furnace's humor was quite barbaric—or at least Hungarian. Plus she had to drive all the way from the beach to Glendale, over thirty miles, every day through freeway traffic.

But she didn't mind.

In fact, she flourished.

The color came back to her cheeks or, rather, came *into* her cheeks—it had never been there before—and she grew strong and lithe.

And then, one night at an art opening, she met Joseph, the demon lover. I had known Joseph for a long, long time, and even when I was twenty, I knew enough to stay away from him. He was too good-looking and too insane. A stuntman type who was actually a musician, he was in the midst of a divorce from a woman who looked totally bedraggled and *farbisson* (Yiddish for embittered) after twenty years of trying to find out where he was, who he was with, and when he was coming home. People say she had once been pretty, but her straggly skirts, motley hair, and hardened frown made it almost impossible to believe.

"I know I'm a sleazeball philanderer and womanizer," Joseph told me, "and Tess is much too good for me."

"You're for damn sure right," I said. "And Joseph, I'm going to kill you if you don't watch how you treat her."

Joseph was drawn to Tess partly because she was so incredibly adorable and sweet and partly because her friends were so loyal to her that they threatened to waste him if he didn't behave.

Joseph was so extremely beautiful that women just followed him out the door and into cars, apartments, and week-ends. But he was madly in love with Tess—as madly as he could fall in love and still be a sleazeball philanderer.

His studio was only five blocks from Tess's apartment. Every time they broke up he would call her at 3:00 A.M., when the West Beach kicked him out, and wind up back in her bed, even when she insisted he would never darken her doorstep again.

Whenever they got into really bad fights, at least Tess still had Clove Furnace. This was lucky. She'd come home too exhausted to care where Joseph was, who he was with, or when he was coming home. When she woke up, of course, she'd remember again.

"I'm just so miserable," she told me, "all I want to do is go somewhere with Clove Furnace forever. Joseph is hanging out with this horrible old hag. It's over. It's ended. We're through. I can't take it anymore."

"Too bad you can't go live with Clove Furnace," I pointed out.

"Well, I can," she said. "I just got offered a job at Burbank Studios, a screenplay about mummies, and it's enough so I can put a down payment on this place with stables and every-thing in my back yard."

"A place with stables?" I exclaimed. "Where?"

"Burbank."

"Burbank? You're thinking of leaving the beach to go live in *Burbank*?"

Burbank is such a loss, I thought. "Beautiful downtown Burbank"—the old "Laugh-In" joke—really is just so smoggy and motley, it's a place no sane person would move to—horse or no horse.

"I like Burbank," she said, "especially where my house is. Six feet from the Equestrian Trail. Not far from the Polo Field."

"Polo?" I perked up. "They've got polo guys in Burbank?"

This was entirely unforeseen, so I agreed to go with Tess to look at the house. What I discovered was a neighborhood so bucolic that everything revolved around horses. They had feed stores and stores that sold horse gear. There was the Equestrian Center, with this enormous polo field covered by a roof. The street signs on Riverside Avenue warned, SLOW DOWN FOR . . . and then showed a girl on a horse in silhouette.

And the house Tess wanted to buy was adorable. It was a Spanish hacienda built in the forties, with tile floors, a woebegone fountain in the back yard, a camellia bush in the front, lots of trees, and—most important of all—stables and small corrals. The works.

We drove over to the Equestrian Center and saw that the Polo Field was overlooked by a divine dining room where they served sort of okay lunches and dinners. We were sure if we could only find the right Argentine polo players, we'd be set for life—even if Burbank was part of the deal.

A week after Tess moved in, I came over and drove her to the feed store and horse supply place, where she bought big rubber galoshes, overalls, and shovels to muck out the stables and also huge trash cans for the horse manure, which the city would pick up if you paid extra.

Clove Furnace was already in his stable when we came back. "It's great," Tess said. "He can watch me get dressed in the morning. He likes it."

"He's a dirty old horse," I sighed, glad I would never have to get on top of anything that big and try to tell it what to do.

As I was driving home, I thought it seemed like an awful lot to go through for a $300 horse—buying a $200,000 house so it could watch you get dressed.

I was totally afraid of Clove Furnace. He was orangey and fire snorted out of his nostrils and he was always in one mood or another, none of them my idea of cozy.

By this time Tess had two new dogs, both of which were constantly running smack into barbed-wire fences and needing to have stitches. Pushpaw, her cat from before, was convinced Tess had moved to Burbank especially for him. All he had to do was learn which season was best for lying under the mimosa tree or the camellia bush or finding shade under a palm frond. (I was in love with Pushpaw.)

Tess had also offered to keep other people's horses in her stables, so she had this white Morgan named Mystic and this ridiculous pony, an old scruffy one named Bear, who had to wear a pink bridle with rhinestones on it if he was going anywhere. "The girl who owns him," Tess explained, "thinks this looks cute."

The idea of this scruffy old man in rhinestones!

Anyway, Tess went on, "The people who used to have him came home one day and he wasn't in the stable or back yard. They found him in their living room, staring into the aquarium."

The image of this old pony staring into a blue aquarium at the fish made me like horses a lot better.

In Cosmo-girl worldly wisdom, a woman giving up an apartment at the beach with an actual view of the ocean for mucking horses in Burbank might seem to be "following your bliss" to a maniacal degree, but for Tess, I thought, it was perfect. At least it kept Joseph from lurching by.

Over the next few months, Tess discovered new amazements.

"I've got chickens," she announced.

"Chickens?"

"You know, for eggs."

"What about the neighbors? Doesn't the rooster . . . ?"

"I give the neighbors eggs."

Tess was never lonely because she always had people around—carpenters building chicken coops, homeopathic vets, gardeners who knew what to feed orange trees to make the fruit sweet, a plumber to fix the fountain.

"Joseph's been calling me," she said one day. "I don't know how he got my number. He wants to come out here."

"Out *there?*" I marveled. Joseph was truly one of those gentlemen surfers who derogatorily referred to anything east of Lincoln Boulevard (the main street about ten blocks east of the ocean) as "the valley." Burbank really *was* the valley. No hip bars to go to at night, no galleries, no restaurants.

"So he's coming tomorrow," she said.

"He is?" I said. "Has he ever met Clove Furnace before?"

And so, the *ménage à deux* that Tess had created turned into an *à trois* on weekends—just Clove, Tess, and born-again Joseph, amazed to find himself happy in the valley with nothing to do but scramble eggs.

"He rides," Tess reported, "especially now that we've got this new horse, Bucky."

"You've got *another* horse?" I gasped. I mean, it seemed quite enough to me with Bear and Clove Furnace and the Morgan. "Pretty soon," I said, "you'll have horses in *your* living room."

"They named him Buck because of Magic Johnson," she said. She knew how I felt about Magic Johnson—I'd go a million miles for one of those smiles. And Buck is Magic Johnson's nickname. "You want to try riding Bucky?" She knew how to get to me.

"Maybe I could ride a horse if I thought of him as my favorite Laker," I said. Up till then, the horse issue had been settled the day I went over to the Beechwood Stables in Hollywood and stared out at the smog on top of this poor old horse who was nevertheless too tall. Once, after that, I had been out to a ranch in Springsville where this magic girl Natalie had put me on top of this Morgan and given me a lesson on an English saddle. That horse had been so magical, I knew no other horse could come close. And especially no horse in the same back yard as Clove Furnace.

So last Wednesday I went out to Tess's and saw Bucky. In fact, he didn't look anything like Magic Johnson. He was a silvery beige with feet so black they looked traced in India ink. What Bucky looked like up close was more like Orlando, my tango teacher. Tender lips full of sad regret.

"Can you believe they paid six thousand dollars for this horse?" Tess said. "This woman bought him for her daughter. Now she never rides, so they left him with me."

"How can a horse cost that much?"

"He's very well trained."

"Maybe he's a thousand dollars worth of horse," I said, "with five thousand worth of lessons."

It was one of those fair February days in L.A. It was still winter up in the hills—you could see snow on top of the San Gabriel Mountains. But a small hot breeze from the Santa Anas had suddenly turned the city from "freezing" (about 55 degrees in the daytime) to a nice 85-degree summer.

Tess, who rode English, put a Western saddle on Bucky for me, for which I was very grateful. But first she made me brush him with a plastic horse comb and a Fuller hair brush. "He loves you for that," she insisted. "Look at how great he looks."

She led Bucky out of the back yard with Bear and into the street, where cars were parked but no one drove fast. Before I knew it, I was on top of this beautiful sweetheart who seemed as resigned as Orlando to having my thighs wrapped ignorantly around him.

For twenty minutes we circled her block and the next one down. I was amazed to realize that horses can not only be made to go forward, they can go right and left, stop, and even go backwards—a truly novel invention, it seemed to me.

Anyway, when we came to the intersection of Valleyhart and Mariposa, Buck came to a complete halt. I knew he would never budge again. This was what all those people were talking about when they said, "I don't know what went wrong with my horse. He just wouldn't go."

"Cinch in your calves," Tess said, "and say giddyap."

"No? Giddyap?" I said. And as soon as I said it, Bucky went—which made me love him a thousand times more. "All I'm afraid of," I said, "is if he suddenly decides to do the Charge of the Light Brigade."

"You know how you told me when you did tango it was like being As One with the music?" Tess said. "Well, with Clove Furnace, it's the same. You're as close as you can possibly be to another living creature—there's nothing between you and it—nothing. And you're As One with the speed."

Compared to the little girl who first arrived with braids looped around her head, Tess was light-years older and more sophisticated that day—an incredible beauty—sitting atop Bear in his pink rhinestone bridle, dressed in baggy sweatpants and this pink Schiaparelli T-shirt and boots, with her thick brown hair chopped right at her chin. Seeing her on Bear, I could hardly believe how elegant and slinky she could look beside Joseph at museum events—now that he's older but wiser.

And so is she.

It suddenly occurred to me, clopping back to her driveway, that the place Joseph filled in her heart now was the same one that had once been occupied by Roux—a poetic connection she never had with Ralph—and that she had found true love at last, home on the ranch.

Devotees of yoga were always trying to convince me that yoga was a way you could make your*self* feel divine, in bliss —that this was something you could achieve, no matter what else was going on in your life or how tragically abandoned you felt.

It now seems to me that what people are looking for in a lover, they'd be better off seeking in yoga, tango partners, or home on the range with animals who have more instinctive knowledge of need and desire than you normally find in

those with flat stomachs who inspire lust with every smoldering gaze.

To be As One with someone, whether to music or to
movement, is what I, anyway, have always wanted—and all
the morals and tenets of Western civilization that try to convince us there are higher things, they've always seemed to
me just a handful of dust. But then, I'm from L.A., and I
have always been what educated people from the East Coast
and England take one look at and think is what's wrong with
this place.

So to me, a flat stomach is still worth it.

DEATH

CITY OF SPECTERS

A teacher here recently gave a vocabulary test in which she asked her students to provide the antonym of *youth*. Over half the class answered *death*.

> Truman Capote, "Hollywood"

They worship death here. They don't worship money they worship death.

> Raymond Chandler on Hollywood

Death is only a word, it is an abrupt absence that has reality.

> John Clellon Holmes

Some mornings, from a majestic set of sooty garret windows, Moss will watch downtown's concrete fall then slowly rise. With black coffee in hand and Joe Turner sassing on the stereo, he daily makes note of the city's slow progress—aborted elaborate projects, radically altered plans. Most evenings he is mesmerized by the strict configuration of windows, light, and ledges that metamorphose into surreal though solemn faces. Like sacred ceremonial masks, they loom stoic and unblinking in the vast night sky.

This warehouse space squats unobtrusively beneath a black argument of electric lines and is cordoned off by a set of railroad tracks that seem to wander nowhere. It's been years since I've settled down on these scarred wood floors, since Moss has opened the door, his mouth, or his heart to friends.

When I first met Moss through his girlfriend Inez, he was new to town. I'd met Inez while I was still shelving and selling best sellers to attorneys and junior film executives at a small bookstore in Century City. Some evenings when I worked late, I'd see her draping mannequins in expensive, exotic clothes. She stopped me one afternoon when she saw me carrying a slim portfolio, while waiting in line for lunch. "Student?" she asked glancing through black-and-white still lifes. I nodded. "Good stuff. It'll get better." She had given up on photography—the smell, the cost. After hours she dressed windows for a chain of Westside department stores; from dawn to dusk she fretted over huge canvases in her downtown loft. With time she offered the use of her forsaken darkroom as well as a critical eye.

In those days, Moss had only just begun curiously prowling empty side streets at all hours, carefully sidestepping limp bodies of homeless women and men. He would stoop to check a pulse at the temple or the rhythm of halting, shallow breaths—once leaning over to share his air with a little girl whose lips and lids had gone blue. This ritual continued until he was shaken down at dusk near Al's Bar at Traction. Now he seldom talks or slows his stride for any thing or one.

Some say now he is a ghost. Standing a shade over six feet, raillike, from a short distance within dusk's half-light, Moss looks like nothing more than a haphazard stroke mark leaning against a gray wall. He hasn't the need for a telephone; even an urgent knock at his door goes unanswered. I've often wondered how, within this shroud of secrecy, of ambient solitude, he spends the measure of his days.

There used to be busy, intricate structures occupying floor-to-ceiling space at four corners of this reconverted warehouse. Dark, heavy pieces of menacing industrial sculpture, fabricated from found fragments of iron, steel, aluminum, old hubcaps or wire hangers. He welded works of art together from piles of castaway remains. On ambitious days, he'd take long rides as far south as Long Beach or as far north as Goleta on "collecting trips." Since there are no trees, he waited to hear the rustle of newspaper skidding across asphalt before beginning his evening's work. At street side, three stories below, you could catch occasional sparks, a warm glow, and flickering shadows as they moved along the farthest wall.

Not much remains of those days: Just a few blistered spots in the floor where the heat became too intense, and a faint gray scar running the length of Moss's arm, starting just above the wrist and terminating at the bend of his elbow.

Only once was I asked along on one of Moss's elaborate scavenger hunts. The invitation surprised me, since he was generally mysterious about his work and seldom had words for me. I'd been downtown working in the darkroom and visiting Inez, who'd been floored with the flu. Moss kept bringing in burnt slices of wheat toast, which Inez rejected with a regal flutter of the hand. When she drifted off to sleep, I gathered my things to head back west. "Where you off to?" he asked over a sink of dishes. "I think I need a second set of eyes." We drove out to the beach, taking congested surface streets, Moss chewing gum and twisting radio knobs all the way. Finding a place a half-dozen blocks from the shore, he pulled out a net, some soiled-stiff work gloves, and slipped out of his shoes. With each step we sank deeper into white hot sand. He rescued odd bits of metals that peeked out from just beneath the surface. The bounty was scarcer than he would have liked; it seemed hardly worth the ride through smog and traffic. "It'd been nice," he said with his eyes on the road ahead, "to save a little bit more."

———

There was the occasional show. There were modest local reviews. There was a community opening up within the shadow of City Hall, as local artists moved from studio spaces near the sea to work spaces just east of Little Tokyo. They settled within a collection of dark suspicious streets— Traction, Rose, Third, Second, Center, Vigness, Santa Fe —that made up an ersatz SoHo, populated by blue- and orange-haired Otis Parsons and Art Center grads.

Moss immigrated from Illinois by hand-me-down Ford Falcon. He flopped in a hole-in-the-wall motel on the easterly fringes of Sunset Strip, with the hourly rates hastily scrawled in pencil and posted on the back of the door. Being an emigré was not information Moss offered freely, but cowboy tans or "pulling calves" would occasionally swirl to the surface in toxically induced reveries. At clear moments he offered instead his sober, polished line: "I was surely dead in Illinois."

Shedding small-town shyness, Moss relaxed gleefully into big-town anonymity, carefully collecting a shimmering cluster of friends. His closest was a painter named Aaron, a native, who had an infectious booming laugh which began somewhere deep inside his five-foot-six-inch frame and ended in a high, maniac titter. Moss met him on a midnight constitutional. Both frequently waged battles with insomnia; they rose at small hours to walk off jangled nerves. In a thin-lapeled, antique tuxedo and black Converse high-tops laced with glittered strings, he would drag Moss to boring Hollywood parties—"B.H.Ps," he called them—where they would stand around in tight private circles laughing and tossing copper pennies into heated turquoise pools. He would then spirit him off again in his pumpkin-colored Rambler to a "real" celebration in Echo Park or Silver Lake where the music, heavy on bass and drum, made the floorboards groan and tremble and the hot air floating in smelled heavy-sweet like ancient gardenias.

Moss lived a few buildings away from the neighborhood's

sole celebrity—singer/songwriter Peter Ivers, the flamboyant host of the cult cable show "New Wave Theater." Ivers, a Harvard graduate in classics, came to L.A. in 1971 to try to break into the music business. Eleven years later, and still far from a household word, he settled into a sixth-floor loft downtown, where he sometimes entertained friends with his own blues harmonica stylings or on a whim invited a random mix of musicians over for a rooftop twilight jam session. He spent many quiet afternoons in meditation or engaged in yoga. Among friends and casual acquaintances he was known as carefree, idealistic, and above all trusting. The first time I saw Ivers, Moss pointed him out at a cramped and smoky downtown party. He was shrugging out of a too-small tailored jacket, as someone put a friendly arm around his shoulder, then ushered him into a distant, darkened room. Moss would often brush against him at noisy openings, or exchange a quick nod behind black shades while traveling in daylight down Traction. The next time I saw Ivers, his grainy face filled the front page of an L.A. free weekly—he had been found on March 3, 1983, bludgeoned to death in his sleep. His body tangled within the folds of sheets damp with his own blood.

Daily patterns changed. An unspoken, unofficial neighborhood curfew was quickly imposed. Residents traveled in loud packs at nightfall, and thin voices offering comfort crossed over thinner telephone wires. People traded stories: about the forty-five minutes it took for police to arrive; about the failure to seal off the murder scene; about the cheap lock on Ivers's front door. Neighbors waited silently for murder motives, for officers to assemble follow-up clues.

But Aaron grew tired. Moss remembers a bristling, electric impatience. After a handful of weeks he was bored with sipping black coffee with friends, waiting to hear if it was safe to roam neighboring side streets at night. After a noisy display, Aaron ventured out of the neighborhood, to the beach, "For inspiration"; his body was found the following morning in a littered alley behind a dumpster, a few blocks from the Venice boardwalk. He'd been relieved of $20, a cracked Timex, and his glittered shoestrings.

Most agreed the streets had gotten mean. "The romance went out of it after that," Moss recalls, "I mean you felt kinda foolish trying to hang on to any of it." The neighborhood began to change after the city re-zoned these industrial work spaces as live-ins. Downtown became a neighborhood in transition. Earthquake proofing and proper plumbing made these last refuges for many local artists financially out of reach. Moss sublet his place to one of the many up-and-coming actors who was venturing into the neighborhood for a "funky place" to throw a memorable grand fete. He rented a U-Haul, packed slides of his work, Levis, T-shirts, hot plate, and books into the trunk of his Falcon and headed east.

"I stopped sculpting," Moss says as he pulls proof sheets, prints, and negatives from black boxes, then spreads them on a gray blanket close to the light. I recognize some faces: Inez, her cotton-white hair pulled away from her face with a foamy smoke-colored scarf, scowls out of frame; Aaron, at the beach in shabby thrift-store layers, shivers through a huge gap-toothed grin.

Moss says, flipping through proofs, that he roamed New York without the energy to pester a soul. He first took a train to Chicago then rented a truck and traveled to Evanston, Illinois, where he says he sat on the day-porch with his father smoking cigarettes, reveling in the scented silence. This was life for a while.

"Just couldn't seem to work with my hands. They just wouldn't cooperate. And when I did it seemed I'd have dreams. Angry dreams. That's why I stay awake."

We wade through more photos. Box upon box of matte-finished black and white images—people, buildings, sky, ragged terrain. Some have amoebalike ocher stains where the fixer wasn't completely rinsed away. Most are underdeveloped and have a somber gray cast. Lack of color, Moss explains, provides necessary distance. "Otherwise it's all too confrontational."

Since these photos remain in narrow black boxes parked beneath his bed, I ask Moss what he does for money. Odd jobs: drawing espresso at local coffee bars, pumping gas, working in darkrooms at professional photo labs in Hollywood. He's grown accustomed to the isolation. "If you drop out of sight in L.A., people don't always assume you're dead, I've learned. Rather they assume you've only moved out of carphone service distance. Or that you're busy . . . thus happy and healthy."

I talk him into taking a walk, to move out of the shade of his living quarters. Maybe pick up a roast beef sandwich at Philippe's, or a warm sake in Little Tokyo—just like old times. We walk along deserted but wide-open stretches of Alameda—the same path we'd take to Aaron's summer evenings just before nightfall. We move slowly toward the cluster of wispy palm trees and stucco clock tower denoting Union Station in the distance. We pass a lone transient with a rusted shopping cart filled with a careful selection of grimy rags and broken glass. He has stripped completely nude. His hair has clustered into a dry forest of auburn dreadlocks, his skin so smooth and dark it looks more like cool onyx than charred flesh. He blesses the corner of Alameda and Second with a wave of open palms, then bends head first toward the sidewalk in an extended stretch that looks more like a mystic yoga posture. Moss and I stand motionless as he pauses for a moment, raises his arms, and shouts into the sun.

In junior high school we went to more funerals than weddings. My friend J. remembers solemn autumn rosaries that began just after sunset, giving us little time to climb out of

dusty chinos and Earth Shoes and into more somber, re-
spectful attire.

These deaths were often careless accidents; macho postur-
ings or random, mercuric moves made in fits of anger, that
most times followed a red blur of words. Best friends played
fatal games with loaded guns, and Cuban "car club" members met with grisly, mysterious demises that drastically re-
wrote the lives of survivors.

The first funerals my classmates attended were for close
friends, all under eighteen. "I didn't go to an old person's
funeral until my grandfather died," J. recalls. By then it was
a ritual that had grown darkly familiar. For shortly before
her grandfather slipped away, her stunned family buried her
older brother, the summer of his sixteenth year.

Around campus, J. was often mistaken for a blond-haired,
blue-eyed Cuban, since her circle of friends except for me,
was almost exclusively Latino. Like the "homegirls," she
adopted a belligerent slur to her speech, a fluid ease to her
style. In her I saw an inner calmness, a worry-free veneer
that I worked hard to master. Yet she, too, like me, possessed
an eager, insatiable curiosity. We both had grand though
pragmatic aspirations of being well respected yet quite possibly only modestly successful writers. We spent weekends
outside of Culver City, a quiet, tidy community just on the
edges of L.A. proper, exploring what lay beyond. We gathered ideas to store in looseleaf notebooks. We collected city
color.

Summer '77, J. and I abandoned Venice Beach and took
to tangled Sunset Boulevard. Of that summer, I remember
an odd jumble of mismatched details—a wash of faces and
light that bloomed on either side of the wide stretch of
boulevard. Music was changing on the radio and in the
streets. Heavy distorted guitars and epic song-cycles were

being replaced by frail, tinny strings backed by even flimsier English voices. These were the new British coif bands that my friend Larry was hyped to join. They would be his magic ticket out of L.A. Others were simply looking to mobilize within city limits, resurrecting junked husks of automobiles to rebuild and eventually call their own. My summer's master plan, to read, eat hothouse tangerines, and watch Lucille Ball four times a day in various sitcom incarnations, was undermined by my parents, who quickly filled afternoons with piano lessons at USC and art classes in the hills above Hollywood where I learned to use a potter's wheel.

What I don't remember about that summer were important details. J.'s actual words—what they were or in what order they were spoken. Those have all blurred and faded with years and numerous tellings and retellings. What has stubbornly remained is the flat tone of her voice—distant, mater of fact—as if she were reporting what was playing at the Culver Theater or reading a list of prices from a coffee-shop menu.

She passed on what little information she had at the time —that her brother's battered body had been found within the tall yellow grass in the canyons behind UCLA just above Sunset. Years later I learned that he had been shot full of heroin and that the coroner found several bullets lodged near his heart.

No arrests were ever made.

At the time I mutely sifted through comfort words. I'm not all that sure if I said that I was sorry, or if I even knew that I was supposed to. For the first time in our friendship, I felt a frustrating, sinking sense of helplessness, uselessness. For I had no words or Lucy Ricardo/Ethel Mertz scheme to change the circumstances or erase this reality. I felt in an unforgivable way that I was letting her down. There was some elusive thing to say, floating and swirling just out of reach, that would, if not change things, alleviate some of the confusion and grief. But I was at a loss to find it.

Her brother remains vague in my mind—an adolescent indifference, an impatient grunt, and a closed bedroom door. His death at sixteen sat uncomfortably within my newly formed fourteen-year-old perceptions of life. Old and very sick people died, not sixteen-year-olds. I assumed they were all mistaken, all wrong. I think in the back of my mind I truly believed that he would reappear and laugh the laugh that softened his eyes into slender crescents like his father's. I never told J. this, but I persistently thought it. Sixteen-year-olds didn't die. They still had too much to do.

Over the years, I know that J. found strength in caring for others, her instinctive need to be strong for everyone else. I'd always been reluctant to ask her how she felt about what happened, but she'd always come to mind when my brother had his own unsettling series of near misses: slipping fifteen feet down an abandoned coal shaft in Colorado; falling asleep at the wheel early one Easter morning just before slamming into a telephone pole. Four A.M. waking nightmares that only confirm how tenuous it all is.

Only recently, just a handful of days before our ten-year high-school reunion—with J. married and with me easing my way into a commitment to journalism—did I sense that there was the distance to beg for closure. Her thoughts materialized slowly in murky fragments, like Moss's jumbled scrapbook stowed in a box: a procession of priests in whispering robes; doves nesting in a front-lawn shade tree; her mother losing a single stone in a ring representing the lives of her children; a teacher who brought by classroom poetry penned in her brother's awkward hand.

With this event, she separates childhood from adulthood. It is her jagged break with innocence. "Because it has to be." It has taken some time, but I realize that I do as well. That it has quickened my pace, skewed my view of the world. Sometimes I run so fast that nothing at all comes into focus.

And at times amid my mind's white noise, I hear well-intentioned but threatening comfort words: "Slow down, you. We've got to slow you down."

J., who's grown weary of being strong for everyone else, in marriage has found an anchor. A peace. Sitting in summer skirts, in winter sun, staring out into the gray sea, I remember J. attempting to call up an image of her brother. "I know he'll never be here the same way I knew him. And not a day goes by that I don't think about him." But sometimes, she confides, no matter how hard she tries, it's difficult to resurrect a face, a form. "It's more like a feeling. A presence. Not a physical shape. More a spirit, I hope to never lose."

Tonight they are dropping poison from the sky. Around the neighborhood there are Xeroxed notices hastily taped to the windows of all my favorite morning haunts—the bookstore near Franklin Avenue, the coffeehouse on Vermont— "Come to the Anti-Malathion Rally at Pioneer Market!" boxy, black letters implore.

At 6:00 P.M. there's a less-than-impressive assembly shaking angry placards at motorists stopped in gridlocked traffic near Echo Park Avenue. By 7:00 P.M., not even remote traces of minor civil disobedience remain. Commuters speed by with air-conditioners blasting. Some pause at the corner and slip folded bills through a narrow opening in the window to purchase plastic covers from sidewalk vendors for their cars.

I wake to the voice of a rabid crackpot who's been doing double duty on the radio recent mornings. He drank down a tumbler full of the solution diluted in water a handful of years ago and is still alive to tell of it. He can't understand why a city whose skies are often a brown smear of smog would be so testy over "a little bug repellent" that just *might* save the state's crop. But as my friend Donna pointed out as I was trying rather unsuccessfully (and against the wind) to

tape down a makeshift plastic cover over my car, "Ever notice they never spray in Beverly Hills." I hadn't made the
conscious connection, not that I was surprised.

I live above one of the less-glamorous stretches of Sunset
Boulevard, just after it snakes belligerently, in fits and starts,
off its course from the shore to downtown. Outside my picture window a decapitated yet otherwise seemingly healthy
palm tree looms. At night when the state helicopters aren't
spraying insecticide, city choppers track the trail of elusive
fugitives with great shafts of white light. During the uncomfortable heat, brought on by a lingering tropical storm
named Fausto, helicopters clip through evening stillness
well into the first cool of morning. These are the summer
evenings, the uncomfortable waves of heat, that usually
don't wrestle with us until the final days of August or early
September. I spend early evening bent over a weary rotary
fan ten years my senior and listen to the humid voice of
Billie Holiday. At night the jasmine, thriving in abundant
clusters near my bedroom window, blooms so strong that it
often enters my dreams.

Friends call late at night without apologies because with
the heat they have lost all hope for sleep. We prepare for the
late summer months when acquaintances from out of town
will descend. At their request, we embark on macabre foot
tours: to the site where a lovely starlet expired after leaping
from her elevated perch atop the Hollywood sign; or to the
barstool at Musso and Frank where F. Scott Fitzgerald swam
in his dry martinis. They want to see just where the noctur-
nal specter takes its noisy ride down Sierra Bonita; where
Marilyn Monroe ate Nembutal and crawled into a final,
dreamless slumber. There is the ride through Silver Lake as
it dips into Atwater, offering a idyllic panoramic view of Forest Lawn Memorial Park in Glendale. For others there is the
obligatory stroll along Hollywood Boulevard near the stretch
where anxious throngs still fit their soles within grooves set
in cement at Mann's Chinese; or those who instead choose

to stare into the now equally famous blank eyes of runaways tirelessly parading the boulevard.

Whipping through the canyons, clipping hairpin turns through arroyo-gashed hills on Mulholland Drive, I explain to my disappointed charges that James Dean didn't take his fatal spill along this stretch of road. They accept with little argument, though I sometimes catch them surreptitiously searching for invisible skid marks in the asphalt ahead. Instead we end up in Griffith Park with the rest of the straw-hatted tourists and bored teens on cheap dates, staring up at the bronze James Dean bust just west of the observatory. They study the inscription, snap a few shots, then ask to move on.

There is a dead-man's curve with which I am more familiar. The one that reckless students risk on any given weekend. Because it is not yet world-famous it is not the one that houseguests ask to see. This sinister, serpentine stretch of gray concrete between Pacific Palisades and Brentwood offers blind curves that open up onto glimmering, startling city views. Sunset becomes a densely foliated backwood pass, and one of the drives most negotiated—tanked up and flying —on a dare. The other, "Top of the World," is a narrow ribbon of road leading up to a flat mesa, where students smoke pot, drink, then extend the rush by driving full speed down this narrow curving grade.

"They are consumed with having fun. Having a good time," local teachers have explained. Many seem oblivious to consequence. "They just want to have a good time. It is their impression of 'The Good Life.' "

A couple of years ago the cover of the *Los Angeles Times* Metro section featured a shot of Palisades High School students slumped in hysterical tears. Four members of the student body had been killed in a automobile accident on Halloween night. The driver had been drinking and ran headlong into a tree on San Vincente Boulevard. The car exploded into a forest of flames that lit the night sky. Those standing close by could hear the screams, but the heat was too fierce to admit assistance. Astonished onlookers heard the cries grow faint then die away.

Most student deaths recorded on this campus perched high above Malibu's palm-lined strand are often fatalities stemming from instances of violence. Too many are DUIs— either unlucky victims or blind perpetrators. Former Palisades administrator Roselynd Weeks puts the average at about five a year: "The Halloween accident seemed to be the most traumatic. There was a longer mourning period. But by junior/senior prom time it was back to business as usual." Bronze plaques go up along main corridors, memorial pages are set aside in class annuals, and classroom discussions spawn promises to mend old ways, but old habits are slow to change.

They've begun bringing wrecked automobiles onto campus to startle errant students, to shock them into some semblance of responsibility. They've placed them conspicuously in the quad for the day—crumpled masses of wrecked and charred metal, that once represented shining pride. They sit stoically in the sun like precious museum pieces on loan. Some students fall by to marvel at the remains, to imagine the condition of bodies pulled from the amorphous mass. At first some parents and faculty wondered about the appropriateness of this gesture. Some saw it as a tasteless sideshow sensation rather than a drunk-driving deterrent. After a more recent fatality, no one blocked the way.

It is sometimes difficult for teachers and administrators to determine whether or not some of these accidents are simply an elaborate way to camouflage a flirtation with suicide. Like an elderly shut-in's failure to take life-sustaining medication, it could be a passive, covert form of taking one's own life.

Teachers and administrators keep careful watch on troubled students and their black moods. They intermittently explore precarious emotional states in constant flux. Close friends will sometimes duck in to alert a trusted teacher or counselor about the words and needs of a distraught friend.

Creative expression is often a key, a hairline artery leading deep inside—a bleak poem composed in a writing class or a brooding pen-and-ink sketch handed in at an art workshop may have subtle allusions to death eloquently stowed between the lines or intricately laced within its borders.

Deep depressions bloom out of everyday disillusionment —disappointment in love, low self-esteem, lack of attention from significant loved ones. These dark moods expand, color existence a sooty gray. Eventually thoughts move from vague indistinct meditations on depression to concrete contemplations of quick ways out.

For many young people of this generation, the concept of life has never been more ephemeral, the scope of a life-span more abstract. Worries hover around the planet—environmental and international issues and the future of the human species. More and more, adolescents construct a blueprint for the future that doesn't carve out a place for spouse and/ or children. "They see the big picture more," explains Roselynd Weeks, "how the system works. And in that sense they are much more mature than generations preceding them."

There is, despite the abundance of sunshine and wealth, an oppressive sense of doom about an indifferent and chaotic world. A profound emptiness and a gray despair are both cradled snugly within this vast lap of luxury. For some, it only becomes increasingly apparent everyday—there is not the need nor time to pace and fret over a future that may never be.

Taking the Harbor Freeway south, the 91 east, I watch a fine drizzle fall. It is the first gray day in months. On the radio, newscasters impart strange tales that seem to wander in from remote dreamscapes: A Latina, after unloading the morning groceries, steps outside of her Huntington Park home and sets herself afire. Across town another woman walks toward a car and into the whirl of smoke and hot flame engulfing it. A skull and bones are found beneath a condemned building along the Wilshire corridor. Another Medfly discovered, this time in the Compton area. To protect the season's crop, there are plans to send helicopters into these skies in strict, arrowhead formation.

Along Santa Fe, in Compton, the sidewalks and structures rising from them emerge in monochromatic grays. These wide stretches of open road and industrial buildings don't offer much consolation. Traveling north, I watch warehouses unfold into boarded-up apartment buildings, then to chain-link fences enclosing lots of full of rust and weeds, and finally plot upon plot of tiny churches boasting grand and inspirational names: Living Water Fellowship, Compton/ Samoa Seventh Day Adventist, Mount Pilgrim Baptist, New Jerusalem Church of God and Christ.

For some time the papers ignored this community and others much like it across the Southland. They ignored the residents who, to avoid a stray bullet, curled near the baseboards to find sleep. They ignored children who stepped over stiff, bloodied, bodies on their way to homeroom. They ignored young mothers who worked themselves to the quick to keep their children in private schools, off the street and hidden from harm.

They ignored the survivors.

Both of my parents taught in these inner-city classrooms. Some Mondays the police would stop by with stills of the most recent "Jane Doe" for my mother to identify. She'd stare at the face, search for a familiar glimmer in the eyes, then shake her head. With a nod of thanks they would quickly depart.

"Those were the most resilient kids," she often recalls.

"They all seemed to be blessed with short memories. Life would jump up and slap them down but they'd quietly collect themselves. They were always ready to take more."

Two years ago, when the "Gang Problem" spilled out of the ever-widening circumscription media-labeled "South-Central L.A.," and into the affluent community of Westwood near UCLA, the papers finally took notice. Police were unleashed on these neighborhoods by the hundreds, to "sweep" the streets clean. City government responded by looking into other vague "emergency programs"—all Band-Aid efforts to cure only one of the many problems that have been chipping away at this community for decades.

In spite of the efforts, the statistics remain chilling: the black infant mortality rate is the highest in the county. Black males in the United States between the ages of fourteen and twenty-five have a one in twenty chance of being shot. In 1990, 364 gang-related homicides were reported in this city alone, almost doubling in 1991.

As a reporter, I've sat in on community meetings held within exquisite eighty-year-old church sanctuaries. After bowing their heads in prayer, the congregation furrows brows and searches sagacious eyes for the answers. From AIDS to random drive-by shootings, they are a people besieged. Some only shrug shoulders. Others whisper genocide.

Here it is sometimes difficult to gauge what is feared most —the ominous threat of death or the uncertain properties of life. "Some put up a front, a bravado, to get them through," I've listened to teachers muse. "They will tell you they're not afraid. I think some of them fear death. Those with conventional values. A good number of them have the loftiest of ambitions—doctors, lawyers, actors, singers, athletes—but then there's also the element that has nothing to lose. Those who simply exist."

You see those empty eyes, those clouded, spiritless faces

all over. Yet I'm still struck by the chill that returns a well-intentioned smile. Along this stretch of East Compton Boulevard, this chill moves through to the core. More gray buildings, more steely faces; the only splashes of color I see for blocks are the Moorish and Byzantine structures containing the mausoleums of Angeles Abbey Memorial Park.

"We've lost the ability to love, especially the black race. We just can't seem to love ourselves," says Jean Sanders, who is vice president/general manager of Angeles Abbey, the second black cemetery west of the Mississippi.

Sanders, on a busy week, sees ten to twelve families in her small, orderly office papered with inspirational messages clipped from magazines, and color snapshots of various government dignitaries. The winter months are the hardest, she says. Especially Christmas. "The joyous times are often the saddest. People just can't cope. The county stats go way high."

Sanders, whose grandfather was a mortician in Arkansas, carries the tradition a third generation. She is the first black woman to be appointed to the state's Cemetery Board. She digs graves, works in the crematory, and when short-handed, operates the tractor, but most importantly she explains, her purpose is to listen and console.

She's grown used to the fact that when families arrive they are often surprised to see her. Those grieving expect instead a grim old man in an ill-fitting gray suit, but when he fails to greet them, they seldom bother to hide their amazement. Soon their faces will relax with her presence, with the gentle cadence of her voice and the sincerity of her eyes.

"I have women who come in to work on their sons' graves. In the process, they will be able to accept their child's death. It's taken one woman seven years. A seven-year death. She's just beginning to focus in on her family. People here die slowly, inwardly for a long, long time."

———

It wasn't too long ago that finding a plot of soil to buy a black body posed a problem in Los Angeles. In some areas, private charters blocked these interments as late as 1966. African-American families, in black veils and ash-gray suits, loaded caskets onto streetcars and rode to Evergreen Cemetery in East L.A. It is where three generations of my family have been laid to rest. Sanders remembers hearing those stories. She has watched this neighborhood change three times— from predominately white until Watts went up in flames in '65, then predominately black, and now Latino.

Angeles Abbey has had to adjust to the community's changing face: the Gypsies who throw noisy feasts and roast pigs in honor of the newly departed; the Vietnamese who fill caskets with the loved one's earthly possessions, then decorate the grounds with ripe fruit and flora. The gang funerals she says, despite what you read in the dailies, have been low-key and uneventful. "They come in, do their thing, and then they leave.

"These kids are more afraid of the known than the unknown," Sanders explains. "They live with the known everyday. Live with a father on crack or a mother on welfare, maybe a brother in the gangs. They take their hostility out on buildings—mark it up with graffiti, break windows. They take their hostility out on people. They take human lives."

Staring in the face of all this can spiritually drain you, Sanders tells me. It is a job which is difficult to term "enjoyable," but Sanders admits she does what she can to strengthen and uplift. She likes people. She gives them hope. "I had a lot of babies coming in recently. A *lot* of babies, and that's hard. Young adults with gunshot wounds —victims of violent crime. The hatred and hostility is troubling. These dying spirits. I sometimes stop and ask them what they're hungry for. And when they answer, it seems so basic, so simple when you stop to think about it—happiness. That's all they want. 'Happiness in the house.' "

———

My old roommate from my days north has recently moved in to town. She is just beginning to get a grip on the rhythm of the city, but its heat and size still daunt her. Just as she traveled two buses with me to buy a proper winter fedora for February's gusts and lightning storms, I carefully instruct her to place cool compresses on her pressure points—at her wrists and temples—then to lie in a darkened room "cadaver still."

We often share notes for survival.

She has taken a movie job, a low-budget travesty that required a scene in a cemetery. The crew set up on a patch of green and started digging a shallow grave. After awhile they turned up dry bones. Caretakers turned their heads. The remains glowed ivory white in the dusky earth.

My mind's eye quickly processes these spare details into flickering clips from campy fifties' horror movies; an endless montage shot from oblique angles and captured in powdery half-light. I visualize men and women intently lobbing sun-scorched bones. Tibias and ulnae sail gently through cloudless skies. Yet as in the movies, in varying shades of gray, the eyes don't look so urgent or frightened, the expressions not nearly as desperate as they would, or often do, in real life.

As my friend imparts her tale, we stand in front of "The Original" Miceli's Italian on Las Palmas. We wait along with a small cluster of others for a table near the bar upstairs where a graying rhythm section runs through an impressive collection of standards—"Night and Day," "Stella by Starlight," "Body and Soul." A bewildered drifter, with upturned palms, slows his pace as he nears the line forming near the front doors. Muttering, he works his way north toward the neon and noise of Hollywood Boulevard, shaking his head, his face stretched into a wild, delirious smile, he is saying, "I'm not dead yet, I'm not dead yet. *I'm not dead yet.*"

GOD

David Reid

THE POSSESSED

1

Los Angeles was the heavenly city of the Jazz Age, almost as famous for its messiahs and evangelists as for the movies, its chief export. Nathanael West, Evelyn Waugh, Aldous Huxley, James M. Cain, have all written about the luxuriance of gods in the thirties and forties, and by 1940, the *WPA Guide to Los Angeles* claimed, "The multiplicity and diversity of faiths that flourish in the aptly named City of Angels probably cannot be duplicated in any other city on earth." Since Los Angeles fifty years ago had a much smaller population than Detroit or Philadelphia, size alone cannot account for all these heavenly mansions.

In the next half-century, Los Angeles became the second city of the Jewish Diaspora. It is probably the largest center of Theravadin and Mahayana Buddhism outside Asia. It is also home to a substantial Muslim population, not to mention enclaves of Santería and Voudon, and colonies of Jains and Sikhs. Rastafarianism, a religion of the oppressed in Jamaica, is a cult among middle-class surfers in Del Mar and Malibu.

The $9 million geodesic "FaithDome" built by the Reverend Frederick K. C. Price, the largest church in the United States, serves a mostly African-American congregation of 16,000 on Vermont Avenue in the South Central district. In Orange County, the glass-sheathed and made-for-television design of the Garden Grove Community Church, the famous "Crystal Cathedral" designed by Philip Johnson, testifies gigantically to the power of positive thinking—as practiced by the Reverend Dr. Robert H. Schuller, the television evangelist whose ministry began across the street in 1955, on the roof of the snack bar of the Orange Drive-In. The "22-acre shopping center for Jesus Christ" where Garden Grove stands is currently being adorned with a 234-foot "Prayer Spire," which will be visible, as the cathedral increasingly is not, from the Santa Ana Freeway.

The hills above Hollywood Boulevard have sheltered a sedate little outpost of Asian mysticism for most of this century. Alan Watts described these precincts as "a district of faded glamour that was once haunted by pandits of the Theosophical Society, where the streets have such names as Temple Hill Drive and Vasanta Way, and where the architecture simulates the wealthier parts of Marrakesh and Fez." Aldous Huxley, Gerald Heard, and Christopher Isherwood, the "British Mystical Expatriates," were familiars here in the days when Swami Prabhavananda of the Ramakrishna mission presided over the Vedanta temple.

Asia has been sending missionaries to Southern California since the turn of the century, to minister to immigrant communities and to proselytize among the natives. Downtown are the elaborate Shingon and Jodo Buddhist temples built by the Issei, the first generation of immigrants from Japan. The Zen Center of Los Angeles (ZCLA), whose bhikkus are mostly Anglo, occupies a whole city block on Normandie Avenue and carries on sidelines in Zen plumbing, carpentry, and publishing. In Koreatown the saffron-colored Buddhist temple of Chua Viet-Nam stands at Ninth and Berendo, a legacy of the war in Southeast Asia. Its founder, Dr. Thien-An, was one of the Buddhist monks in Saigon who rallied opposition to President Ngo Dinh Diem in 1963. A Zen master with a doctorate in Oriental literature, Thien-An came to Los Angeles during the war to teach. Persuaded by his American students to stay, he was waiting at Camp Pendleton in 1975 when the first wave of refugees arrived.

City of shouting churches, marabouts, brujas, dervishes, and desert prophets—how "aptly named"!—what is it about Los Angeles that inflames so many prophetic souls?

If the diversity of world religions in Los Angeles is simply explained by the fact that it has always been a racial and ethnic "archipelago," even during the Anglo ascendancy, its spiritual extremism is usually blamed on geography. Or as John Gunther wrote in *Inside U.S.A.* (1947), "The hills around Ventura, let us say, are the last stop; California is stuck with so many crackpots if only because they can't go any farther." Edmund Wilson said that Southern California offered a taste of every faith "from Theosophistry to Christian Sirens," and his friend Nathanael West had the same idea, assuming that the cause for all the strangeness was the great immigration from the Midwest of 1880–1930—"the people who come to California to die," as West calls them in *The Day of the Locust.* But now, with the millennium approaching, the traffic in strange gods is as brisk as ever. The "radical rentiers" of the thirties are mostly resting in Forest

Lawn, but the same sort of cults that diverted their sunset years now lure their firm-bodied great-grandchildren. The Church of Scientology has a Celebrity Centre International in Hollywood, and another new religion, Nicheren Shoshu, a Japanese derivative of Buddhism with roots in the thirteenth century, has some claim to being the fastest-growing sect in the city.

Ancient Alexandria (the city in history Los Angeles most resembles), was obsessed—like Byzantium—with the mystery of Christ's real nature. Was His substance partly human? wholly divine? The mystery that typically consumes Southern Californians is personal transformation, and what "technologies of the self" should be used to achieve it. As a vale of soul-making, Los Angeles represents a heightened, intensified version of the national cult, for it is a Pelagian city, "Pelagianism" being that most dangerous and seductive doctrine, anathematized by Saint Augustine, that says a man can save his soul by his own exertions. Los Angeles is the voice of Rilke's "Archaic Torso of Apollo" saying, "You must change your life."

The drama critic Kenneth Tynan saw this heresy enacted in the ordinary activities of the day when he discovered the automated car wash. "It is in fact a purification in which it is not so much the car that is purified as the owner," he wrote. "It is he who feels morally and spiritually cleansed, as his machine emerges gleaming from the assembly line. And for an extra dollar he can subject it to a further ordeal: an inundation of hot wax. This represents the annealing fire through which the soul must pass."

Rebirth—metamorphosis, transfiguration, second acts—here is the key to all Southern California mythologies, and the promise held out by its gods, goddesses, avatars, and messiahs. Of the cults invented or revived by Southern Californians (native and born-again) some have flourished like the bay tree; most are born merely to bloom and drop. As

T. E. Lawrence says of the Arabs, "Their failures they kept to themselves. The fringes of their deserts were strewn with broken faiths."

2

Angelus Temple, Sister Aimee Semple McPherson's establishment in Echo Park (dedicated January 1, 1923), is sunk in slightly frowzy old age, the Norma Desmond of Los Angeles churches. Once, it was the most famous stately mansion of all. McPherson herself designed it, in the shape of an immense concrete wedding cake. Now it has a musty, abandoned air. The "Miracle Room," filled in apostolic times with cast-off crutches, wheelchairs, and trusses, has been reduced to a display case. (Shown similar wonders at Lourdes, Anatole France is supposed to have said; "What, no wooden legs?") Most poignantly, the Prayer Tower, where relays of worshipers used to pray around the clock, women by day, men by night, in two-hour shifts, now closes sensibly at dusk. The sea of faith has receded and left the great dingy monument at 11000 Glendale Boulevard marooned in memories of the twenties, like the resort hotel where Jack Nicholson goes mad in *The Shining*. How glorious it was when Sister would preach in her admiral's uniform or dress up as a motorcycle cop and speed to the pulpit in a motorcycle: "Stop! You're on a one-way street to Hell!" H. L. Mencken came all the way from Baltimore to scoff, and young Richard Nixon and his family all the way from Whittier to pray.

Since no one at the temple could tell me, I telephoned the church's curia on Sunset Boulevard to ask exactly when they had broken the spell and begun shutting down the Prayer Tower at night.

"You will have to ask Mr. Causabon [not his real name] about that," the receptionist said.

"Do *you* remember?"

"It was a long time ago." The tone implied an event not quite so long ago as the Flood—more like the dissolution of the monasteries. "Anyway, you'll have to submit your question in writing. We have been burned by the press before, you know."

Angelus Temple was built toward the end of four decades in which Los Angeles had transformed itself from a squalid little town into the largest city on the West Coast, the decades of the great migration from the Midwest. The Theosophical colony at Point Loma, from which Southern California's reputation for religious weirdness can be dated, materialized like Oz in 1900. Commanding a windswept promontory across the harbor from San Diego and facing the sea, Point Loma was soon adorned by an Aryan Temple, the ninety-room green-domed Homestead, and "a School of Antiquity, a Theosophical University, a Greek Theater, a Raja Yoga College, and the Iris Temple of Art, Music and Drama." Its spiritual dictator was Katherine Tingley, known as the "Purple Mother." According to Carey McWilliams, the presence of this occult humbug within his sphere of influence deeply troubled General Harrison Gray Otis, publisher of the *Los Angeles Times.* Engaged in the serious enterprise of empire-building, General Otis regarded yogis from out of state as the worst sort of advertising for his Southland. He was infuriated by rumors that the Theosophists worshiped a sacred dog, Spot, believed by them to be the reincarnation of one of the Purple Mother's husbands. But when the *Times* ventured to denounce their midnight orgies, "gross immoralities" as practiced "by the disciples of spookism," Tingly sued and to general astonishment eventually collected.

In 1906, William James took notice of a religious revival,

going back to the nineties, comparable, it seemed to him, to the early days of Christianity, Buddhism, and Islam. In the piney woods of the South and the big cities swarming with immigrants, there was a spiritual quickening, an enlarged will to believe. Either the religious were becoming more intensely whatever they already were, as in the Holiness movement within Methodism, or they were finding new gods. "New Thought" and Christian Science swept through Boston. As long ago as 1893, popular interest in Asian religions had been excited by the World Parliament of Religions in Chicago, the great new metropolis of the age. For the first time the pandits of the East had presented themselves in person to a large American audience. The greatest crowd-pleaser was the glamorous and commanding Swami Vivekananda, disciple of the antic Bengali mystic, Sri Ramakrishna. Vivekananda, who went on to found the Vedanta Society in 1897, missionized on the West Coast at the turn of the century. The occult, Easternizing doctrine of Theosophy attracted a national following, and an earnest handful of intellectuals undertook a serious study of Buddhism. All of these movements had soon converged in Southern California.

In April 1906, the *Los Angeles Times* reported a "Weird Babel of Tongues" at a revival on Azusa Street. The participants were mostly washerwomen and other African-American laborers at the start, but included in time some middle-class whites who had come to gape and stayed to pray. The evangelist leading the revival, William Seymour, was a black minister from Texas who had not spoken in tongues before the revival in Los Angeles. Together, he and his flock "prayed their way to Pentecost." Though following on earlier Holiness revivals in the heartland, including episodes of glossolalia (the learned name for the gift of tongues) in Kansas, the Pentecostal moment on Azusa Street was something new under the sun; it was in Los Angeles that the movement, which is now the fastest growing part of Christianity, was launched as a worldwide phenomenon. For believers, the gift of tongues—dismissed by the newspapers as "jabbering"—signified baptism in the Holy Spirit, as the Apostles had experienced it, and the approaching end of the world. According to the prophet Joel and the Book of Acts, it was in the "last days" that the Spirit would be poured out, and "your sons and daughters shall prophesy, your young men will see visions, and your old men will dream dreams." The sense of an ending was dramatically confirmed by the San Francisco earthquake of 1906. Fallen was Babylon, that great city.

Believing there was little time, the first generation of Pentecostals threw themselves into missionizing. In these early days, most of them believed that when the "tongues of fire" descended on them, they were actually speaking in languages that they did not know—Chinese, Swedish, Russian, Hebrew, and so on. This phenomenon, which linguists assert does not exist, is technically called "xenoglossy," and the early missionaries who poured out of Azusa Street believed that their speaking in unknown languages would become permanent once they arrived at their destinations—in China they would speak Chinese without learning it, in Rumania Rumanian, and so on. Within a year or two, evangelists were said to be reporting from Syria, Australia, Tibet, Africa, Cuba, and Japan. Robert Semple, a boilermaker by trade, carried the word to the farm country of Ontario, Canada, where he converted a seventeen-year-old schoolgirl, Aimee Elizabeth Kennedy. "Oh, Mr. Semple, what a blessed privilege it would be to bear the light into the darkest corners of heathendom," she had exclaimed. The strapping man of God took the hint. Almost at once, they were married and bound for China.

In 1905 William James's "younger and vainer and shallower" brother Henry had arrived in Los Angeles from Chicago. To his immense surprise, the Master found himself enchanted, especially after he checked into the glittering Hotel del Coronado in San Diego, and he confessed as much in a letter to his sister-in-law in Cambridge: "California . . . (Southern C. at least—which, however, the real C, I believe much repudiates) has completely bowled me over—such a delicious difference from the rest of the U.S. do I find in it. (I speak of course all of nature and climate, fruits and flowers; for there is absolutely nothing else, and the sense of the shining social and human inane is utter.)" "Such a delicious difference" summarizes the appeal and the interest of Los Angeles at the turn of the century and for many years after. As L.P. Jacks wrote: "Here, it seems, is the place where harassed Americans come to recover the joy and serenity which their manner of life denies them elsewhere, the place, in short, to study America in flight from itself."

In the nineteenth century, the Gold Rush and the rise of San Francisco—for James in 1905, still the capital city of the "real" California—had accelerated the tempo of American life; Marx himself said that "nowhere else has the upheaval most shamelessly caused by capitalist centralization taken place with such speed." For most of the twentieth century, as the UCLA geographer Edward W. Soja observes, this has been even truer of Southern California. And yet the enduring mythology of Southern California grew up in the interval when it seemed to be the place not to encounter but to elude the ordeal of change. In a remarkable book, *No Place of Grace* (1981), the young historian Jackson Lears described the diffuse movement—it might better simply be called a "mood"—of "antimodernism" that developed in response to the enormous changes that occurred between 1880 and 1920 in Europe and North America—the railroads reticulated across continents, the cities electrified; radio, movies, phonograph records; psychoanalysis and the death of God; the European age of empire and the Great War. . . . By way of comparison, how little the West changed in the forty-five years of the Cold War! To Henry James, his countrymen seemed "dancing, all consciously, on the thin crust of a volcano": an odd description of America in the confident years when Theodore Rex was in the White House, but underneath the confidence was an epidemic of nerves. It was the age of the nervous breakdown and the fashionable disease of "neurasthenia," a sense of psychological and physical enfeeblement, of "weightlessness" and unreality, that plagued the affluent housewife and the harassed tycoon alike.

Representing on the one hand a longing for intensity and authenticity, on the other a need for escape and repose, "antimodernism," says Lears, was manifest in such disparate forms as Theodore Roosevelt's cult of the strenuous life, the Arts and Crafts movement, the exploration of alien faiths like Buddhism and Vedanta, environmentalism, and the discovery of moral uplift in Native Americana, spiritualism, and the Middle Ages. In Pasadena during the Progressive Era, so well evoked by Kevin Starr in *Inventing the Dream*, antimodernism reached a pitch of refinement. The literary bohemians of the Arroyo set, led by the master publicist Charles Fletcher Lummis, went in for Indian blankets and Mission furniture, while their grander neighbors, the "Tory bohemian" rich commissioned bungalows from the Greene brothers, Henry and Charles. (Charles was a Buddhist.) Antimodernism was the crucible of what Michel Foucault would call the "California cult of the self." *You must change your life.*

The craving for novelty, in religious dogma as in any other sphere, was perfectly comprehensible: what was there to lose? In contrast to San Francisco's virile past, the settlers who made Los Angeles were typically unyoung and often infirm. If San Francisco had been an American exploit in the 1840s and '50s, then Los Angeles, in the decades brack-

eting the turn of the century, was symbolically an escape—
from the nerve-wracking industrial society of the East, from
the boredom and drudgery of farm life in the Midwest, from
aging and pain. Those not busy being reborn were busy
dying.

3

On the last page of his first novel, *This Side of Paradise*,
accepted by Scribners' in 1919, Scott Fitzgerald declared "all
wars fought, all Gods dead, all faiths in man shaken." Nowhere was postwar disillusionment really as comprehensive
as all that. A better prophet, William Butler Yeats, had
begun the new year by writing "The Second Coming," with
its famous vision of a "rough beast slouching towards Bethlehem to be born." In Southern California, far from being
dead, the gods were stirring in their stony sleep.

That spring, Yeats himself, as he tells in *A Vision*, was
contacted by spirit "communicators," late in the night as his
train was speeding between San Bernardino and Los Angeles. In Hollywood, where he had a lecture date, he might
have seen the Babylonian fertility goddess Ishtar reborn in
lath and plaster, looming seventy feet tall at the corner of
Sunset and Hollywood, on the crumbling set of D. W. Griffith's superepic, *Intolerance*. *Intolerance* was a very long
movie depicting in detail modern industrial unrest, the Fall
of Babylon, the Saint Bartholomew's Day Massacre, and
somewhat more sketchily the Crucifixion. Even coming
from the demigod director of *Birth of a Nation*, it failed to
enrapture the ticket-buying public. Anita Loos remembered
viewing the rough cut, and thinking as the lights went up in
the projection room, "D. W. had lost his mind." Nonetheless, the gargantuan sets (falling to pieces in 1919, with the

city pleading with Griffith to pull them down) suited the mood of the movie capital, which was overweening and ozymandian. At last concentrated in Southern California, the American movie industry accounted for almost 80 percent of the world's ticket sales. How many of the living gods in history ever commanded the awe or compelled the ravening curiosity aroused by the new Hollywoodian gods and goddesses?

The shopgirls, ribbon clerks, whores, cowboys, college kids, and gin-soaked vaudevillians who had unexpectedly become gods on the movie Olympus understandably craved reassurance that their amazing and bewildering transformation belonged, after all, to the natural order of things. Chaplin, though the greatest god of all, was almost alone in playing the skeptic. "Douglas [Fairbanks]," for example, "believed that our lives were ordained and that our destiny was important," he writes in his *Autobiography*. "I remember one warm summer's night both of us climbed to the top of a large water tank and sat there talking in the wild grandeur of Beverly. . . .

" 'Look!' said Douglas fervently, making an arc gesture taking in all the heavens. 'The moon! And those myriads of stars! Surely there must be some reason for all this beauty? It must be fulfilling some destiny! It must be for some good and you and I are part of it!' Then he turned to me, suddenly inspired. 'Why are you given this talent, this wonderful medium of motion pictures that reaches millions of people throughout the world!'

" 'Why is it given to Louis B. Mayer and the Warner brothers?' I said."

In religions, as in the movies, there was an immense market for old wine in new bottles. The proletarian writer Louis Adamic avidly prowled the holy bazaar. "I discovered all sorts of churches I had never heard of before—churches of Divine Power, of Divine Fire, of Advanced Thought, of the

Higher Things in Life," he writes in *Laughing in the Jungle* (1932). He met the prophet of "Maz-daz-Lan," known as the Universal Genius, who preached "a weird concoction of sun-worship, phallicism, Oriental philosophies of all kinds, health, and breath culture." Once he attended a Sunday service at which Rin-Tin-Tin, the dog movie star, appeared "in person."

"On Saturdays I saw church advertisements in the *Times* and the *Examiner* announcing sermons apparently by the leading preachers in the city on such topics as 'What Would Jesus Do if He Were a Great Movie Director Like Cecil de Mille? or If He Were President of the Advertising Club?'." One minister was self-described as an "ex-gambler, now a mighty hunter before the Lord," and his subject on Sunday was "Who Killed the Dead Sea?" Pentecostalism escaped his notice, but Adamic seized on the "fantastic human muddle" that explains, to the unbeliever, why such a movement could catch fire here, and not on the prairie where it was born. It was not that Los Angeles was "cosmopolitan," as some church historians have ventured—rather, he explained, that it was an "enormous village."

4

Of the messiahs of the city, Jiddu Krishnamurti was the most puzzling. He arrived, at the start of the twenties, in a blazing nimbus of publicity, proclaimed by the elite of the worldwide Theosophical Society as the future World Teacher, destined to be possessed by the same divine spirit that had formerly been incarnated in Jesus Christ and, two thousand years before that, as the lute-playing Hindu god Krishna. Worshiped and manipulated since boyhood, Krishnamurti was expected to emerge as a god, a hero, and a sage—and there would be those who believed that he actually did become each of these things. In the course of one of the strangest careers in the history of religion, he was messiah and apostate. He was active for almost seventy years—decades of incessant lecturing and publishing—after his arrival in Southern California, and, when he died in February 1986, even those closest to him were still unsure who or what he had been.

Krishnamurti's coming had been expected in Los Angeles almost since his "discovery" on a beach near Madras in India in 1909. A leading Theosophist, famous for clairvoyant powers, had picked him out of a crowd of swimmers, saying he had the most wonderful aura he had ever seen, "without a particle of selfishness in it."

His discoverer, a former Anglican curate named C. W. Leadbeater, was notoriously fond of the company of handsome boys, but Krishnamurti could not have appealed to him on that ground. The boy on the beach was unkempt and sickly, with crooked teeth, a moronic expression, and lice in his eyebrows, and so timid and dim it seemed he might be mentally retarded. The eighth son of a poor Brahmin, he was then fourteen years old.

Theosophy taught an esoteric version of evolution supposedly learned from a Great White Brotherhood of "Masters" or "mahatmas." The Masters were believed to live in a hidden ravine in Tibet, and therefore had to be visited on the astral plane. It was essential to Krishnamurti's early acceptance that within the society no one was more adept at making such journeys than "C.W.L." No one was more adept or as skillful at imposing his version of what ostensibly was happening in the spirit world. The president of the society, Annie Besant, though a great political force in Indian affairs, deferred to the ex-curate in all matters of the occult, and embraced Krishnamurti as the avatar from the moment they met.

In the ten years after his theophany, the physical and social changes in Krishnamurti were almost supernatural. The lice-ridden boy in danger of starvation was miraculously transformed into the exotically handsome "New Messiah in Tennis Flannels" who was a newspaper sensation in London and Benares, Bucharest and Montevideo, New York and, at last, Los Angeles. Fencing with reporters in a vast suite at the Waldorf-Astoria, presiding over annual "camps" on three continents organized with military precision, speaking in French from the Eiffel Tower to a radio audience of 1.2 million—in almost all his public appearances, he was a composed and enigmatic figure, whose golf clubs and London suits, tennis rackets and aristocratic offhandedness seemed calculated to contradict every standard expectation of an Indian guru. The Order of the Star, an international organization essentially dedicated to his deification, enrolled over 40,000 members in forty countries.

At stage center beside the messiah himself was Annie Besant, the former militant feminist, Fabian socialist, freethinker, rumored lover of George Bernard Shaw, and labor agitator, who had forsaken all that in favor of astral planes and "Ascended Masters." Besant was acknowledged by most Theosophists (but never by her poisonous rival, the Purple Mother) as the legitimate heir of the society's founder, the great Russian spiritualist-adventurer, Madame Blavatsky. Nor was Krishnamurti, "our Krishna-Christ," as she called him, her only cause. Until Gandhi supplanted her, she was the leading figure in the movement for Indian independence.

In the summer of 1922 when he came to California, Krishnamurti had not yet shown any evidence of a spiritual vocation, in spite of all the occult initiations he had undergone. Even Mrs. Besant murmured, "Oh dear, what is to become of you?" On the verge of his voyage across the Pacific, he wrote to his confidante, Lady Emily Lutyens, "Lord! how I

hate it all. . . . It all goes against my nature & I am not fit
for this job." Yet another message from the Masters was
"brought through," and he resolved to do better. In California, he and his younger brother, Nityananda, took the train
from San Francisco to Ventura, and were driven straight to
the upper end of the Ojai Valley, where a cabin had been
rented for them. Nitya was tubercular, and it was hoped the
dry air would be good for him.

It was a visit long overdue. Since the turn of the century,
years before Krishnamurti's discovery, Annie Besant had
been lecturing around the world on the theme of "The Coming Race and the Coming Christ," building on Madame Blavatsky's secret prophecies of a new messiah. For a time,
Australia had been promoted as the cradle of the new race,
only to be replaced by Southern California, with its superior
spiritual vibrations. These expectations dovetailed nicely
with the "racialist" nonsense about Southern California becoming the new "Aryan" homeland that had been popular-
ized years before by such figures as Joseph Widney, one of
the first presidents of the University of Southern California.

In Ojai, Krishnamurti experienced the first of the seizures,
kept secret for many years, that he called "the process" and
which continued intermittently for the rest of his life. These
were intensely painful "out of body" experiences during
which he would trash and writhe, call his own name aloud,
and, in a child's voice, talk of visions and strange night journeys. He told his brother it was "like being tied down in the
desert, one's face to the blazing sun, with one's eyelids cut
off." His entourage naturally interpreted these events as the
mystical awakening of the kundalini.

The public sequel was equally dramatic. Though devas-
tated by Nityananda's death in November 1925, which he
learned of while passing through the Suez Canal on the way
to India, Krishnamurti became persuaded that he was the
World Teacher. Speaking in the shadow of a huge banyan
tree in Adyar, he said at last: "*I* come to those who want

sympathy, who want happiness, who are longing to be released."

The next four years were very curious. Many Theosophical luminaries either failed to notice or disbelieved in the Second Coming—perhaps Krishnamurti was bewitched. Even true believers entertained theological quibbles, usually centering on whether he would be permanently occupied by the god, or only intermittently. On the other hand, the divinization of a "Dusky Messiah," as one headline writer called him, especially one who was proud of his golf handicap (plus two), was just the sort of nine-day wonder the twenties reveled in. Typically, the *New York Times* reported (August 25, 1926) that the young god would arrive on the *Majestic*, "like any other celebrity." Mrs. Besant arranged the purchase of almost a thousand acres in the Ojai Valley, stating that she was acting "as a servant of the Great Hierarchy," and gave a statement to the Associated Press that declared unequivocally, "The World Teacher is here." Krishnamurti took to commuting between Hollywood and Ojai in a blue Packard convertible, usually in the early morning to elude speed cops. He was luckier with automobiles than another avatar, the silent sage Meher Baba ("Don't worry, be happy"), who also boasted a great following in Hollywood, and was almost killed in a crack-up near Sunset Boulevard. On May 15, Krishnamurti gave his first public talk in the United States, speaking to a crowd of 16,000 in Hollywood Bowl.

Around this time he was offered $5,000 a week to appear in a movie about the life of Buddha. He was interested enough in movie-making to visit the set of Cecil B. De Mille's *King of Kings*, where he was photographed standing between the director and the beautiful, alcoholic H. B. Warner, who had been cast as Christ. Krishnamurti told his friend John Barrymore, "I left soon after this, as I thought three Saviors on the same lot was a little too much."

Among two thousand listeners who paid the $45 entry fee

to attend the week-long Star Camp held in Ojai between May 27 and June 4, 1929 were the seventeen-year-old Jackson Pollock, recently expelled from Manual Arts High School for disciplinary offenses, and his friend Phil Goldstein (Philip Guston). According to his biographers Steven Naifeh and Gregory White Smith, Pollock was understandably taken with the rebellious, instinctive, antiauthoritarian, and anti-intellectual themes that Krishnamurti was emphasizing in those days. "Each one has to make his own path."

Naturally, the same themes bewildered or affronted old-school Theosophists. Secretly, Krishnamurti had always disliked the mumbo-jumbo associated with Theosophy. He was now free to confess that he had never finished a Theosophical book, nor understood any of what he now called the society's jargon. But it was not merely that the old doctrines were superseded by the arrival of the messiah. If truth could be apprehended directly, the whole society, with its elaborate rituals and initiations, was a positive hindrance to liberation.

"But supposing that Krishnamurti was indeed the *jagadguru*, the world teacher," Alan Watts wrote many years later, "how would he have responded to such adulation? He would have done exactly what he did, which was—in 1928—to dissolve the Order of the Star, and to proclaim that he was not a guru and acknowledged no disciples." It was actually in August 1929, at a Star Camp in Ommen, Holland, where his order owned several thousand acres, that he finally renounced his followers:

"You can form other organizations and expect someone else. . . . My concern is to set men absolutely, unconditionally free."

It appeared he had led his disciples into the wilderness and left them there.

5

Trapped inside Angelus Temple was another prisoner of fame. Aimee Semple McPherson was twenty-six when she followed the sawdust trail to the sea in 1917, already an experienced revivalist who had been blessed with her own "foursquare" revelation. Widowed in Hong Kong at nineteen, when her missionary husband died of "Eastern fever," bored and restless back on the Canadian plain, she had quickly seen where her vocation lay. Her first revival in Los Angeles packed Philharmonic Auditorium, and then, in San Diego, where pale invalids thronged the streets, she discovered a gift for faith healing. She would not return to Los Angeles until 1921, but already she had determined to build her own tabernacle by the lake in Echo Park.

Angelus Temple was dedicated on New Year's Day, 1923. The Nixon family was entirely characteristic of the lower-middle-class "folks" who flocked to the services held three times a week and twice on Sunday: "small shopkeepers, barbers, beauty-shop operators, small-fry realtors, and the owners of hamburger joints," according to Carey McWilliams's inventory in *Southern California Country*. Sister, as she was known, satisfied their inchoate longing for pageantry and fellowship—Christianity with no chiaroscuro and a warm neon glow. Her evangel, polished on the road, was one of "joy, joy, joy," and in this sign she conquered Los Angeles.

Like many conquerors, she found herself alone at the moment of triumph (except for her mother, Minnie Kennedy, who in a highly unusual arrangement, was co-owner of the church's many enterprises). After losing one husband to fever, she forsook her second, a colorless grocery clerk named Harold McPherson, to evangelize. He divorced her on grounds of desertion in 1921, adding that he hoped never to see her again and hinting darkly of "wildcat habits" that belied her smiling public face. Evidently, Sister did not deeply feel his loss, either. Still, Foursquare Gospel theology did not permit the remarriage of divorced persons so long as the former mate was still living, and though swiftly forgotten, Harold McPherson persisted in remaining alive.

Then, in May 1926, the faith of Angelus Temple was sorely tried, and the circulation of the nation's newspapers vastly enlarged, when Sister Aimee Semple McPherson disappeared in the waves of Ocean Park and surfaced some weeks later in Douglas, Arizona, with a breathless story of escaping from kidnapers so far gone in depravity they had threatened to sell her into white slavery in Mexico. The press soon discovered that in reality she had spent the interval secluded in a "love cottage" in Carmel in the company of an electrician, Kenneth G. Ormiston, employed by her radio station, KFSG, the "Glory Station of the Pacific Coast."

As Carey McWilliams and others have reconstructed the story, Sister intended her disappearance to be permanent. By dying, she would be delivered from an increasingly intolerable celebrity, the Church of the Foursquare Gospel would be preserved, and Mr. Ormiston would be hers. However, she had not reckoned on the frenzied devotion of her followers, who lit bonfires on the beach and staged vigils (one committed suicide, another drowned); nor did she anticipate the exertions of the authorities, who sent out search planes and divers, or the vigilance and mean suspiciousness of the newspapers. Continued flight was not the answer. It had become clear that her fame would eventually have discovered her somewhere, in Rangoon or Reno (there was a close call near San Luis Obispo), and her followers would be cruelly betrayed. To save her church, Sister had to be reborn. A crowd of 100,000 was at the railroad station to greet the prophet when she returned from the desert.

Almost immediately, her story began to unravel. Though

the hard core of her following never wavered, her ruin seemed complete when the district attorney's office announced it would prosecute her for the perpetration of a hoax. "Her great success raised up two sets of enemies, both powerful," Mencken wrote. "One was made up of the regular clergy, who resented her raids upon their customers. The other was composed of the town Babbitts who began to fear that her growing celebrity was making Los Angeles ridiculous. So it was decided to bump her off, and her ill-timed morganatic honeymoon with the bald-headed and wooden-legged Mr. Ormiston offered a good chance." More like the wildcat than the lamb to which she compared herself, McPherson fought back, alleging that she was the victim variously of a Roman Catholic vendetta, a cabal of vice-lords, and the jealousy and malice of her fellow prelates. In the midst of her trial, whether worn down, frightened away, or, as many believed, paid off, the district attorney dropped all charges.

There would be no escape from Angelus Temple. For privacy, she acquired a fourteen-room Moorish castle near Elsinore. In 1931, dispensing with theological scruples, she even acquired a mate, a radio technician named David Hutton, but her third marriage quickly failed. The evangelist now escaped her troubles and restored her nerves with retreats to Malibu, Asia, and London. Over the years, the crowds at her homecomings dwindled. From 35,000 souls in the twenties, her flock diminished to 8,000 or 10,000 in the Depression years.

Throughout all her troubles, McPherson seemed quite incapable of rancor or vindictiveness, says McWilliams, who often wrote of her. "There was not a trace of snobbery in this woman. She conducted no 'vice crusades,' engaged in no snooping, and baited no radicals." All this was in striking contrast to her hateful rival, the Reverend Bob Shuler, a great book-burner and red-baiter, maker and unmaker of politicians, whose army of spies was constantly searching out high-school students who drank, pharmacists who sold contraceptives, and millionaires with guilty pasts. Conscientious churchgoers like the Nixons found time for Angelus Temple and Shuler's Trinity Methodist as well, finding "joy, joy, joy" in one and indulging their voyeurism and instinct for moral superiority in the other. Of course, it was the Reverend Bob Shuler, whose radio station, KGEF, was devoted to "spreading the gospel and advancing civic betterment, and no modernist or evolutionist shall be allowed to speak over it," who was the truly prophetic figure.

6

The Great Depression enlarged the scope of fear and credulity in the City of Angels. A hundred cults were born, and if most died young, others would prove to be amazingly resilient, triumphs of hope over experience, like Samuel Johnson's description of second marriages.

One of the leading spiritual celebrities in Los Angeles was the Ascended Master, Count de Saint-Germain, who will be familiar to readers of *Foucault's Pendulum*. The historic Saint-Germain was one of the odder figures of the Age of Reason, a Cagliostro-like intriguer who was a "chemist, alchemist, and wonder worker, the alleged founder of Freemasonry," and who died or disappeared in 1780. Voltaire is supposed to have called him "the wisest man in Europe," and Madame Blavatsky gave him a place in the Theosophical pantheon. His Californian prophets, Guy W. Ballard, a former paperhanger and unsuccessful mine promoter, and his wife, Edna, met him in 1933, when the Ascended Master introduced himself to Guy, who was hiking near Mount Shasta. The amazed paperhanger was soon swept along on a whirlwind tour including "the buried cities of the Amazon, France, Egypt, Karnak, Luxor, the fabled Inca cities, the Royal Tetons, and Yellowstone National Park," and shown buried treasures at each location. An account was published of his adventure. Within a matter of months, Saint-Germain had attracted thousands of worshipers in Los Angeles, New York, Chicago, West Palm Beach, Philadelphia. At the height of the movement there were 350,000 enrolled devotees of the "Mighty I AM" presence. The cult built its principal basilica in Los Angeles and bathed it in neon light; neon, in those days, was the Southern California equivalent of the odor of sanctity.

"Mighty I AM" must qualify as the prototypical New Age cult-enterprise. The Ballards sold a voluminous line of publications (the "I AM" discourses, adorations, affirmations, and decrees), recordings of spiritual elevating music (advertised as "the music of the spheres"), cosmetics and unguents including a "New Age Cold Cream," charms, and crystals. All these thriving product lines emphasized personal "empowerment" meshed with thaumaturgic and hermetic themes. Rather than an escape from the material world of getting-and-spending, "Mighty I AM" promised, like so many New Age evangels, power and competitive advantages. Doctrinally, "Mighty I AM" was simply a minor derivation of Theosophy, at least so far as its more occult teachings were concerned, although the pantheon of Ascended Masters was enlarged and rearranged to give it a more Christian tone.

Rivaling or exceeding "Mighty I AM" in absurdity and numbers was "Mankind United," whose founder Arthur Lowler Osborn Fontaine Bell claimed to have several doubles "all capable of thinking as one," *Time* reported in 1945, and whose spiritual guides belonged to "a superhuman race of little men with metallic heads who dwell in the center of the earth." Arthur Bell was an Axis sympathizer, and he or one of his doubles found himself in jail after war broke out. The widowed Mrs. Ballard (Guy Ballard abandoned his "etheric body" in 1939) was sent up for tax fraud in 1945.

The taint of fascism clung to many of the leading California cults, if not as a matter of actual politics, then in terms of their aesthetics. McWilliams's description of a typical "Mighty I AM" morning service, with "buxom middle-aged usherettes, clad in flowing evening gowns" and adorned with orchids and gardenias, bustling around a tabernacle "literally" steaming with perfume, sounds rather like a scene from Leni Riefenstahl being reenacted by the chubby club women in the cartoons that Helen Hokinson used to draw for *The New Yorker*. But then, as Susan Sontag says in *Under the Sign of Saturn*, fascist aesthetics typically "endorse two seemingly opposite states, egomania and servitude. . . . The fascist dramaturgy centers on the orgiastic transactions between mighty forces and their puppets, uniformly garbed and shown in ever-swelling numbers." Even after Edna Ballard endured martyrdom at the hands of the IRS, the affirming and decreeing could be witnessed at the sanctuary on South Hope Street, "repeated over and over again, rising to an almost intolerable shrillness and vehemence as the initiates demand[ed] radios, automobiles, perfumes, and pressure-cookers of Saint-Germain." Fascinating Fascism!

William Dudley Pelley was one of the seedy and bizarre demagogues who flourished in the early thirties. Though based in Asheville, North Carolina, Thomas Wolfe's hometown, his pro-Nazi Legion of Silver Shirts recruited most successfully in Southern California. Pelley himself had worked in Los Angeles as both a realtor and a screenwriter, thus combining in one résumé experience in the region's two most lucrative industries. In 1929, according to his own account in *American Magazine*, he died and was resurrected. The interval, "seven minutes in Eternity," was spent becoming acquainted with the Theosophical mahatmas. Along with imparting much astrological lore (would-be Silver Shirts were required to state the time and day of their births), these luminaries alerted him to Adolf Hitler as a man of destiny. Hitler's rise to the chancellorship in 1933 was the cue for Pelley to launch his own movement in the United States. Besides drilling his followers in their colorful uniforms, Pelley published a magazine and founded a college, both devoted to "Christian Economics." His principal political demand was that Jews be disenfranchised, beginning presumably with the president of the United States, whom he called Rosenfelt. In 1936, Pelley himself ran for president, although his candidacy was not widely noticed. FDR did not scruple to send the FBI or the IRS out after seditious cultists (the House Un-American Activities Committee went into action around this time as well), and of course their civil rights were not observed any more nicely than those of actual or alleged Communists would be after the war. Pelley was soon in legal trouble, and after 1941 in jail, leaving "Mighty I AM" to pick up what remained of the bereft Silver Shirts.

Plainly, the confusion of politics and mysticism, or politics and piety, was no more limited to Southern California then than now, as witness the radio demagogue Father Coughlin, broadcasting from his Shrine of the Little Flower in Royal Oak, Michigan, who for a time in the early thirties commanded a bigger audience than "Amos n' Andy" and received more mail than Franklin Roosevelt. Still, the political movement with messianic overtones, the mystical sect with a political agenda, flowered with a sort of lurid hothouse vigor in Southern California—Technology, the Utopian Society, Social Credit, Plentocracy, the Townsend Plan, Upton Sinclair's admirable EPIC ("End Poverty in California") campaign for governor, and the sinister and ridiculous Ham and Eggs—which for a time was the largest organized political movement in California—not only because of the deracination and despair of Southern Californians, but also because anything like normal political development had been thwarted, deformed, and turned into subterranean ways by what McWilliams calls "the despotic dominance of reaction."

In *The Day of the Locust*, Todd Hackett is a witness one night at the "Tabernacle of the Third Coming" to the testimony of a crazed old man from the desert, with "the same countersunk eyes, like the heads of burnished spikes, that a monk by Magnasco might have. . . . He was very angry. The message he had brought to the city was one that an illiterate anchorite might have given decadent Rome. It was a crazy jumble of dietary rules, economics and Biblical threats. He claimed to have seen the Tiger of Wrath stalking the walls of the citadel and the Jackal of Lust skulking in the shrubbery, and he connected these omens with 'thirty dollars every Thursday' and meat eating." The rest of the congregation is equally furious, and Todd repects their fury, "appreciating its awful, anarchic power and aware that they had it in them to destroy civilization."

In contrast to West's feverish alarm, c. 1940, is the dispassionate retrospect of James Q. Wilson's "The Political Culture of Southern California," an essay published in 1967. By 1940, the date of West's novel, half the population of Southern California were immigrants or the children of immigrants—largely from the midwestern heartland, but also in substantial numbers from the border states, the upper plains, and the mountain states—and the tide of newcomers "brought an essential ingredient of Southern California life —fundamentalist Protestant individualism. We like to think of the store-front church as being a Negro invention; not so," Wilson writes. "I remember scores of white store-front churches—mostly of small Pentecostal and Adventist sects —lining the main streets of Long Beach. Most people went to established churches, but these were only bigger and slightly more orthodox versions of the same thing—Baptists, Methodists, Mormons, Church of Christ, and so on. *Church was a very important part of life, but hardly any two people belonged to the same one* [italics my emphasis]."

7

Beside the gorgeous cult of Saint-Germain and the hallelujahs thundering over Echo Park, the Buddhists of Los Angeles were a subdued if growing presence. By the late 1930s the several Buddhist temples downtown included the Kong Chew Chinese Buddhist Temple in New Chinatown, and in Little Tokyo, the Daisha Mission of the Shingon sect, and the Jodo Shinshyu Hongwaji Temple—all conscientiously noted by the WPA canvassers, down to the "joss sticks smouldering in peanut oil" at Kong Chew and the fluttering strips of white paper, each bearing the name of a generous worshiper, at the Daisha Mission. Entirely off their map was the tiny *zendo* or meditation hall on Turner Street, where the monk Nyogen Senzaki, the "homeless mushroom" or "happy Jap" as he called himself, taught the dharma to a handful of Japanese and white Americans.

Nyogen Senzaki's "floating zendo" was furnished with battered folding chairs. Like almost all Japanese Zennists at the time, he was convinced that the lotus position was beyond the capacity of Westerners. Meetings at Turner Street were simple and austere—a brief dharma talk, sitting, no socializing afterward.

He had studied with the famous Soyen Shaku, the first Zen master ever to visit the United States. He and a fellow student, D. T. Suzuki, joined the master in San Francisco in 1905, where he had accepted an invitation to stay with the wealthy Russell family in their house on the Great Highway.

Suzuki, who had already launched himself on his legendary career as a writer and scholar, was put to work translating his talks. One was delivered to an audience of a thousand in Los Angeles. (At this time the entire Japanese population of Southern California was less than five hundred, so presumably interest among the Anglos accounted for the size of the audience.) Senzaki worked as a houseboy at the Russells', proved to be inept, and was sent on his way by the cook. "This may be better for you instead of being hampered as my attendant monk," Soyen Shaku said as they walked through Golden Gate Park, master lugging disciple's suitcase. "Just face the great city and see whether it conquers you or you conquer it," he said, cautioning his disciple not to teach, not even to "utter the 'B' in Buddhism," for seventeen years.

Supporting himself as porter, houseboy, cook, and finally as part-owner of a hotel, Senzaki obediently waited until 1922 to open his first floating zendo in San Francisco, hiring halls for Zen sitting and scheduling talks when he could afford to, moving to Turner Street in 1931.

In spring 1942, Nyogen Senzaki was among the 37,000 Japanese relocated from Los Angeles to internment camps throughout the West. On the train to Heart Mountain, Wyoming, he found himself reflecting on how Buddhism had always grown in the direction of the rising sun. Why did Bodhidharma come from the West? "This morning the winding train,/like a big black snake,/Takes us as far away as Wyoming./The current of Buddhist thought always runs eastward./This policy may support the tendency of the teaching./Who knows?" Who knew?

8

In popular memory (never long in God's country), the religious revival that swept over the United States after the Second World War has left little trace, its modest positive-thinking, churchgoing satisfactions quite eclipsed by the ecstatic and colorful Third Great Awakening that Tom Wolfe discovered in the 1970s. Claims of a personal acquaintance with Jesus were somewhat rarer than today; yet by 1956, 96 percent of Americans professed a belief in God and in 1960, when the wave crested, 62 percent were formally affiliated with a church. In that year, over $1 billion was spent on church construction at a time when the entire federal budget was less than $100 billion. "Our government makes no sense unless it is founded on a deeply felt religious faith," President Dwight D. Eisenhower said firmly, "—and I don't care what it is."

In November 1949, two days after a shaken Harry S Truman disclosed that Russia had exploded an atomic bomb, the Tarheel evangelist Billy Graham launched his "Crusade for Christ in Los Angeles" in a mammoth, three-poled tent pitched on a downtown lot. The tradition of urban revivalism, languishing since Aimee Semple McPherson's probably accidental death by an overdose of sleeping pills in 1944, on the second day of a planned "magic carpet crusade" in Oakland, California, was reborn. Not all at once.

Naturally, the evil empire's acquisition of the bomb did not go unremarked in Graham's sermons. (No one had imagined the Kremlin's scientists to be capable of such a thing; the president himself, whose behavior alternated spells of hypomanic self-confidence with shows of humility that would have shamed Uriah Heep, had only recently told Robert Oppenheimer that he knew exactly when the Soviets would develop their own bomb: "Never.") "Do you know the

area that is marked out for the enemy's first atomic bomb!"
Graham cried. "New York! Secondly, Chicago! And thirdly,
the city of Los Angeles! Do you know that the Fifth Colum-
nists, called Communists, are more rampant in Los Angeles
than any other city in America?" As usual, Los Angeles was
in the midst of a witch-hunt, but now, with the Russians'
bomb and China recently "lost" to Mao Zedong, Harry Truman busy purging the State Department of homosexuals
and other "security risks," and the House Un-American Activities Committee, including the member from Whittier,
Richard M. Nixon, rampant on the heights, so was the rest
of the nation. "God is giving us a desperate choice, a
choice of either revival or judgment. There is no alternative!
If Sodom and Gomorrah could not get away with sin,
if Pompeii and Rome could not escape, neither can Los
Angeles!"

Unhappily, attendance had been sparse and unecstatic at
Graham's two preceding crusades, in Baltimore and Altoona, Pennsylvania; and though he had been invited to Los
Angeles by a committee of prosperous Christian businessmen, "headed by the president of a sportswear company
called Hollywood Toggs, Inc.," there was a tatterdemalion
feel to his revival, with its school-of-Billy-Sunday banners,
mildewy sawdust, and louche surroundings. To just such an
event might Dreiser's Clyde Griffiths have been dragged by
his pious parents. According to his biographer, Marshall
Frady, Graham himself had been afflicted in recent weeks
by doubts about his intellectual capacities, doubts that
emerged when a friend urged that they enroll at Oxford or
Cambridge for a potentially dangerous study of the Higher
Criticism; he was also troubled by doubts about the value or
acceptability of doubts as such, particularly as they related
to the literal inerrancy of Scripture. Fortunately, all these
perplexities had been dispelled by a long prayer session at a
Bible Camp near San Bernardino, within sight of the promised land.

Then, for more than three weeks, the revival in the "Canvas Cathedral" obstinately failed to catch fire. Would the City of Angels be as unreachable as ungodly Baltimore and faithless Altoona? Perhaps. As *Life* magazine later explained, "Though loud-voiced and powerfully persuasive, Graham frowned on flashy, crowd-drawing showmanship." Fortunately, "Jane Russell sent a message: 'It looks like Billy Graham has started a worldwide revival. Praise the Lord!'" Then, toward the end of his scheduled four weeks, Graham was edged into the limelight, as, in succession, he converted an alcoholic singing cowboy with his own radio show; an alcoholic former Olympic track star and war hero; and, most alluring to the newspapers, a wiretapper named Jimmy Vaus, employed by the renowned gangster Mickey Cohen. When Graham's face was on the cover of *Time* a few years later, he testified that Mickey himself was among the notables moved by the spirit—"I am sincerely convinced that he wanted God."

Even so, Graham's celebrity might have remained small and local. The crusade was drawing to an equivocal close when a single Godlike edict abruptly elevated Graham into the pantheon of celebrities. As Frady writes in his fine Confederate-general prose, it was

the direct hand of William Randolph Hearst, unexpectedly extended forth out of San Simeon, that translated Graham at last into an instant in the pop-mythic life of the nation. . . . Even at eighty-six, some fifty years after Havana Harbor and *The Maine*, now ponderous and filmy of eye, withdrawn into his own private American Xanadu along the misty sea cliffs of northern California, he was still given to vagrant guttering of that old Faustian hubris to personally choreograph the destiny of the whole Republic.

Actually, Hearst's doctors had exiled the aged press lord from his private paradise on the central coast two years before. In 1949, he and Marion Davies were living in reduced circumstances on an eight-acre estate in Beverly Hills. So it was not from a cloud-capped tower in San Simeon but more prosaically from 1007 North Beverly Drive that Hearst dispatched to his newspapers the curt thunderbolt commanding them to "Puff Graham" that announced the advent of a global icon of Protestantism, preacher to the millions and intimate of presidents from Dwight Eisenhower to George Bush. Forty-one years after the transfiguration in Los Angeles, Graham was the warrior-king's guest in the private quarters of the White House on the night the ground war was launched in Iraq, formerly Babylon.

By 1954, according to the tally published in *Time*, Graham had "personally preached to 12 million people" and converted 200,000. But rather than reviving revivalism—it is now clear, approaching a half-century later—his historic role was to capture revivalism for the new medium of television, the "home altar" in Gore Vidal's apt phrase. In strict accordance with the paradigm soon to be announced by the oracle Marshall McLuhan (who published *The Mechanical Bride* in 1951), the old medium, in this case the sermon addressed to a throng in a tent, is transformed into the content of a new medium, a televised media event wherein the penitent crowd is reduced to mere decor. Like Sister Aimee Semple McPherson (despite her own Pentecostal background), Graham has never countenanced any distracting crowd participation in his liturgy—let alone outbursts of glossolalia or "xenoglossy." Even audible "amens" and hallelujahs are discouraged. As Sidney A. Ahlstrom writes in *A Religious History of the American People*, Graham's following was destined to be among the more conservative, culturally alienated membership of the older denominations who were appalled by what compromises with modernism, neo-orthodoxy, and the ghost of Charles Darwin had done to the old-time religion. Yet even in the Canvas Cathedral it was obvious that he had a rendezvous with respectability. Nothing could be more distant from the mood of his ministry than the Pentecostal "third force," historically radiating from Azusa Street, whose growth has been the great global fact of Christendom in this century but which, in 1949, was still emerging from a long, latent, catacombesque phase.

9

In 1954 the prolific young Gore Vidal published his sixth book, *Messiah*, a science-fiction novel that described how a new religion arose in Los Angeles at mid-century and conquered the world—except, prophetic touch, for obdurate Islam. The new faith, Cavesword, is founded on the worship of death.

In fact, a global religious movement from the Coast did arise, announcing itself in this way:

> That famous "revival of religion," about which so many people have been talking for so long, will not come about as the result of evangelistic mass meetings or the television appearances of photogenic clergymen. It will come about as the result of biochemical discoveries that will make it possible for large numbers of men and women to achieve a radical self-transcendence and a deeper understanding of the nature of things.

As Nathanael West imagined, a prophet had risen in the desert, whose vision threatened civilization itself—at least in the eyes of the most alarmed observers. He was, of all people, Aldous Huxley.

After Pentecostalism and the contemporary New Age cults, the third religious movement to emerge from Los Angeles was psychedelia. That the psychedelic movement began as an earnest effort to cleanse the doors of ordinary perception cannot be doubted, however carnivalesque it became; and for a season LSD and the other mind-expanding drugs added the aloeswood scent of mysticism to the now-distant but still bankable turbulence of the 1960s. Like Cavesword, the imaginary religion in Vidal's novel, this revolution was at the beginning the work of a cabal, or in this case a visionary company, gathered in Los Angeles.

"Art and religion, carnivals and saturnalia, dancing and listening to oratory—all these have served, in H. G. Wells's phrase, as Doors in the Wall. And for private, for everyday use there have always been chemical intoxicants," Huxley wrote in *The Doors of Perception*, after his first experience with drugs. The extraordinary properties of lysergic acid diethylamide-25 were discovered in 1943 at the Basel laboratories of the Sandoz company. Their discoverer was Albert Hoffman, the same methodical Swiss research chemist who had synthesized LSD-25 five years before. Hoffman had a "peculiar presentiment" that he had overlooked the full potential of this particular ergotamine molecule. "Miracle" drugs were being encountered all the time in the thirties and forties: might this be the long-sought cure for migraine headache? What was thought to be a safely minute dose of 250 millionths of a gram soon convinced him that the interest of the drug lay in another direction, and by 1949 Sandoz was distributing small doses of the LSD to American psychological researchers as a means for inducing "model psychoses of short duration."

As Huxley tells in *The Doors of Perception*, he was initiated into the mysteries of mescaline by a young English psychiatrist, Dr. Humphrey Osmond, who was using the drug in his work with schizophrenics at a mental hospital in Saskatchewan. Huxley, who read everything, happened on an article by Osmond in the *Hibbert Journal* and wrote an interested letter; Osmond, an admirer of Huxley, though wrongly imagining him to be "disillusioned, cynical and even savage," accepted a rare invitation to stay with Aldous and Maria Huxley at their house on North Kings Road while he was in Los Angeles for a meeting of the American Psychiatrists' Association. On May 4, 1953, Huxley, casual in blue jeans (refined into gray flannels in his book), "swallowed four-tenths of a gram of mescaline dissolved in half a glass of water and sat down to wait for the results." Osmond wondered fleetingly if the great man would go mad. Ninety minutes later, Huxley realized, all at once it seemed, that the world was appareled in celestial light.

In the 1920s he had been the brightest of England's Bright Young Things. The blood of T. H. Huxley, "Darwin's bulldog," and Matthew Arnold mingled in his veins, and his brilliance and promise were so apparent that Proust dropped his name in *Remembrance of Things Past*, before Huxley had published his first novel. As a young writer, he traveled incessantly, though, as he wrote, "To travel is to discover that everyone is wrong." After 1938, he lived in various places in and around Los Angeles: Hollywood, Pacific Palisades, Llano del Rio, Wrightwood, Hollywood again. Elizabeth Hardwick once remarked, "Huxley is one of the oddest figures in European literature: brilliant, credulous, something of a wizard. He is not Californian." Perhaps, but he stayed on until he died, in 1963, in a house on Mulholland Drive, below the first "O" in the HOLLYWOOD sign.

For five years, beginning early in 1942, he and his wife Maria were mostly living in an oasis in the Mojave, at Llano del Rio, site of an abandoned socialist utopia. Huxley was studying the literature of mysticism for his anthology, *The Perennial Philosophy*, and he found himself deeply drawn to the silence and radiance of the desert—"this great crystal of light, whose base is as large as Europe and whose height for all practical purpose is infinite." Toward the end of the decade, they moved into their large, comfortable house in Hollywood, between Santa Monica and Melrose. Assuming a grave air of credulity, they would invite friends to join them in investigating nostrums and saviors, both thick on the ground in the pregnant atmosphere of mid-century. In the winter of 1950–51, for example, the subject was Dianetics, a "new science of mind," whose discoverer, L. Ron Hubbard, had announced *his* evangel in the pages of *Astounding Science-Fiction*. Hubbard was duly invited to North Kings Road, where he unfolded the mysteries of "engrams" and "auditing."

Tuesday nights were generally set aside for such ventures. "First the participants would eat dinner at the counter of the World's Largest Drug Store, then assemble in the long main-room of the house, the music-room," according to Huxley's biographer, Sybille Bedford. "Here—always game to try anything that might come up, and what did not come up in Southern California—they would flash bright lights, make magnetic passes, turn on records of strange sounds, put the visiting hypnotist or medium through his paces."

Dr. Osmond's bundles from Saskatchewan, first mescaline and then LSD, to which Huxley and his fellow wizard Gerald Heard were introduced at Christmastime 1955, not only released the frustrated mystic in Huxley, they intoxicated the social engineer. Increasingly, they brought into plain view the aspiring messiah that had all the while been hidden, even to himself. Huxley's experience on mescaline persuaded him to adopt Henri Bergson's theory of the brain as a kind of filter for the infinite range of possible stimuli. When the doors of perception were flung open, even the traffic on Sunset Boulevard, which Huxley imagined himself to be parting as if it were the Red Sea, or the cheap merchandise in "The World's Biggest Drug Store" became surpassingly beautiful and significant. It was as if he were inside a jeweled Persian miniature. Remembering William James's realization that most drunks are failed mystics, Huxley at first promoted mescaline as a safer means of self-transcendence than alcohol or the legal forms of dope. By the time he wrote "The Drugs That Shape Men's Minds" for the *Saturday Evening Post* in 1958, he had experienced LSD and become persuaded that the ultimate significance of the psychedelic drugs (Humphrey Osmond's word; Huxley preferred "phanerothyme") was religious. "That men and women can, by physical and chemical means, transcend themselves in a genuinely spiritual way is something which, to the squeamish idealist, seems rather shocking. But, after all, the drug or the physical exercise is not the cause of the spiritual experience: it is only the occasion. . . ."

With its odd mixture of torpor and terror, the age of Ike was expansive about mind-altering drugs, from the ancient standbys alcohol and tobacco to Librium and Miltown, even LSD. Witness the fact that Huxley's messianic pronouncement was published in an ultrarespectable venue like the old *Post*. For a time the nascent psychedelic movement was a sort of mystery religion with all priests and no believers, and it was largely confined to Los Angeles, though the Beats, the CIA, the psychiatric establishment in the Bay Area, and after 1960 various mavericks at Harvard University were also pursuing parallel paths leading to the drug culture of the sixties.

Jay Stevens's meticulous history, *Storming Heaven*, shows how the circle of psychedelic initiates in Los Angeles was enlarged by psychologists such as Oscar Janiger, known as "Oz," and Sidney Cohen (who gave LSD to Herman Kahn, one of the models for Dr. Strangelove)—and by perennial bohemians like Anaïs Nin, who was recruited by Janiger. In Alan Watts's rose-colored retrospect, as of 1972, "something else was on the way, in religion, in music, in ethics and sexuality, in our attitudes to nature, and in our whole style of life . . . an energy that's in the air that cannot *entirely* be attributed to the revelations of LSD [my emphasis]," but was plainly amplified by it. For years Watts had been driving from San Francisco to Los Angeles, preparing the ground, presiding over seminars in a cottage in Carmel, a glass palace in Montecito, a Neutra house in Ojai owned by a disciple of Krishnamurti—and now, practically within the precincts of old Krotona, the old Theosophical utopia in Hollywood, the free-lance mystic would enjoy "far-into-the-night parties at which the guests might include Aldous and Laura Huxley, Marlon Brando, John Saxon, Lew Ayres, Anaïs Nin, Zen master Joshu Sasaki, and a fascinating cast—this is Hollywood—of psychiatrists, physicians, artists, writers, dancers, and hippies who, in this context, somehow managed not to bore each other."

Like so many intellectuals, Huxley was entranced by the idea of an "open conspiracy." He would redeem the time by introducing psychedelics to leading artists and writers, publicists and intellectuals, and letting their effects spread by osmosis. Early on, he even sought a Ford Foundation grant for this purpose and was indignant to be turned down. However, the logic of his position committed him to the near-universal availability of "mind-expanding" drugs.

Anaïs Nin doubted whether the net should be cast quite so widely. "These experiences should have remained esoteric," she reflects in a passage from her *Diaries, 1955–1966*. But it was as if the long-suppressed blood of Huxley's hymn-singing ancestors was at last asserting itself. At a cocktail party in a "glass house at the very top of a Hollywood mountain," he "disagree[d] vehemently" with her cautious attitude.

"You happen to have direct communication to your unconscious," Huxley admitted, "that is rare, but most people do not and for them drugs are necessary." Nin accepted the tribute as only her due. "He has a vehement attitude against Europe. He seems to be finished with it. I had no time to find out why he felt this."

Another doubter was Krishnamurti, who had simply gone on as a secular sage after his renunciation of 1929. He was a friend of Huxley's since the thirties whom the novelist revered, writing of one of the sage's talks, "It was like listening to a discourse of the Buddha—such power, such intrinsic authority, such an uncompromising refusal to allow the *homme moyen sensuel* any escapes or surrogates, any gurus, saviors, fuhrers, churches." Since Krishnamurti's atttude really was utterly uncompromising, psychedelics naturally did not appear to him in the light of a panacea.

"Well, Aldous used to discuss it with me, but of course the whole thing is meaningless," he said. "Why go so far? An alcoholic drink will do that much for you."

One of their last meetings was at Gstaad in 1961. Huxley and his second wife, Laura Archera, had gone to see him speak in the nearby village of Saanen, as Krishnamurti did every year. Huxley had just published his psychedelic utopia, *Island*, and Archera, a pioneer in the Californian self-help movement, had completed a book of "Recipes for Living and Loving" that would eventually be an international best seller. "We spoke about vitamins and imagination, solitary confinement, LSD, alcoholism, and the congress on extrasensory perception that Aldous had recently attended in the South of France," Archera writes. After luncheon, their hostess suggested she might want a private moment with Krishnamurti. Evidently he wanted one with her. Were psychedelics of any value? he asked when they were alone. She replied that even a single session might cure alcoholism, a popular claim at the time. Krishnamurti considered this for a moment and then, as it seemed to Archera, he "exploded" in a tense, strained voice, "You know, I think that those people who go about helping other people, those people . . . they are a *curse!*"

10

The historian William L. O'Neill claims that "American religious life was probably more fertile and diverse in the sixties than at any time since the nineteenth century. . . . The established churches became more secular, unchurched youths more religious." By then, black Pentecostal churches claimed almost as many believers as the Baptists. The largest, the Church of God in Christ, traced its lineage directly to the presence of its founder, Charles H. Mason, at Azusa Street. With the Van Nuys revival of 1960, Pentecostal or "charismatic" practices began to be seen in the predominantly white, mainstream Protestant denominations. Before the end of the decade, the charismatic movement reached into Roman Catholicism.

Of course, the enthusiasms of the counterculture leaned heavily to the occult or at least the unfamiliar: Tantra, Ghost dances, Tarot cards, the *I Ching* . . . "Even the religious traditions of the European past were to become acceptable . . . so long as they were sufficiently cleansed by antiquity and irrationality from any taint of association with Christianity or scientific rationalism," Godfrey Hodgson wrote in 1976. "Young Americans who could not conceivably be persuaded to read Milton or Pascal pored with scholarly patience over theses on the Druidic cults at Stonehenge. . . ."

The "Jesus people" who appeared like some medieval apparition at decade's end, represented the discovery of Pentecostalism by many typical citizens of the sixties who had fled in disillusionment from ashrams and crashpads.

The famous Third Great Awakening of the 1970s was another Alexandrian "tutti-frutti," an immense spectacle of staid Episcopalian and Methodist congregations reborn as Pentecostal shouting churches; evangelists banging tin cups on television; Air India flights choked with enterprising pandits, babas, and bhagwans; clamorous encounter groups (earthly paradise for grievance collectors); Carlos Castaneda's exemplary tales about Don Juan; urban revivals of Santería, Voudon, and Rastafarianism; goddess worship; and thaumaturgical, occult, or esoteric sects new, like Scientology and Arica, and improved, like Elizabeth Clare Prophet's neo-Theosophy.

To the extent that these movements found national followings, they may be seen as representing what the historian John Lukacs called the "Californization" of American life. An unscientific survey of persons involved in the human potential movement conducted around 1980 showed that almost half lived in California. Their preferred spiritual disciplines and "growth modalities" were "Zen, 40 percent; yoga, 40 percent; Christian mysticism, 31 percent; journals and dream therapy, 23 percent; Tibetan Buddhism, 23 percent; Transcendental Meditation, 21 percent; Sufism, 19 percent; Transactional Analysis, 11 percent; the Kabbalah, 10 percent." Forty percent acknowledged using psychedelics at some point (a large percentage declined to answer questions about drug use), and the preferred body therapies were T'ai Chi and Rolfing.

But how large was this venturesome lot? The U.S. Census does not inquire into religious affiliations. In *The American Condition* (1982) by Edward Fawcett and Tony Thomas, correspondents for *The Economist*, we are told, "There are about 1,500 major and minor religious cults in the United States, with a total of about 3 million members." A more recent survey concluded that only 28,000 Americans were professedly involved with New Age religions. The overwhelming majority of Americans were Catholic, Protestant, or Jewish; and church attendance was growing as the population aged. Obviously, definitions are more than usually dicey. The human potential movement, more often chemically elevated in the seventies than now, with its scientific pretensions and weakness for the occult, is obviously much larger than the explicitly non-Christian New Age sects; and the self-help movement is much larger again.

In the 1990s the principal technologies of the self used in Southern California are the oldest ones, like meditation, confession, diet, and exercising. Obviously, Aldous Huxley deeply underestimated the appeal of mortification. The flourishing self-help cults modeled after Alcoholics Anonymous, practicing ritual confession and rigid abstinence, the ethos of good-bye to all that, are the liveliest churches in town.

The latest Californian New Age clearly represents a series of variations on standard themes. Amid the shamans, aura readers, channelers, neuro-linguistic programmers, rebirthers, magnetic healers, hypnotherapists, herbologists, polarity therapists, spellcrafters, and psychics are perennial favorites from the golden age of credulity in the twenties and thirties, and back to antiquity. Saint John the Divine, Nostradamus, Saint-Germain, Madame Blavatsky, Annie Besant, Guy and Edna Ballard, the Mahachohan—all the great names appear in the pantheon of such New Age prophets and mediums as Judith Z. Knight and Elizabeth Clare Prophet, "Guru Ma" of the Church Universal and Triumphant. Prophet attracted worldwide attention in March 1989 when two thousand of her followers poured into Paradise Valley, Montana, looking for places in underground shelters built in anticipation of nuclear war. Essentially, Prophet's church is "Mighty I AM" redux; however, the choir of "Ascended Masters," borrowed in the first place from Theosophy, seems to have been enlarged again. At least, the appearance of two new female faces, Nada and Thérèse de Lisieux, looks suspiciously like a concession to changing times.

Real-estate prices being what they are in Southern California, a fair number of premillennial cults have moved their sanctuaries to places like Yelm, Washington, and Medford, Oregon, where the entity Mafu speaks in the voice of Penny Torres Rubin, "who was a housewife married to a Los Angeles policeman until Mafu descended and their bed levitated in 1986," according to Don Lattin in the *San Francisco Chronicle*. Increasingly, Terror, Decadence, and Renewal, the familiar themes of preapocalyptic anxiety, are given urgency and topicality by the supposed "death of nature," and the approach of a new millennium.

11

Krishnamurti's biographer Mary Lutyens could never reconcile the mature sage with the "vacant, childish, almost moronic" boy she had known, "interested really in nothing except golf, and mechanical things such as cameras, clocks and motor-bicycles. I could not see how this being could ever have developed the brain to expound Krishnamurti's teaching." Perhaps he *had* been used by something since his "awakening" in 1922, and his consciousness was permeated with the other's, like a sponge. Lutyens occasionally felt this power herself. Once, at the English manor house that the Krishnamurti Foundation had purchased to use as a school, she opened the door of an unused ballroom and a great wind arose in the empty room and began to howl. "He does not even call himself a swami," wrote the Indian writer Aubrey Menon, who used to see Krishnamurti in Rome, "although he is the most famous of all."

Sometime in the twenties, a photographer caught the World Teacher reading a copy of *Elmer Gantry* and lounging on a deck chair aboard one of the ocean liners where he spent so much of his youth. That snapshot inevitably comes

to mind in connection with the publication of Radha Rajagopal Sloss's deliberately iconoclastic memoir *Lives in the
Shadow with J. Krishnamurti* (London, 1991).

For almost two decades—in the intervals between his travels and during World War II—Krishnamurti lived in Ojai at
close quarters with Sloss's parents, D. Rajagopal, who scheduled his travels and edited and arranged the publication of
his talks, and Rajagopal's wife, Rosalind. Rosalind had
nursed Krishnamurti during the "process" in 1923 and had
once been in love with his brother Nitya. According to Sloss,
her parents ceased to have sexual relations soon after she
was born in 1931. A few months later, she says, her mother
and Krishnamurti began an affair of almost thirty years. Rosalind Rajagopal believed that her husband was a silent
partner in the menage, but apparently he was merely
unobservant. Business frequently kept him in Hollywood,
and in Ojai he was a night worker who lived a life apart from
those around him. Learning of the affair after twenty years,
he was shocked and hurt. Sloss is convinced that the terrible
legal wrangle over copyrights and archives that developed
between Krishnamurti and Rajagopal in the sixties, dividing
their friends into two camps, was a result of Krishnamurti's
fear that Rajagopal would expose him.

Radha Rajagopal Sloss says that from earliest childhood
she realized that the true marriage in her home was between
her mother and Krishnamurti. "Krinsh" was playful and romantic, and capable of bold stunts like waiting for nightfall
and then leaping "Errol Flynn style" between his balcony
and Rosalind's at the old Peter Pan Inn at Carmel. This was
in the thirties on the same holiday when he was quibbling
with the writer Rom Landau about his divinity. "I never
either denied or affirmed that I was Christ or anyone else,"
he said. "Such attributions are utterly meaningless to me."

"Krishna possessed almost all the qualities that make a
person attractive (to both sexes and also children and

animals). Outwardly, when he was younger, he was beautiful, charming, gentle, physically courageous and compassionate," Sloss writes. But he was also, she insists, vain, manipulative, ungrateful, disloyal, fearful (mostly of unpleasantness or opposition), and consequently untruthful; in fact, an inveterate liar. Even the strengths that she ascribes to him—including a trained verbal intelligence and a cool capacity for long-range planning—are almost as much at odds with his reputation as the faults, and his lifelong capacity for metamorphosis is made to seem either sinister or fraudulent. Obviously, if Krishnamurti brightened many lives, he seriously darkened some as well.

Of course, he was not a randy clergyman or a holy fool. (However, it is interesting that one of the few serious novels he ever read carefully was Dostoevski's *Idiot*.) Nor, if it happened, does his affair with Rosalind Rajagopal amount to the Last Temptation of J. Krishnamurti. (Mary Lutyens has already promised a reply.) He did not preach chastity after his Theosophical days, and if his public image remained chaste, his teachings were so completely antinomian and contemptuous of conventional morality that it would be difficult to convict him of hypocrisy. "That is the only way to judge," he said in 1929: "in what way are you freer, more dangerous to every society that is based on the false and unessential?" In the end, *Lives in the Shadow* deepens, rather than dispels, the mystery of his life. Perhaps, we read, he was an aspect of Shiva the Destroyer; perhaps, as the author says her mother came to believe, he was "more than one person"—literally, a divided soul. That he was a sage, neither of them seems to have doubted.

For almost seventy years he had been saying something like what he told Alan Watts one day at Ojai. "Look, on the one hand there must be the understanding that there is nothing, nothing, nothing, absolutely nothing you can do to improve, transform, or better yourself. If you understand this completely you will realize that there is no such entity as 'you.' " He dropped a cushion he was using as a prop, and held up another. "Then, if you have totally abandoned this ambition, you will be in the state of true meditation . . . wave after wave after wave of amazing light and bliss." It was like Rilke's Apollo as rewritten by Beckett. *You must change your life. You cannot change your life. You must change your life.* He was quite clear about the fact that liberation could only be achieved by this kind of spontaneous mutation, and also quite certain that no one had ever achieved such a transformation as a result of his teaching. "But nobody has done it," he said toward the end, meaning no one anywhere. "Nobody. And so that's that."

Individuality was an illusion. Consequently, everyone was responsible for the condition of the world, with its evils. All systems of value were equally mistaken. His favorite term of contempt was "mediocrity." In the seventies, when he was staying in Malibu, he was visited by Sidney Field, a former Disney screenwriter and a friend since old Hollywood days. Mary Zimbalist's house, where he stayed, was near the new dun-colored campus of Pepperdine University, which he passed on walks. "They could not have made them uglier," he said. "The triumph of mediocrity." They paused to watch the football squad at spring practice. Krishnamurti was briefly entranced, but soon recovered himself. "Educated morons!"

He talked about the condition of India, where he was still mobbed by idolatrous crowds. He despised Gandhi's memory, regarding him as a violent man at heart whose fame had unjustly eclipsed Mrs. Besant's, while seeming to admire the Nehru family, whose members sometimes sought him out for advice. Still, Indian government was rotten from top to bottom, and it was madness to repose any faith in politicians. One day when the beach was deserted, Field, who had been raised a Theosophist, ventured that to a clairvoyant it would not look so bare. "People, sea elementals . . ."

"The place is full of them. I pay no attention to them," said Krishnamurti, dismissing the spirit world.

"Do you see them every time you come out here?"

"Only when I want to."

In September 1985, in England, he told his Indian friend Pupul Jayakar, "The manifestation is starting to fade." There was a final circumnavigation of the globe. He spoke for the last time in public in Madras, afterward retiring to the compound of the Krishnamurti Foundation at Adyar. On January 10, he walked on the beach where his strange body of fate had come upon him the better part of a century before. That night, changed from Indian clothes into a tweed jacket and slacks, he left for Los Angeles, flying by way of Singapore and Tokyo. Five weeks later, he died of pancreatic cancer at his cottage in the upper Ojai Valley. His body was cremated in Ventura at the other end of the valley, and the ashes divided and scattered—in Ojai, at his school in England, and in India at the source of the Ganges in the Himalayas, near Varanasi at midstream, and at a place in the ocean off Adyar, where they were taken by catamaran.

The death of Krishnamurti marked an epoch, the completion of a cycle of mysteries and messiahs that began with the arrival of Theosophy in Southern California. Spengler says somewhere that the sage in the garden is the ultimate expression of a *rational* age. "The sage goes back to Nature—to Ferney or Eremonville, to Attic gardens or Indian groves—which is the most intellectual way of being a megalopolitan."

In the orange groves at Ojai, nothing could seem more distant than the great Babylonish city that in reality surrounds it, if not yet in a sea of houses, then in census tracts and fantastic developers' schemes—the city that has thronged in pursuit of so many strange gods, that brought the sage to the garden and pilgrims to the sage, and resurrected Ishtar at a crossroads where a visiting poet might see her.

Our towns are copied fragments from our breast;
And all man's Babylons strive but to impart
The grandeurs of his Babylonian heart. *

A Note on Sources

Anyone who writes about Southern California cults in the first half of
this century, or for that matter about any aspect of Los Angeles in that
period, will be indebted to Carey McWilliams's classic study, *Southern
California Country* (New York, 1946), though it does contain a few
errors and exaggerations. Some additional material appears in his 1947
magazine article "California: Mecca of the Miraculous," reprinted in
The California Dream, edited by Dennis Hale and Jonathan Eisen
(New York, 1968), a very useful collection; and in "Aimee Semple
McPherson: 'Sunlight in My Soul," written for *The Aspirin Age, 1919–
1941*, edited by Isabel Leighton (New York, 1949). Apart from the
overview he provides, I have relied most on McWilliams for his account of Theosophy, McPherson, "Mighty I AM," and other cult
movements of the Depression Era, and for a sense of the atmosphere
in which they flourished.

   Three other books I relied on for historical overviews as well as
factual matter are Rick Fields's *How the Swans Came to the Lake: A
Narrative History of Buddhism in America* (Boulder, Colorado, 1981),
Sydney E. Ahlstrom's magnificent *A Religious History of the American
People* (New Haven and London, 1972), and Jay Stevens's *Storming
Heaven: LSD and the American Dream* (New York, 1987). Two valu-
able memoirs are Alan Watts's *In My Own Way* (New York, 1973), and
Christopher Isherwood's *My Guru and His Disciple* (New York, 1980).
The WPA Guide to Los Angeles (1940) contains a useful sketch of
religious life in the city.

   The coverage on religion in the *Los Angeles Times* by Russell Chandler and John Dart is superb, and for the opening survey I have drawn
on the coverage in the *Times* of such events as the opening of the

---

* William Butler Yeats, in "The Symbolism of Poetry" (1900).

"FaithDome." Articles by Don Lattin, the religion correspondent of the *San Francisco Chronicle*, have been helpful as well. The founding of Chua Viet-Nam is described by Rick Fields in *A Vietnamese Buddhist Temple in Los Angeles* (Los Angeles, 1988). The quotation from Kenneth Tynan appears in *Kenneth Tynan*, by Kathleen Tynan (New York, 1989).

Two studies of Pentecostalism I found useful were *Fields White Unto Harvest: Charles F. Parham and the Missionary Origins of Pentecostalism* by James R. Goff, Jr. (Fayetteville, Ark., and London, 1988), and *The Charismatic Movement: Is There a New Pentecost?* by Margaret Poloma (Boston, 1972).

Jackson Lears's *No Place of Grace: Antimodernism and the Transformation of American Culture 1880–1920* is a provocative and original study of *mentalités* during the decades when Southern California became metropolitan; there is a valuable section on the "White Buddhists" of Boston.

On Yeats's spiritual encounter in Southern California, see *A Vision* (second edition, revised, New York, 1937; reprint 1965). On Griffith, see Richard Schickel, *David Wark Griffith*. The making of *Intolerance* is also discussed in Kevin Starr's *Material Dreams: Southern California Through the 1920s* (Oxford, 1990). Michael Rogin's "The Great Mother Domesticated: Sexual Difference and Sexual Indifference in D. W. Griffith's *Intolerance*," in *Critical Inquiry* (Spring 1989), is a remarkable essay about the sexual politics of the film. Louis Adamic's *Laughing in the Jungle: The Autobiography of an Immigrant in America* (New York, 1932) contains a vivid account of cultism in the twenties; on the Reverend Bob Shuler, see Edmund Wilson's 1932 essay "The City of Our Lady the Queen of the Angels," reprinted in *The American Earthquake: A Documentary of the Twenties and Thirties* (New York, 1958). The career of William Dudley Pelley is part of the "Theology of Ferment" described in Arthur M. Schlesinger, Jr.'s *the Politics of Upheaval* (Boston, 1960); it is also covered briefly by Ahlstrom. James Q. Wilson's essay is reprinted in *The California Dream*.

On Krishnamurti, see the three-volume life by Mary Lutyens, *Krishnamurti: The Years of Awakening* (New York, 1975), *The Years of Fulfillment* (New York, 1983), and *The Open Door* (New York, 1988); and

Krishnamurti: A Biography by Pupul Jayakar (San Francisco, 1986). The second volume of Arthur H. Netheroot's biography of Annie Besant, *The Last Four Lives of Annie Besant* (Chicago, 1963) is invaluable. *Krishnamurti: The Reluctant Messiah* by Sidney Field, edited by Peter Hay (New York, 1989), is a slight, charming memoir.

On Nyogen Sensaki, I have relied on the account in Fields's book and on Helen Tworkov's *Zen in America: Profiles of Five Teachers* (Berkeley, 1989).

On Billy Graham I am indebted to Marshall Frady's biogaphy, *Billy Graham: A Parable of American Righteousness* (Boston, 1979); and to contemporary magazine coverage in *Time* and *Life*.

Sybille Bedford's *Aldous Huxley* (New York, 1974) is the standard life; the *Letters of Aldous Huxley* (London, 1969), edited by Grover Smith, is useful on the psychedelic epoch, which is discussed in David King Dunaway's *Huxley in Hollywood* (New York, 1989), and in Laura Archera Huxley's *This Timeless Moment: A Personal View of Aldous Huxley* (New York, 1968), which contains the superb rebuke from Krishnamurti. "The Drugs That Shape Men's Minds" is reprinted in the *Collected Essays* (New York, 1958). Peter Conrad's *Imagining America* (New York, 1980) has acute things to say about Isherwood and Huxley's mystical turn.

The quotation from William L. O'Neill appears in *Coming Apart: An Informal History of America in the 1960s* (New York, 1971); the quotation from Godfrey Hodgson, in *America in Our Time* (New York, 1976). The unscientific survey appears in Marilyn Ferguson's *The Aquarian Conspiracy: Personal and Social Transformation in the 1980s* (Los Angeles, 1980), a characteristic document of the human potential movement.

LA PLACITA

Newspapers, photos, diary notes, articles, stat sheets, and books—Christopher Isherwood's *A Single Man*, Rudy Acuña's *Occupied America*, Raymond Chandler's *The High Window*, Susan Kelly's *Mastering Word Perfect 5*—and family heirlooms surround me in piles across what was once my father's bedroom. He stood at the picture window to my right during the air-raid blackouts of World War II, watching searchlights crisscross skies just like tonight's when a rusty-gray blanket hides the handful of stars that can survive the city glare.

And I begin by lighting a votive candle emblazoned with the image of San Martín de Porres at the altar where I've gathered together the objects of the living and the dead: grandmother's finely molded hand mirror with the Deco engraving on the back (if I look into it now will I see her face instead of mine?); the wallet-sized photo of my girlfriend, her stare questioning my soul from three thousand miles away in Guatemala City where maybe I'd rather be; the brittle, yellowed leaf from Palm Sunday at the Old Plaza Church, where Father Luis Olivares showered the thousands of Mexicanos and Centroamericanos surrounding him with holy water; the calling card that Hector Oqueli handed me three months before he was kidnapped and assassinated in Guatemala City; the cassette sleeve with the red-black-yellow slogans that Dago the ardent revolutionary gave me a month before a Salvadoran army bullet pierced his lung and he convulsed into his final breath during the FMLN guerrilla offensive of 1989 in downtown San Salvador.

I continue by turning off the overhead light so that the candle flame transforms the shadow of the crucifix into a pair of outstretched arms. The faint, wavering light glows upon the photos of my late grandparents.

I do this alone, in my grandparents' house in the L.A. neighborhood north of downtown known as Silver Lake. I do it because my grandmother once did it, each night with me before I said my prayers. I do this and many other things like it, here in this house, because I feel as if somehow my grandparents were living through me when I do. This is important—it is my history. There is much else that is my history, too; the things that pertain to my particular generation, which I experienced directly or indirectly and that make up my cultural and political vocabulary. Everything from Watergate to the Flintstones to Robert Kennedy's assassination and the time the white hippie from Marshall High spit on me, the brown scrub, while I walked home from Franklin Elementary; to the earthquakes and dozens of *noir* and war movies I watched with my father; to Rubén Salazar's

death at the Chicano Moratorium and later on my own be-
lated encounter with Revolution via Nicaragua and El Salvador and the subsequent disillusionments, and the sex, lies,
and performance art of the eighties, and now The Walls
Coming Down.

And this is as close as it gets to home, right here in Silver
Lake on this cool L.A. summer night looking down on a
deserted Glendale Boulevard, a block above where my
grandparents worked themselves into alcoholism and heart
attacks at La Ronda, the Mexican restaurant they owned in
the fifties and sixties and that now is a gay bar. "As close as
it gets," because my home is L.A. and L.A. is an antihome.
So, this journal is an attempt to gather together the strewn
shards of my identity scattered like the beads of broken glass
across the Golden State Freeway three miles north of here,
where a few days ago a big rig hauling fifty thousand pounds
of tomatoes crushed a trailer home, killing three of four
members of a tourist family who'd come all the way from
Canada to visit Disneyland.

What surrounds me is my history, I repeat to myself. The
words become my mantra: I must have a history.

"Baptism Souvenir," it says, in badly printed, kitschy cursive
on the cardboard frame. "Our Lady Queen of the Angels
(Old Mission Plaza)." A smiling kid swathed in virgin white,
laid out horizontally before the silver-haired priest (horn-
rimmed glasses, lips pursed), who the frame catches right at
the moment he's letting the water fall on my head.

Our Lady Queen of the Angels Church, popularly known
as La Placita, is the historic center of the city: where the city
began, where I began. Every Sunday, at this modest mission
founded in 1781, an average of 250 Mexicanos, Chicanos,
and, increasingly, Centroamericanos, bring their babies to
be baptized in the chapel christened Nuestra Señora la

Reina de Los Angeles de Porciúncula—the original, over-wrought Catholic name for L.A. They come, dressed to kill in rented suits and home-stitched silk dresses, and the photographers swarm around them, exactly as one George A. Pérez (whose name is printed on the back of the cardboard frame) accosted my family one Sunday twenty-eight years ago. I am cradled by my grandfather, whose hair is just beginning to turn gray. His aquiline, northern Mexican nose gives him an air of dignified *mestizo*-ness, right on the border between the *indígena* and the Spaniard; my grandmother (softer features, light-complected, large eyes, less *indígena*) holds my hand.

It is 1962, just before the October Missile Crisis. My grandparents' restaurant has taken shape on Glendale Boulevard. Elvis Presley stopped by not long ago (my grandparents had no idea who he was) and wrote, "Nice place, great food. Elvis Presley," on a napkin that is now my younger sister's prize possession.

My father is doing litho work at a place called Rapid Blue Print, making very good money ($1.50 an hour) for a first-generation Mexican. He likes to slick his hair back but is not a *pachuco*—he's proud to speak an accentless English as well as a perfect Spanish. And, as he will still say thirty years later, is proud to be better off than the *chusma*, the recently arrived immigrants who gather in squalor in the barrios to the south and to the east of La Placita. My mother's English is still awkward and heavily accented; she's doing her best at playing the classic housewife, watching a lot of TV (which inspires her to do her hair up Jackie Kennedy–style), singing nursery rhymes to me in Spanish in the afternoons, and probably still thinking a lot about her native El Salvador, which she left only a few years before.

My parents live in their newly built house in Silver Lake (only five minutes away from my grandparents). It's all very idyllic and I'm the model firstborn son; my parents have representatives of the fledgling Latino middle class over to the house often for martinis and cha-cha dancing, the men with Brylcreamed hair wearing sharp suits and thin ties and the women with their knee-length solid-colored or polka-dotted dresses and teased, Roman-arched hair.

Father must work eighteen, sometimes twenty hours a day, and this begins to take its toll on my mother. Late one night, alone in the house with her son fast asleep, the isolation, her longing for the comfort of the large family she left behind in El Salvador and the vastness of a city she doesn't understand bring her to the verge of a breakdown. She locks herself in the bathroom. My father comes home and finds her still there, shaken and wordless, in the early morning hours. From this moment on, I begin to have nightmares about monsters lurking outside in the darkness of the city, poised to leap out and tear my family apart.

Nearly thirty years later, and I'm still hanging out at La Placita. Something in or about that baptism water.

Today, a piercing blue sky. The famous "Santa Ana winds" have returned with their dry cowboy heat and blown the smog out to sea. Y.—who is here for a month before she returns to Guatemala—and I awake, slightly hungover, in my father's old bedroom. (Father told me recently that sleeping with a woman who is not my wife in my grandmother's house is probably enough to make her turn over in her grave.) Last night, we partied with what's left of the Salvadoran revolutionary cadres-in-exile. Famous guerrilla-salsa band Chiltic-Istac played (they're nine-year veterans of the L.A. scene) and without a trace of irony led the crowd in slogan-spiked *cumbias* ("Si Nicaragua venció, El Salvador vencerá! Y Guatemala!"). I make a point of not mentioning the Nicaraguan election. Nobody does. What is unspoken is that we all know that things have changed forever. No, there will not be a *victoria final*, no triumphant FMLN entry into San Salvador and the subsequent return of the exiles to work in mass literacy programs or to wield machetes alongside the *campesinos*. Y. and I weave home drunk and make love in the same room where my father once pinned up magazine shots of a leggy Betty Grable next to a B-52 bomber.

We straggle out of bed and arrive at La Placita just in time for the eleven-thirty mass. La Placita today is not the church it was before the arrival in 1981 of Father Luis Olivares. Back then, it still leaned toward a touristy quaintness and was mainly attended by the Chicano and Mexicano middle class. Today, shrines paying tribute to the various Latino communities that make up the parish adorn the walls of the church —*El Cristo Negro de Esquipulas* (Guatemala), *El Santo Niño de Atocha* (El Salvador), *El Señor de los Milagros* (Peru), and, Olivares's favorite, the expressionistic lithograph depicting the assassination of Salvadoran archbishop Oscar Arnulfo Romero. Surrounding the church and in the interior patio, Olivares has allowed dozens of Latino street vendors to sell their wares, everything from bootlegged cassettes, tamales and *champurrados* to blinking plastic roses. The vast majority of the parishioners are recent arrivals— Mexicanos and Centroamericanos who come to La Placita because they already knew of the church and its controversial pastor long before they began their dangerous journeys north. La Placita has become a mythic haven on the well-trodden path to the American Dream; hundreds sleep in the church's shelter every night. In 1985, Olivares declared La Placita—in public defiance of the Immigration Reform and Control Act—a "sanctuary" for Central American refugees and the destitute undocumented from Mexico.

Whether or not La Placita will remain a haven for the poor is now in question, however. Months ago, Olivares's superiors of the Claretian Order announced that he would be transferred to a Fort Worth parish. And then, only two weeks before his scheduled departure, he fell gravely ill with what was initially diagnosed as meningitis with complications.

This Sunday was to have been his farewell. We enter the church, squeezing in with the typical overcapacity crowd. To everyone's surprise, Olivares is at his usual post, beneath the large image of the Vírgen de Guadalupe to the left of the altar. His head is bowed with exhaustion, and he is still wearing a hospital I.D. bracelet (his condition is listed as "serious" at Cedars-Sinai Hospital, and he will be rushed back immediately after the service). All eyes are fixed upon the now-fragile Olivares, whose voice once boomed out from the pulpit, challenging his parish to confront its enemies: the *migra*—the Immigration and Naturalization Service agents who flash their badges and ask for green cards—the LAPD, the U.S. government. He cradles his head in pain.

Associate pastor Michael Kennedy officiates the mass, but when it comes time for the homily, he hands the microphone to Olivares, who is so weak he can barely hold it. His voice begins in a weak whisper, but soon he is weaving a powerful and emotional sermon. He confides that the doctors have given him one or two years of life. "But I do not fear death, my brothers and sisters. One must accept the will of God. If He wants me stay on in this, this," he says, summoning a weak, somewhat ironic smile before going on, "vale of tears, then I will stay. If He wishes me to leave, I will leave."

Father Luis Olivares bids La Placita farewell with these words: "Like John the Baptist was called . . . so each of us, upon being baptized, is called to be a prophet of love and justice. I ask the Lord for a special blessing for this community that has fought so hard for justice, not only here and in Central America, but all over the world. May it continue to do so, to live out the true meaning of the Gospel." After saying this, he sinks back into the wheelchair, exhausted.

After the recitation of the Lord's Prayer, and during the traditional mutual offering of peace, an old Mexicana painfully canes her way up to the altar to touch Olivares. Next, a communion-aged boy does the same. Soon, a steady stream of parishioners is tearfully laying hands upon him. But suddenly a tall, attractive blond woman who has been standing near Olivares (he has a bastion of support among the Hollywood in-crowd) puts a stop to this. Towering over the children and *ancianos* with tears in their eyes, she tells them to go back, "No más, no más," in a thickly accented Spanish.

Five days later, during my morning ritual at the Silver Lake house, I open the front door and pick up the morning edition of the *L.A. Times*. I scan the Metro section . . . That page is now torn out, gathering dust on the floor along with all the other clippings:

ACTIVIST PRIEST SAYS HE HAS AIDS

Father Luis Olivares, the activist Roman Catholic priest and long-time champion of Central American refugees who had been hospitalized for the past month with meningitis, revealed Thursday that he has AIDS. Doctors said they believe that he contracted the disease from contaminated needles while undergoing treatment for other ailments while traveling in Central America . . .

L.A. history begins at La Placita, and ends at La Placita. I cross the city dozens of times in a single week, but I must always return there—*I must always go home.* Just as the successive waves of Mexicano immigrants have inevitably been drawn there since the battle began in the eighteenth century to see who would win control of the Los Angeles basin.

La Placita itself was founded on September 4, 1781, by a ragtag band of forty-four Native American, *mestizo*, and African subjects of Spain (only one of the original expedition could claim pure Spanish blood), who stuck a flag in the dusty chaparral where two centuries later Father Luis Olivares would assume the pastorship of L.A.'s largest Catholic parish. For decades, L.A. pop history held that our past was a romantic, Spanish Colonial rose-stem-in-teeth story and ignored the fundamental, pluricultural fact.

Such is L.A.'s acute case of amnesia. Better to think that Spanish troubadours on palomino horses swept castanet-snapping *señoritas* off their feet rather than accept the fact that the *Californios* were actually *mestizo* Iberophiles who exploited the region's majority population of poor Mexicanos and smattering of Native Americans.

Though official romanticization of the false Spanish mythos has waned in recent decades in favor of an equally Hollywoodized version of a Mexican past (mariachis are invited to play at virtually every official city welcoming ceremony), remnants of the former remained imbedded in the city's psyche during my school years. Enough so that every time the Los Angeles Unified School District conducted an "ethnic survey" and I was presented with the choice of "Anglo," "Mexican," "Asian," "Black," or "Other," I would check this last box and pencil in "Spanish." At a young age, I learned to try to be anything other than a "dirty Mexican" (as the little blond girl with ponytails whispered to her friend while pointing at my father at Allesandro Elementary School in Silver Lake, circa 1946). My Salvadoran consciousness, during that time, was hardly an issue: Central America did not exist as far as L.A. was concerned until the Sandinista army rolled into Managua and the FMLN appeared close to achieving a similar triumph in San Salvador. The turmoil of 1979 and '80 also began the mass pilgrimage of Central Americans to Los Angeles.

Back then, when I watched images of the Sandinistas taking Managua on NBC, Y. was still in high school. They had just given her her first weapon—a 9mm piece of shit, but there was that whole mystique about arms in the guerrilla organizations and it meant a lot to her. She carried it in her purse wherever she went. But intrafactional revolutionary intrigue would lead her to disillusionment before very long. The war sucked her in, spat her out, and she landed in L.A. —where we would finally meet.

Thunderheads towered over the mountains today and a Central America–like humidity engulfed the city. At nightfall, lightning flashed over Glendale, Silver Lake, Los Feliz, and Echo Park—a virtually unheard of occurrence during the L.A. summer. The storm clouds that cut the full moon in half took me back to San Salvador where every afternoon I used to love watching thunder showers descend upon the city, rushing down the slopes of the volcano accompanied by the wild wind and lightning that both fascinated and terrified me as a child. Because of this, I had to call Y.

She tells me that thousands of poor families displaced by the hyperinflation have camped out on her street, as a sign of protest in front of the building that houses the Governmental Human Rights Commission. First they had been forced to abandon their rented shacks. Then they erected a shantytown on the edge of one of the city's huge garbage dumps. The authorities descended upon them and gave them half an hour to leave, citing health codes. Within ten minutes, the police were dousing gasoline on whatever belongings that the poor hadn't been able to carry away. By now they have spent nearly two weeks camping out on the street in front of the commission, demanding whatever open space is available. Every night, it rains. The children are coughing with bronchitis.

I give her the latest chapter on the story of La Placita. After Olivares's departure, the street vendors have once again fallen prey to an overzealous LAPD, suddenly eager to enforce municipal health codes against cooking outdoors (merchants from the nearby Olvera Street, a mini-tourist mecca, complained that the vendors were unfair competition). The sanctuary Olivares founded is being dismantled. In the courtyard where hundreds of destitute *jornaleros* huddled together each night, sometimes singing songs accompanied by guitars and harmonicas as if out of some pastoral scene from the Old West, there are now NO LOITERING signs. And the new pastor has taken down the altar to Archbishop Romero.

After hanging up the phone, I kneel before the altar where I'd lit the San Martín de Porres candle immediately before dialing her number. Her photo is there, her eyes are as piercing as ever. She is there, alive, among all the dead.

I pick up another photo from the parquet floor to begin writing again. It's a pretty black-and-white glossy, in which my Mexican grandmother is decked out in classic Spanish Romantic attire: nineteenth-century-style chiffon crown on her head, white flowers in her hair, a ruffled, floor-length dress. Similarly, my grandfather's silk-trim vest and black trousers, with a red kerchief spilling out from the left pocket, loosely approximate a Spanish don. They are both standing, cradling their guitars and holding down a D-7 in the first position. Seated to their right at a dinner table is a white gentleman in an expensive, bureaucratic-conservative suit. He is smiling. He is also holding a gun. It looks like a quite real standard police issue of the period (he is not identified anywhere on the photo . . . he could be LAPD, but then again also has the looks of mid- to high-level DWP—Department of Water and Power). The gun is pointed at my grandparents. This is a funny joke. My grandmother smiles effusively, with those perfect teeth of hers (cavityless her entire life) and my grandfather plays along also—he is cowering away from the pistol even as he, too, smiles.

I walk into my grandmother's room now, which I have recently repainted and am using to store the boxes of books and files of subversive Salvadoran literature that you left me, Y. Were I living in San Salvador, the stuff would have to be hidden under the floorboards.

I remember what *abuelita* used to say about the Paris Inn, where she and my grandfather were part of Bert Rovere's grand floor show throughout the 1940s. (The place was on Market Street, only a few blocks away from La Placita, and was completely razed in the fifties in a development project.) "The patrons were so rich, that they used to throw money away for fun. One time in the parking lot your grandfather and I picked up hundreds of dollars that these people threw out into the air from the top of the stairs, laughing . . ."

I need walk only a few feet back through the small, arched hallway flanked by two cedarwood closets to return to my father's old bedroom where he is eight years old and staring out the picture window that frames the concrete oval filled with water that we call Silver Lake (actually, it can look kind of sparkling-nice when they superchlorinate the water periodically to kill off the larvae that sometimes pour through local faucets into residents' glasses of water). Searchlights are crisscrossing the sky as father stares at the photo on the wall above the window of a P-38 fighter floating above cottony cumulus (no flak in the air). Tonight, I imagine, he hung out at the Paris Inn with my grandparents (no babysitter available), and snuck into the dancing girls' dressing room to catch glimpses of supple dance-girl flesh.

I walk into the living room now, past the kitchen where

my grandmother is opening cans of dog food for Escout (that's Spanish for "Scout"), the family's collie. There is rice on the stove, boiling in a sea of blood-red tomato sauce. And now I hear my grandfather, bedridden with a bad heart, listening to the ballgame in the bedroom (the Dodgers are losing yet again to the Giants): "*¡Mamarrachos!*" he spits out bitterly.

In the living room I open up one of the floor-level cabinets and am greeted with a waft of what I will remember for the rest of my life as my grandmother's aroma: Jabón Maja, a fragrant soap from Spain. There are hundreds of photos here in a scrapbook: my grandparents, smiling, cradling their guitars, playing for the city players. I go over to the cream-colored console and put on one of the old 78 demos they recorded with the Paris Inn band. "Allá en el Rancho Grande, allá donde vivía / había una rancherita, que alegre me decía / que alegre me decía . . ."

My grandparents were paid well to play to the *gringo* notion of Latin romance—well enough to buy this Deco house in Silver Lake, nothing to sniff at. And they were the only Mexicanos within a five-mile radius of this Anglo middle-class Shangri-La . . .

I'm back in my father's bedroom at the computer. On my lap, Carey McWilliams's *North from Mexico*. I read:

August 12, 1942
C.B. Horrall,
Chief of Police.
Sir:
   The Los Angeles Police Department in conjunction with the Sheriff, California Highway Patrol, the Monterey, Montebello, and Alhambra Police Departments, conducted a drive on Mexican gangs throughout Los Angeles

County on the nights of August 10th and 11th. All persons suspected of gang activities were stopped. Approximately 600 persons were brought in. There were approximately 175 arrested for having knives, guns, chains, dirks, daggers, or any other implement that might have been used in assault cases. . . . Present plans call for drastic action.
Respectfully,
Joseph F. Reed
Administrative Assistant

Hollywood donned Latino garb throughout the thirties and forties: Rudolph Valentino's Latin Lover image was the rage, the tango was popular among the wealthy, and who can forget Carmen Miranda with ruffled sleeves and the fruit on her head? Mexican popular music, rancheras and corridos, were in too.

But the reality off-screen was much different, as Joseph Reed's memo indicates. The *migra* and the LAPD worked together to deport hundreds of thousands of Mexicanos (the euphemism used at the time: "Repatriation"). Hundreds of Latino youth were pummeled by police and armed forces personnel during the Zoot Suit Riots of 1943. Restaurants employed segregationist policies and public swimming pools typically announced "Tuesdays for Mexicans and Negroes Only." The *L.A. Times* and other downtown power brokers bulldozed barrios at an alarming rate to pave the way for their high-stakes redevelopment schemes. The city would rid itself of its seedy past—the various bloody sieges, virtual enslavement of Mexicanos, vigilante lynchings, etcetera—*by repeating it.*

Foremost on the city's agenda regarding the Mexicano community was the "gang problem." The LAPD barrio raids were only one instance of whipping up state-of-siege sentiments to mask the questionable constitutionality of its actions. They were also typical of the department's methods:

as McWilliams points out, the "implements that might have been used in assault cases" were tire irons, hammers, wrenches, and jack handles found in the youth's cars—not knives or guns. The Mexicano gangs of the time were hardly more violent then than they are now—the number of youths involved in serious crimes was exceedingly low. The rest were "kickin' it," belonging to a group, the only group they felt at home with, safe with, in the face of constant hostility from the *gringo* world and its authorities.

But the "war" on the "hoodlums" (*L.A. Times* terminology of the time) played well with the press and a paranoid wartime public eager for scapegoats. Among the "solutions" to the problem proposed during the era:

- LAPD: that all gang members be imprisoned, and that all Chicano youths under the age of eighteen be given the option of working or enlisting in the armed forces.
- Los Angeles City Council: a thirty-day jail sentence for the wearing of a zoot suit.
- LAPD: in cases of gang violence, jail the entire gang, even those members who had nothing to do with the committing of a given crime.

And, just in case the foregoing was thought to be an exercise in mere nostalgia, I have gathered here on the floor some of the "solutions" for the gang problem in Los Angeles, 1990:

- Street Terrorist Enforcement and Prevention Act (STEP): allows for prosecution of "any person who actively participates in a criminal street gang with knowledge that its members have engaged in a pattern of criminal activity . . ."
- The National Concern Network: gang members should be enlisted in the armed forces instead of sending them to prison, since that way many youths would be given a

chance to "straighten out their lives" and "escape from the vicious circle of violence."
· Gang-Related Active Trafficker Suppression program (GRATS): promotes raids by 200 to 300 officers under orders to "stop and interrogate anyone who they suspect is a gang member, basing their assumptions on their *dress* or their use of gang hand signals . . ."

McWilliams said it best: "One thing must be said for the Los Angeles Police: it is above all consistent. When it is wrong, it is consistently wrong; when it makes a mistake, it will be repeated."

When California achieved statehood in 1850, Mexicanos comprised over 90 percent of Los Angeles's population.

By 1890, after the Gold Rush and expansion of railroads that brought a torrent of easterners and midwesterners into the Southland, the Mexicano population had dropped to 10 percent.

The bloody Díaz dictatorshop and the subsequent revolution in Mexico reversed the trend in the early part of the twentieth century. Between 1900 and 1930, the Mexicano population exploded from approximately 5,000 to almost 200,000, the majority of which was clustered around La Placita. This demographic revolution drove the Anglo middle class out of the parish. By the 1900s, affluent Catholics attended mass at St. Viviana's, closer to what was then a more affluent section of downtown (today, homeless line the sidewalks alongside it); La Placita was the Church of the Poor.

Mexicanos were by and large employed in the construction and industrial sectors. Shantytowns rose up near railroad lines and factories. Living conditions for the immigrants were terrifyingly close to what they had left behind in Mexico: infant mortality ranged from two to eight times higher than for Anglos in the L.A. Basin. (Flash forward: "[Los Angeles] County figures show the Latino infant mortality rate has risen by more than a third since 1987. Stillbirths during the same period rose by 45 percent."—*L.A. Times*, July 20, 1990.)

But the battle for the control of the Old Plaza area was just beginning. Downtown development players like the *L.A. Times* began to bulldoze the old barrio and rapidly built up what by the twenties would be a thoroughly modern commercial district, replete with high-rises. "Nativists" and Social Darwinists led an anti-Mexican campaign to justify the necessary displacement of the old barrio residents. One observer noted in 1914 that "all races meet the Mexican with an attitude of contempt and scorn and they are generally regarded as the most degraded race in the city."

Almost a century later, after two massive deportation campaigns (in the thirties and fifties), boom again: the 1990 census shows Latinos at 40 percent of L.A.'s total population, Anglos are now the minority at 37 percent. The response from the authorities? 846,622 apprehensions of undocumented immigrants by the INS (year to date total—a rate double that of 1989's final tally).

I turn the tape player on.

"The authorities would have us or force us to do something against the will of God, and when we don't do as they wish, they punish us or murder us, all because of our fidelity to the law of God," says Olivares. I remember the mass clearly. The church was filled to capacity, with the overflow crowd spilling out onto the courtyard, where a speaker crackled with his voice. The air was hot, humid; the scent of human sweat was in the air and dozens of parishioners fanned themselves fervently with folded parish announcement sheets.

"In our times, we have the example of Archbishop Oscar Arnulfo Romero," he continued, his voice booming through the church. "Romero said things that didn't sit well with the government and with the military. . . . Three days before he was assassinated, he asked President Carter to stop sending more money to the military. Three days later, while he officiated the holy mass, he was brutally assassinated before the altar of the Eucharist, and the blood of Romero mixed with the blood of Christ.

"This community of La Placita has distinguished itself by its preferential option for the poor. And the *migra* doesn't like it, and the FBI doesn't like it, and many civic authorities don't like it, and many times our very own ecclesiastical authorities don't like what this community proclaims: the defense of the poor, of the rejected, of the undocumented. But it is because of this—precisely because of this—that this Christian community deserves respect. They can kill us, they can reject us . . . but this community will continue faithful in its commitment to the poor."

As I continue listening to the old tape, the images of Olivares and his sometimes ingenious, sometimes quixotic quests come to mind: Olivares sitting at a table crowded with tape recorders and in the glare of the TV cameras pointing to a map of El Salvador and decrying the repression by the Salvadoran army (with not a little air of FMLN *commandante* about him); Olivares leading a memorial service in memory of the six Jesuit priests assassinated in El Salvador during the FMLN's November 1989 offensive; Olivares on the street in front of La Placita, standing between the LAPD and the unlicensed street vendors he'd befriended; Olivares in his study at La Placita, framed by images of Augusto Sandino, César Chávez, and Emiliano Zapata on the wall behind him, lambasting the *migra*; Olivares called a "Communist son of a bitch" and threatened by an L.A. Salvadoran death squad; Olivares marching alongside day laborers demanding they be allowed to solicit work on the streets of Los Angeles; Olivares called a "renegade" by INS Regional Commissioner Harold Ezell; Olivares and assistant pastor Michael Kennedy leading a highly emotional campaign in which they converted a young Salvadoran refugee who returned to El Salvador around the time of the FMLN offensive (and who quite probably was FMLN himself) into a virtual human-rights martyr upon notice of his disappearance, only to have him turn up alive a few months later; Olivares at yet another press conference, declaring La Placita a sanctuary for Central American refugees and the undocumented, saying: "To the extent that we openly aid, abet, and harbor the undocumented, we indeed are breaking the law. The Gospel would have us do no other." Olivares on the steps of the Federal Building downtown, shouting out revolutionary slogans ("¡El pueblo, unido, jamás será vencido!), and later going limp in the arms of LAPD officers who handcuff him and drag him away . . .

Far away, I hear walls shuddering and wood splintering. Finally: the Big One. I will myself out of a deep sleep and up into my preplanned escape route, out of my father's bedroom (which I am certain will collapse because it leans out over the open space of the laundry area below).

But halfway out towards the living room, I realize it is not the Big One that we're all waiting for. I have been awakened instead by a crew of Japanese carpenters who are sledgehammering the walls of the kitchen where my grandmother cooked thousands of meals. The remodeling of the house begins. A project that my father is certain will bring in higher rent when I move out and some yuppie couple moves in a couple of months from now.

"The past is all well and good," my father says. "But it's not *practical* . . ." He's thinking of cutting corners on cost. I take a preservationist stance. This puts father and son into curious roles: the son is intent on preserving the past; the father, on wiping it out.

The kitchen will be completely redone. It has been targeted for total destruction/construction because of its "impractical" layout: barely eight by ten, there is virtually no counter or cupboard space. The saving grace of the room is its fine Mexican-style blue-green, black, and yellow tile, and a large mirror curiously placed above the sink. A beautiful Deco archway divides the room down the middle of the ceiling and there is a small half-oval altar carved into the wall near a picture window with a panoramic view of Silver Lake.

The workers take sledgehammers to the tile and the mirror and the arch and the walls. Something unexpected occurs as the kitchen is pulverized—the kitchen smells of sixty years are released as the wood splinters and plaster crumbles. Sixty years of grease, spices, saliva, crumbs, dirty dishwater, farts, particles of mud tracked in during the winter of 1939, smoke from candles and matches and rice burning on the stove, the oily sweat of young hands on which there slowly and inexorably appeared liver spots, and where blue veins began to show through the increasingly pale, fragile flesh. Inside the walls and deep in the wood of the cabinets and shelves, inside the prongholes of the electrical outlets, underneath the floorboards and on the underside of the water tap, there are millions of particles of long dead or still slowly decaying matter. *This is the soul of the house*, I whisper to myself, out loud, as I write this. Because every meal, every glass of wine, whiskey, or vermouth, every step, every conversation (and argument), is imbued with an emotional charge—the mundane acts of sixty years gather together and compose the life of a family and its ultimate meaning. That meaning is now in the thick dust that hangs heavy in the air of 2411 McCready Avenue.

Late last night, I entered the gutted kitchen to get a glass of water. A chill ran up my spine as soon as I opened the door. Because, in addition to the pungency of the aroma that has refused to leave the house from the moment the workers began their demolition, I smelled my grandmother.

It was her favorite soap and perfume, her clothes impregnated with the cedar closet smell, the phlegm she coughed up in the mornings of her middle age.

I stood motionless in the middle of the kitchen lit only by the block of light slanting out from the refrigerator, hemmed in by the smell, fascinated and terrified. As I peered into the darkness, faint images began to dance before the exposed lathing. There's grandfather, who can barely walk—after a life of hard drinking and singing and traveling North and South and North and South; his heart has finally betrayed him. My father appears, head bowed before his father. I cover my ears against the bitter shouts; my father is holding my grandfather in his arms as he convulses and dies his horrid, painful death; my grandparents in the living room, listening to one of the old 78s, softly singing along with tears in their eyes. I am ten years old, watching a rare thunderstorm toss lightning down on the hills of Silver Lake. And there is grandmother, who is nearly blind eight years after my grandfather's death. She stands alone in the kitchen, alone in the house of memories, pouring herself a glass of grapefruit juice and staring out the window at the Silver Lake Reservoir.

All the smells—particles of matter—I sense immediately in that moment, are entering me through my nostrils, and they will never leave me. These smells are leading me back into my own history—an endless spiral of conquests, exiles, and pilgrimages in search of, by turns, the American Dream and Old Mexico . . . through revolutions, racism, and meldings of Norths and Souths—the history erased by the nonhistory of growing up in Los Angeles.

In yet another pile of papers, in between the Paris Inn menu
and a pocket-sized photo of my mother when she was still in
El Salvador, there is this document:

> Dear Sirs:
> We, the Salvadoran artists-in-exile, communicate to you
> our deepest concern upon the invitation extended by the
> Festival to Salvadoran writer David Escobar Galindo . . .
> he is a faithful representative of the ARENA government
> of Alfredo Cristiani, whose government is recognized as
> violator of the human rights of the Salvadoran people . . ."

A few days ago, in a sixties minimalist box on Flower
Street south of downtown, the exiles plotted revolution. The
Los Angeles Festival, the Peter Sellars–directed spectacle
billed as the event that will prove to the world once and for
all that L.A. is no longer a cultural backwater devolutioniz-
ing the human race with Rambos and Valley Girls, com-
mited a grave error: Galindo, poet and, according to the
exiles, apologist for repressive Salvadoran regimes dating as
far back as the early seventies, was invited to participate in
the poetry component of the festival.

Roll call. Rigoberto "I studied with the big ones" Rey
(sculptor); Roque "Fuck the *gringos* and fuck English" San-
tana (poet); María "I'm really an *indígena*" Virginia (writer);
Pablo "Fuck the revolution but I'm still progressive"
Paz (writer); Fidel "Orthodoxy or death" Cienfuegos . . .
¡Presentes!

The ideological spectrum sports everything from Fidel-in-
the-mountains true believers like Cienfuegos to social democratic wimps like me. It is a wonder that we can stand each
other. But we do—barely. We have—for over five years
now.

The draft of the protest letter (which will eventually arrive on Sellers's desk and spawn a controversy that will make the front pages of the *L.A. Times*'s Arts section) gets a once-over by the committee.

"*Compañero*," somebody says, "don't you think the rhetoric is a little harsh? I mean come on, this is nineteen-ninety."

"What are you talking about, *compañero*," responds a hardliner. "Last week, we started out radical. Now you want to soften the tone of the letter. By next week, we'll be begging *them* for forgiveness!"

Eventually, the debate reaches critical mass. Shouts of "Point of order!" become more frequent. And then, the inevitable, "Just what is this group about, anyway?"

Depending upon the speaker, we are, *a*) a perennial ad-hoc committee destined to always lag behind History by regurgitating sixties slogans; *b*) an ideologically infirm band of Salvadoran bohemians who'd rather be at one of Salvador's stunning dark-sanded beaches, drinking Pilsener (the national beer) and slurping down oysters while arguing about the whereabouts of the remains of Roque Dalton, the country's revolutionary-poet-martyr; *c*) cultural workers that need only reiterate their allegiance to the Movement and stop dreaming of drinking Pilsener at the beach so as to contribute to the forging of New El Salvador; or *d*) exiles stuck between countries, epochs, political junctures, and desperately in search of a home.

It is moved that the discussion be adjourned and continued at the next meeting. Motion seconded. Unanimously approved.

Immediately afterward, a contingent of the group enters the La Tecleña #3 restaurant/nightclub on Olympic Boulevard, in the heart of the sprawling Salvadoran barrio just west of the downtown scrapers. They ask the pretty Salvadoreña waitress for Pilsener beer.

"Solo tenemos Budweiser o Miller Light," she says.

At Point Fermin above the harbor in San Pedro the multi-colored silk of Balinese fertility poles whips in the wind as Peter Sellars, wearing African pants and Nike Airs, bangs a Korean bell. The L.A. Festival has begun!

More than any other event since the 1984 Olympics, the L.A. Festival is a grand attempt to define L.A.

The next two weeks will be frenetic—some 1,400 artists at about a hundred venues all over the city. Do we "get it," as the festival organizers say in their transformational seminar-like lingo, or do we remain cynical and indict the dominant culture's hopping on the multicultural bandwagon as nothing more than cultural tourism to ensure that grant monies continue to flow to the status quo?

There are moments during the festival when I do "get it."

I'm at Griffith Park, where one of the big free outdoor events takes place. Surreal puppets with kids in tow; an Argentine tango group; New Age Andean folkloric winds; jazz percussion . . . though I note that the crowd is mostly Anglo —in a part of the park that is generally heavily Latino on weekends—waves of nostalgia wash over me. For what, I'm not sure, because I've never seen anything quite like it. Maybe for the rare festivals I attended as a youth, school or church affairs.

There are moments during the festival when I feel like spitting. I am at the Santa Monica pier, where El Gran Circo Teatro de Chile, an amazing theater ensemble which renders a theatrical version of Roberto Parra's ode to a prostitute, *La Negra Ester*. A trendy magazine editor (with a monocle on one eye!) is sitting next to me and saying how "extraordinary" the festival's Third World exotica is—it's enough to convince me that the whole thing is a sham that will reinforce stereotypes and patronizing liberal attitudes. But suddenly I'm immersed in *La Negra Ester*, a beautiful

work brimming over with nostalgia and I'm back home again
—willing to consider even yuppie magazine editors col-
leagues in the great Multicultural Project.

I witness dozens of events—hundreds of moments; a Festival of Moments. I go from the Million Dollar Theater (a
historic Latino hangout downtown), where a performance
spectacle is staged, to Griffith Park on the same day, and
then on the next check out Latin American poets declaiming
their verses; then it's on to witness Thailand's Likay dancers,
whose improvisational techniques turn what I thought
would be mere folklore into something much closer to open-
ended, topical popular theater.

I fan out across the city—from the Arboretum in Pasadena to Sunset Canyon at UCLA to Point Fermin (we're
talking about five freeways, seventy-five miles, and about six
hours driving time), forced to visit places that I've never
visited despite the fact that I'm a "local." My cynicism begins
to crack: its dying gasps cry out: "You've been co-opted by
Sellars and Co.!" The *L.A. Weekly* has hired me to cover the
festival and I turn in extremely schizophrenic copy. I will be
criticized by both Chicanos and Anglos—and my father,
who tells me that I extol racist attitudes—for what I write.

There is a moment at the Artists Village at UCLA near the
end of the festival when a Japanese dancer is celebratorily
drunk and asking everybody to sign his Bruins sweatshirt in
the language of their choice. Soon, everybody is writing on
each other—on shirts, on skin—in different scripts. There
are Chileans jamming the blues with Cambodians; Eskimos
dancing alongside Aborigines. It's real and it's a parody; it's
superficial, kitschy, deceiving, fun, invigorating, debate-
sparking. Maybe, just maybe, it's what we are.

The saga of the Silver Lake house's remodeling continues;
Father and I are still at odds.

He calls the new layer of stucco freshly splattered on the house Desert Rose. I call it Pan Dulce Pink. He calls the new coat of paint on half of the trim on the balcony and window frames Seaweed. I call it Agua Caribeña Blue. He calls the other half of the trim Sedona. I call it Cantinera-Puta Pink.

Gone is the lovingly textured plaster that had adorned the house since its construction. Gone the off-white coat of paint that came forty years later, and gone the thick *serape*-brown trim—sandblasted away. It has been nearly impossible to write these last two weeks, what with the blasting and the reek of oil-base paint, the hammering away in the kitchen, ladders slamming against the wall of my father's old bedroom, inside which there is the last refuge of *serape*-brown trim and lovingly textured plaster. The texture of the new stucco is like cottage cheese. What's left of the old plaster is a fine dust that now coats the leaves of the rose bushes my grandmother once tended to in the garden.

Even my father's uncertain about the new color scheme: today he said, "It kind of shocked me at first. It's kind of gaudy . . ." Precisely because of that gaudiness, I am over-joyed. Perhaps it was a conspiracy between my grandmother's spirit and the Mexican day laborers who did the work: the house has braved an attempt at Southwest Pastelization . . . and come closer to Mexican Kitsch. I feel at home.

We take over La Placita for a day with *La Raza en la Calle*, part of the L.A. Festival. The dream just about comes true: we have mimes, social-real street theater, avant-garde per-formance, gay/lesbian poetry . . . and the nightmares, for the most part, do not materialize (the possibility that the day laborers would start shouting "¡Maricones!" at the gay artists, for example).

For this one Sunday, the street vendors are back at La Placita, selling bootlegged Marlboro cigarettes, *tamarindo*, *limonada*, and *piña* juices, tamales and fruit salads. The vendors' crises of "Pepino, mango, papaya!" in the midst of the art festival make me terribly nostalgic. Our only problem through most of the afternoon is a 100-degree sun, that drives our audience into the bushes at the sides of the stage area, leaving the seats in front of the stage empty. But our audience is exactly what we wanted it to be: a combination of street people, Latino churchgoers from La Placita, a smattering of Anglo tourists.

The performance would not have been complete, however, without an appearance by the LAPD. Seems that some of the Olvera Street merchants (who sell curios to tourists and whose complaints that the street vendors were unfair competition led to the LAPD raids in the first place) called in a complaint. Two towering Anglo officers enter the performance area late in the afternoon, checking the vendors for health and safety permits. All are in order except for one.

I am M.C.-ing on stage when this occurs. My co-M.C., local peformance artist Elia Arce, tails the cops as they go from vendor to vendor, until they reach the teenage girl who did not have her papers in order. The cops started in— "Should we give her a ticket? Should we confiscate the goods? Or should we just take her to jail?"—clearly enjoying their work. Elia did everything she could, offering the officers tickets to other festival performances, acting coquettish, etcetera. From the mike on stage, I began a speech gleaned from years of listening to FMLN spokespersons rallying crowds to the Cause. I guess I did a good job; within a few minutes, the homeless were chanting, "¡Qué saquen a la policía!" And I had to wonder how far this thing should go— I envisioned orders to disperse and police batons in that moment. But the Angels of La Placita intervened; the cops left after a verbal warning. Were they touched by the thick sentimentality of *La Raza*? I'd like to think so, but probably a 100-degree-inspired laziness to fill out paperwork was the real reason.

Our participation in the L.A. Festival finished off with a golden light glowing on the brick buildings of La Placita in the late afternoon, people dancing to Latin rock by the local group Umbral, and the idea that *cultura popular,* for at least a few hours, had won out over *la cultura dominante* at La Placita.

> We're a people who walk
> and walking together we'll arrive
> at another city where there's no pain nor sadness,
> the eternal city . . .
>
>   La Placita Church hymn
>   (accompanied by mariachis)

"Bring Olivares back" slurs the homeless Mexicano near the bus stop, under the shade of olive trees probably as old as La Placita itself. "What have we done to them? Why are they doing this to us" he says, rocking back and forth on his heels.

A few seconds before, I had seen him walking through the courtyard next to the church, begging. Then the LAPD was on him, pushing him out onto the street, where many homeless now sit, watching two white officers patrol the sidewalk, where now they roust a street vendor who has not heeded the order to disperse.

What Olivares brought to La Placita is all but gone. The stirring sermons are gone too. Today's was offered by an aging Spaniard, in that Castilian accent that grates harshly on the Latin American ear.

"The peace of the Lord be with you," he said. "And also with you," we mumbled. "Wait a minute," he said. "Where's the enthusiasm? This is a celebration of our faith before the Lord. He wants to see your enthusiasm, feel your energy!

Louder! Say it louder! THE PEACE OF THE LORD BE WITH YOU!" "And also with you," half the parish says, slightly louder. Many don't even bother. I stop in mid-phrase.

There are newcomers to mass these days. During today's 9:00 A.M. service, once offered by Father Michael Kennedy (Olivares's assistant pastor and fervent liberation theologian, who also left the parish when Olivares fell ill), two LAPD officers stormed into the church in pursuit of a young home-less Latino whom they'd told to vacate the courtyard. In the middle of the liturgical reading, the officers chased the kid *across the altar*. The aging Spaniard did not even blink. The kid escaped through a side entrance, with the cops on his heels. A few seconds later, he ran back through the church, this time down the side aisle towards the main entrance. The cops barged their way through the crowd after him. They never did catch him.

"If there's criminal activity," LAPD sergeant Barry Staggs, a barrel-chested, silver-haired man with Jesse James eyes tells me, "we're going to chase 'em right into the church or anywhere else."

Staggs is standing on the grass in the middle of a small park across the street from La Placita. A few Latino couples lounge in the shade. The homeless and the vendors are no-where to be seen. "All that [Olivares] did was draw crimi-nals," he tells me. "Now, I love this," he says, his hand sweeping over the impressive panorama of the three quiet and obviously uneasy couples on the grass. "You see these families, shoot. They can stay here all day long, go into the church, do anything that they want.

"Olivera [sic] was trying to make a political statement. And this is not the place to do it. This is where L.A. started. This was once a Mexican village, I hear. I mean, Jesus Christ," he says, mouth open and eyes wide, a look of overwrought disbelief, ". . . here they are, all these scumbags from Nicaragua, Salvador, and Honduras, every one of 'em are damn thieves.

"Now that it's cleaned up . . . boy, I tell ya, it's a breath of fresh air, and I feel a lot better."

A full moon rises above the downtown scrapers that surround the plaza across the street from La Placita. They've fenced off the kiosk tonight. Tables surround the stage and well-dressed Angelenos talk in small groups and sip wine and beer.

Father Luis Olivares is returning to La Placita for the first time since he fell ill and left the parish. It is an official affair: the dinner for "Father Louie," as he is known in activist circles, is sponsored in great part by the city itself, and the politicos are out in force. Ditto the radical chic of L.A.— progressive Hollywood actors, Left university professors, Central America solidarity activists and labor organizers (half of them dressed to kill, others—the students mostly— extremely prole). There is just a touch of irony that Olivares is being saluted by some of the very authorities who have supported the development plans which are rumored to have made his departure necessary. With Olivares out of La Placita, gone is the figurehead of the local progressive community. And gone, once again, are the poor from La Placita. Enter the developers.

The organizers of tonight's event thought it wise to put up a portable chain-link fence around the kiosk area (tickets for the dinner were $30 to $75) so that everyone can feast on their catered Mexican dinner and honor Olivares without the hassle of whatever homeless party-crashers are still left in the plaza area after the recent, very effective LAPD raids.

Suddenly, while a local quasi–New Age *folklórico* band does garish renditions of spacey *indígena* music (a big hit with the *gringos*), a group of poor immigrants rushes from the church shelter area up to the fence around the kiosk. They start making noise. "¡Queremos al Padre Olivares!" they shout. They love Olivares, they want Olivares. They can barely be heard over the sound system, but heads begin to turn.

Their fingers curl around the gray metal of the fence.

"Father Olivares helped us economically, socially, and spiritually," says one day laborer across the fence to me.

Recognizing me as a journalist, the group begins to talk all at once, a collage of voices:

"The LAPD is taking us out of La Placita, they're harassing us and treating us like dogs!"

"Olivares, Olivares, Olivares," the group begins to shout, in chorus.

Their fingers poke through the chain links. "Olivares, Olivares, Olivares!"

An organizer opens the gate, and about twenty men enter the kiosk area, with their paint-flecked shoes, torn shirts, and dusty hair. After being given some food, they mill about the table area. The radical chic crowd does double takes. A few get up, offering their chairs to the homeless. Some of the men accept.

Olivares himself is now being introduced on the stage. A standing ovation. He has lost weight, and his skin still has a deathly pallor to it. But he walks, unassisted, up to the podium and addresses the crowd in a voice just a notch below the one that once boomed out over the pews across the street, recalling the words of Simeon to Mary, upon the birth of Jesus.

"Behold," Olivares quotes, "this child is destined . . . to be a sign that shall be contradicted . . ."

VISIBILIA

Thomas S. Hines

MACHINES
IN THE GARDEN:

Notes Toward a History of Modern
Los Angeles Architecture, 1900–1990

The major theme in the history of Los Angeles architecture since 1900 has been the city's and the region's encounter with "modernism"—that evocative, but ambiguous concept that did seem to characterize the century's most significant avant-garde architecture. In the 1960s and early 1970s, the tenets of modernism would come under attack from the tentatively named movement of "Post-Modern Eclecticism." Yet throughout the 1970s and 1980s, the work of such architects as Frank Gehry and the younger architects of the Gehry orbit would confirm that the rumors of the death of modernism had been greatly exaggerated.[1]

"While Southern California has been called a place of

'cultural confusion' and an urban Disneyland," the historian
Leslie Heumann has argued, "it is more importantly a place
of experimentation, an invitation and a challenge of fertile
imaginations to create the ultimate and the easiest, the most
fantastic and the most functional, the best and occasionally
the worst, in architecture. Out of this amorphous, chame-
leonic atmosphere have emerged pioneering manifestations
of architectural thought and practice."[2]

Four highly vulnerable concepts best categorize this development: first, the idea of "Craftsman" or "Mission Modernism" as epitomized in the work of Irving Gill; second, the
concept of "Romantic Modernism" as exemplified primarily
in the Los Angeles buildings of Frank Lloyd Wright and,
briefly, of those other architects who worked in the modes
contemporaries called "modernistic" and that came to be
labeled "Art Deco" and "Streamlined Moderne"; third, as
opposed to Romantic Modernism, the idea of Machine
Modernism, or as they liked to call it, "Rational Modernism," as illustrated primarily in the work of Richard Neutra
and his sympathetic contemporaries in the International
Style; and fourth, the extension of modernism after the critique of Post-Modernism—into the movement that some
have labeled "Mineshaft Modern" or "Deconstructivist" as
exemplified in the work of Frank Gehry and his school.

The blessing and curse of time and space provide the essential rationale for using Gill, Wright, Neutra, and Gehry
as examples and for virtually ignoring such important figures
as Charles and Henry Greene, Rudolph Schindler, Charles
Eames, and Charles Moore. I regret that I must mention
only in passing those significant architects and their numerous gifted contemporaries, as well as the monuments of the
mimetic pop vernacular from the Brown Derby to Disneyland. The latter architecture is significant as both stimulant
and comic counterpoint to the more consciously "serious"
architecture of modernism.

"The new art is a world-wide fact," wrote the Spanish philosopher José Ortega y Gasset in 1925. "For about twenty years now the most alert young people of two successive generations . . . have found themselves faced with the undeniable fact that they have no use for traditional art. . . . With these young people one can do one of two things: shoot them, or try to understand them. . . . Who knows what may come out of this budding style? The task it sets itself is enormous; it wants to create from nought."[3]

The effects of the "new art" that reverberated from the 1910 Post-Impressionist show in London moved the novelist Virginia Woolf to make the blunt assertion that "in or around December, 1910, human nature changed radically." The literary critic Robert Adams used Woolf's cryptic pronouncement as the focal point of a lecture in 1977 with the significant title "What Was Modernism?" He believed she was right about 1910: "Within five years either way of that date," he asserted, "a great sequence of new and different works appeared in Western culture, striking the tonic chords of modernism. Ten years before that fulcrum of December 1910, modernism is not yet; ten years after, it is already. Mind," he cautioned, "I'm not talking about 'the modern world' or anything like that; just about a particular stylistic period in Western art, literature, music. . . ."[4]

Adams then answered the title question of his lecture by admitting that the label "modernism" was "an inaccurate and misleading term applied to a cultural trend that's most clearly discernible between 1905 and 1925. When it is understood to refer to distinct structural features that some artistic works of the period have in common, it's got a real meaning. [But] as it departs from that specific meaning, it gets fuzzier and fuzzier. . . . Still it's been a prevalent and widely accepted stopgap term, with a loose emotive tonality."[5]

Though its life-cycle in architecture stretched considerably beyond Adams and Ortega's 1905–1925 parameters, modernism in architecture shared with the other arts similar problems of taxonomic imprecision. Etymologically, according to the *Oxford English Dictionary*, the term "modern" and its derivatives evolved from the late Latin sixth-century *modernus*, roughly meaning "just now," but it was not widely adopted before the sixteenth century, when it became increasingly necessary to distinguish the period since the Renaissance from the ancient and medieval worlds. In addition to that large but relatively specific meaning, it continued from the sixteenth into the late twentieth century to convey, as well, a more floating identity with things "characteristic of the present and recent times . . . not antiquated or obsolete." But in the late nineteenth century, the floating term quickened into a harder specificity as the term for the new art of the incipient new century.

Though most architectural modernists would continue to insist that they followed no "style," they opted for what ultimately came to be a cluster of new styles—from the hot, exotic plasticity of Expressionism to the elegantly cool austerity of Rationalism. Yet almost all avant-garde twentieth-century architects were willing to accept the "modernist" label. In 1894, when the Viennese pioneer Otto Wagner entitled a lecture and treatise "Modern Architecture," the term was not yet in common usage. By 1932, when New York's recently established Museum of Modern Art staged its epochal "Modern Architecture" show, the appellation was unquestioned. By 1966, when the same museum published Robert Venturi's seminal critique of modernism, *Complexity and Contradiction in Architecture*, architectural "modernism"—the term and the movement—was beginning to experience increasingly serious identity problems, problems which did not abate with MoMA's "Deconstructivist" show of 1988, which featured, among others, the work of Frank Gehry.

In 1921, the critic Eloise Roorbach published in *House Beautiful* an article praising Irving Gill and his house in Los Angeles for the businessman, Walter Dodge, built six years before. The house, she believed, "holds to the Spanish spirit as far as the plain walls, arches, and patios are concerned and thus is in harmony with the romantic inheritance of the West," but, she averred, "in all else it is distinctly modern." Roorbach's dualities, the historian Thomas Jimmerson has noted, "established what would become the critical consensus, describing the work of Irving Gill as oscillating between two poles, a romantic regionalism rooted in the revival of the California Mission style, and a scientific modernism characterized by simplification, standardization, and technological innovation."[6]

As the modern movement, particularly the International Style, gained ascendancy in the 1920s and 1930s, historians of that development tended to emphasize the latter part of the Gill equation. Lewis Mumford in *The Brown Decades* (1931) argued that Gill's houses were "the best early statements of the essential or *sachlich* house: in his deliberate absence of ornamental effect, he anticipated both the polemics and the practice of Le Corbusier and the de Stijl group. . . ." Gill's "clarity of form and simplicity of means," observed Henry-Russell Hitchcock, "is more premonitory of the next phase of modern architecture than any other American work of the period."[7]

In the 1970s, not surprisingly, Post-Modernist architects and critics would deemphasize Gill's modernist leanings and focus on his use of "traditional effects," particularly his "Hispanic" arcades and loggias. By the 1990s, however, as "Post-Modernist" architecture fell increasingly from favor, critics and architects found themselves returning to an appreciation of Gill's boldly "abstract" geometric form making. In characterizing his work, Gill, himself, embraced the same dualities, though with a definite tilt toward the modernist components. This was conditioned by his own early life and professional training.

Born into a Quaker family in Syracuse, New York, in 1870, Gill had no formal education beyond high school, learning his trade by observation of his father's work as a building contractor and by apprenticing with a local architect. In 1890, however, sensing like so many of his peers, that his fortune lay in trekking west, he moved to Chicago and managed to land a job in the prestigious office of Louis Sullivan and Dankmar Adler. There, alongside Frank Lloyd Wright, another Sullivan apprentice just down from Wisconsin, Gill worked on various projects including the great arched "Golden Door" of Sullivan and Adler's Transportation Building of the 1893 Columbian Exposition. In 1893, concerned about his declining health, he ventured farther south and west to San Diego, California, then a sleepy town of 25,000 people. There, and to the north toward metropolitan Los Angeles, Gill opened himself fully to the built and natural southwestern environment.[8]

In California, he wrote, "We have great wide plains, arched by blue skies that are fresh chapters as yet unwritten. We have noble mountains, lovely little hills and canyons waiting to hold the record of this generation's history, ideals, imagination, sense of romance and honesty. . . . The West has an opportunity unparalleled in the history of the world for it is the newest white page turned for registration."[9]

The Spanish missions had been built a century before Gill arrived in California, when the page was even whiter. Finer than most of the buildings that followed them in the nineteenth century, the missions and the related Spanish houses of the era should, Gill believed, be preserved and honored, for in "their long, low lines, graceful arcades, tile roofs, bell towers, arched doorways and walled gardens, we find a most expressive medium of retaining tradition, history, and romance." The missions, however, should not be caricatured.

He was certain, in fact, that "more crimes have been committed in their name than any other unless it be the Grecian temples." The mission forms, he argued, in their "charming proportions and graceful outline have been distorted to adorn tall buildings, low railway stations, ornate hotels, cramped stables and minute private houses in the most . . . pitiable way." California's Hispanic buildings were useful therefore as models for contemporary building chiefly as simple abstract embodiments of the basic geometric forms. [10]

To this regional source of inspiration, Gill instinctively added the old devotion to simplicity of his Quaker forebears as fostered in the American cult of "the simple life" by such nineteenth-century secular oracles as Henry David Thoreau. The idea of contemporary "efficiency experts" such as Frederick Winslow Taylor also influenced Gill's commitments to functional, laborsaving devices particularly inflected toward the housewife-caretaker and, in larger homes, the servants. These included coved surfaces connecting the walls with floors and ceilings so as to minimize dust-catching surfaces, as well as vacuum-cleaner outlets in every room taking dust to the furnace. These values of simplicity, functionalism, efficiency, and cleanliness were connected to the era's reformists' goals of sounder mental and physical health, preoccupations, indeed, of the "modernist" way of life and of the next generation of modernist architects. In fact, Gill spent his entire career "experimenting with the idea of producing a perfectly sanitary, laborsaving house, one where the maximum of comfort may be had with the minimum of drudgery." [11]

Gill expressed his credo most succinctly in a 1916 article in *The Craftsman*: "The Home of the Future: The New Architecture of the West: Small Homes for a Great Country." "If we, the Architects of the West," he wrote, "wish to do great and lasting work, we must dare to be simple, must have the courage to fling aside every device that distracts the eye

Los Angeles in the 1850s by an unknown artist.

from structural beauty, must break through convention and get down to fundamental truths. Through force of custom and education," he argued, "we, in whose hands much of the beauty of country and city is entrusted, have been compelled to study the style of other men, with the result that most of our modern work is an open imitation . . . of another's idea. To break away from this degradation we must boldly throw aside every accepted structural belief and standard of beauty and get back to the straight line, the arch, the cube and the circle and drink from these fountains of Art that gave life to the great men of old."[12]

Among his many buildings in Southern California, three projects in Los Angeles County best reified Gill's ideas: the Dodge House, Hollywood, 1916; the Horatio West Court, Santa Monica, 1919; and the Lewis Courts, Sierra Madre, 1910.

Little is known about Walter Dodge, the manufacturer of patent medicines, whose fortune was shaped by his best-known product, "Tiz for tired feet." The gulf between that banal slogan and the sophisticated house Dodge commissioned from Irving Gill is, in fact, hard to explain. Did he or his wife live a secret life that craved artistic fulfillment which was partially realized in their collaboration with a regional architectural genius? In any case, the building was Gill's masterpiece.

The main south entrance led from the arched porte-cochere into a grand reception stair hall with living room and billiard room to the west, and dining and breakfast rooms to the east, the latter of which looked onto a walled open court. The long arm of the east wing included kitchen, servants' quarters, garage, and swimming pool. Upstairs bedrooms led onto decks and balconies as the downstairs areas led onto courts and gardens. Though abstract exterior arches reminded contemporaries of the vestigial mission forms, the most prophetic elevation was the north garden side, where

Irving Gill, Dodge House, 1915.

dramatically cubistic protrusions and recessions worked with
the creative tension of the occultly balanced window group-
ings to form an astonishingly abstract architectural composition. Of this elevation the historian William Jordy has
observed, "As in modern European architecture typical for
the twenties, we feel an equilibrium on the very brink of
disintegration, which yet retains a taut stability."[13]

Despite its status by the 1960s as a modernist icon of immense significance, the Dodge House was demolished in
1969 by no less a body than the city of Los Angeles, to whom
it had been bequeathed for use as a school. The shock waves
unleashed by its destruction, however, led indirectly to the
strengthening of the region's preservation consciousness and
to the establishment in the 1970s of the Los Angeles Conservancy, an activist preservation lobbying and educational
group.

Much of the same equilibrium between regional references and international modernism provided Gill's more

populist designs for people of modest means. This included housing for Mexican workers of the Riverside Cement Company (1911), later demolished, as well as only partially realized housing for workers in the new industrial town of Torrance, near Los Angeles (1913). Later, in the 1930s, Gill would design housing, again only partially implemented, for an Indian resettlement project at Lakeside, California. In 1910, in the Lewis Courts he completed a fully realized village of small, juxtaposed, low-cost apartments, which hugged the property lines along the street sides and opened onto a spacious central courtyard containing pergola, sitting, and recreational areas. Yet the arched-door, flat-roofed one-story apartments, with their easy indoor-outdoor spatial patterns, were so attractive that they soon began to appeal to a more up-scale clientele. The resulting rise in rents, therefore, gradually forced out many of the lower-income residents for whom the building had been designed. Then, in a still further effort to capitalize on his investment, the owner made a self-destructive move as he filled in the central court with additional rental units, *not* designed by Gill. This largely destroyed the appeal of the place for its middle-income residents and it again became, ironically, a working-class enclave. The court would continue to exist but only as a ghost of its former self.[14]

The four-unit, two-story, middle-class Horatio West Court near the beach in Santa Monica (1919) achieved the same initial success that most Gill buildings did, but after a period of decline, in contrast to the Lewis Courts, it was brilliantly restored in the 1970s. The same bold "Hispanic" arches graced the entrance porches, though the rest of the complex contained fewer historical references than even the Dodge House did. A walled patio off living and dining rooms, and upstairs sleeping porches, later enclosed by Gill, furnished the familiar inside-outside circulation patterns. Spectacular views of mountains and oceans were favorite features of the upstairs rooms.

Irving Gill, Horatio West Court, 1919.

By the late 1960s, the Horatio West had become an urban ruin, infamous as a center of the neighborhood drug traffic. A group of imaginative, young Gill enthusiasts, however, bought the units for a modest price and restored them to their former crispness. One of the restorers was the film-maker Margaret Bach, who, appropriately, became the founding president of the Los Angeles Conservancy.[15]

Gill's commitments to simplicity and functionalism, in his low-cost housing as in his grand expensive villas, brought him, Jordy argued, "to the brink of the modern as this came to be defined in Europe in the next decade," an architect "who literally invented his way in an isolated situation toward so much of what came to be the future."[16] As such, Gill became the undisputed godfather of twentieth-century Los Angeles modernism.

The year 1921 was important in the history of Southern California modernism because it marked, with the completion of the Barnsdall house, the West Coast emergence of Frank

Lloyd Wright. Born in Wisconsin in 1867, venturing to Chicago in 1887 and building a studio residence in Oak Park,
Wright had, by 1910 established himself, nationally and in-
ternationally, as a leading practitioner and prophet of modernism. His so-called Prairie Style epitomized what he called
"organic" design, architecture conceived from the inside
out, with a deference to the nature of materials and a marriage of the building to the site. Finally, Wright recognized
the possibilities and imperatives of the machine and used it
to help provide shelter and comfort for life in the machine
age.[17]

Between 1910 and 1920, however, Wright's life and architecture underwent dramatic changes. In 1909, in his early
forties, he acknowledged the failure of his first marriage and
escaped to Europe with a client, Mamah Cheney, both of
them leaving spouses and children in Oak Park. In Berlin,
he oversaw the publication of the great German Wasmuth
editions which introduced his work to Europe. With neither
of the abandoned spouses willing at that time to grant a
divorce and finding Oak Park hostile and scandalized by
their behavior, Wright and Mamah retreated to his roots in
Wisconsin and built a great house on the ancestral family
farm. "Taliesin," he called it, after the old Welsh bard. At
"Taliesin" he and Mamah and various of their alternately
visiting sets of children lived happily until 1914, with Wright
commuting between there and Chicago to supervise his
steadily declining number of commissions.

It was while working on the great Midway Gardens, a fes-
tive outdoor restaurant-cabaret, that he received a call to
return to Taliesin to confront an almost unbelievable calam-
ity. A deranged servant had run completely amok, setting
fire to the house, and then brutally murdering with an axe
seven of the occupants when they attempted to flee, including Mamah Cheney, her two visiting children, a draftsman,
and three servants. The house was virtually destroyed as was

Wright's own emotional stability. Both would be restored, the house relatively quickly, Wright's personal life more slowly and painfully. The two were intertwined, of course. But the rebuilt Taliesin was later struck by lightning, causing another fire and another rebuilding. It also caused more than one pious Wisconsin minister to remind the faithful that such was the fate of sinners like Mr. Wright, who obviously was being punished by a just and angry God.

But God also smiled on Wright and aided his recovery with two vast new commissions in the teens: the Imperial Hotel, Tokyo, and the Barnsdall complex in Los Angeles—fortuitous diversions in more ways than one. For a time at least, Wisconsin and the Middle West held too many sad and sordid memories and Wright knew that he was destined to drift and to roam, to "get away" and stretch himself. And he was thankful that he could escape to the sunnier climes of Japan and California. The personal travail influenced the work, of course. In the Los Angeles houses more than ever before, Wright built aloof and impregnable bastions to protect him vicariously through his extended family of clients from the tongues and intrusions of a hostile world. They were wonderful houses in many ways, but houses which, with their guarded access routes, seemed to place a greater premium on privacy than ever before in his earlier work. It was a trenchant example of the historical intersection of culture and personality.

The Los Angeles buildings and the Imperial Hotel, however, not only reflected the vicissitudes of Wright's personal life; they reflected concurrent changes in his architectural interests as well. The personal problems both predicted and reflected a related restlessness in Wright's artistic nature as he seemed to be tiring of the formulas and patterns of the Prairie School gestalt—so influenced by the tenets of the recent Arts and Crafts movements in Europe and America and the timeless aesthetics of Japanese design. Wright had always been pulled toward a certain cultural nationalism, drawn, like his heroes Emerson and Whitman, to find and create an "American" culture. And his search for the roots of a distinctly American architecture led him naturally to the buildings of the first Americans: the Indians. Later he would use the teepee as a reference, but in the teens and early twenties, he seemed drawn to the pueblos of the American Southwest and to their even grander Mayan cousins of pre-Columbian Mexico, buildings which also placed a premium on privacy and difficulty of access. He never publicly acknowledged the obvious Mayan sources, though he used them throughout the twenties as he had even earlier in certain Prairie fragments. Surely they appeared in Unity Temple, Oak Park; in the Midway Gardens, Chicago; in the A.D. German Warehouse, Richland Center, Wisconsin; and even in the Japanese Imperial Hotel, but never so strongly as in the complex of buildings he designed in the late teens for the intriguing oil heiress Aline Barnsdall.

A complex creature, Wright wrote of her perceptively, "neither neo, quasi, nor pseudo . . . as near American as any Indian, as developed and traveled in appreciation of the beautiful as any European. As domestic as a shooting star." Her detractors called her a socialite socialist, a rich parlor Communist, as she built her grand shelter for plotting the revolution, not only in the arts but in politics as well. For years along the Hollywood Boulevard side of her property, great billboards pleaded the cases of Sacco and Vanzetti, Tom Mooney, and other of her heroes. Barnsdall and Wright had met in Chicago in the middle teens via various mutual "Little Theater" interests, but Barnsdall, preferring more exotic Los Angeles, decided to establish a not-so-little theater in Hollywood. Norman Bel Geddes agreed to be her art director and Frank Lloyd Wright her architect. For various complex reasons, partially having to do with her peripatetic restlessness and the unfortunate choice of certain

Frank Lloyd Wright, Hollyhock House, 1921.

other associates, Barnsdall's theater projects went largely unrealized, but the house and its accouterments became one
of Wright's masterworks.[18]

Built primarily of hollow tile and stucco richly tinted in a
pinkish beige, the house formed the shape of a rough letter
U. The main north entrance led east to dining room,
kitchen, and servants' rooms; southwest to the library and
living room; southeast to the bedroom wing for Barnsdall,
her guests, and her only child, a daughter, nicknamed
Sugar-top. Aline Barnsdall never married and the identity of
the child's father would always remain a mystery.

The fireplace at Hollyhock, with Wright's elegant abstract
sculpture, was topped by a skylight and was surrounded by a
fish pool whose water was circulated to the outside basins.
Sugar-top's nursery had indoor and outdoor play areas with
fine glass and miniature fairy-tale balconies above miniature
water moats leading to a courtyard with a lintel so miniature

that anyone but Sugar-top and her friends would bump his oversized adult head. The larger courtyards were particularly significant spaces—extensions of the house onto the California landscape. From there, and even better from the higher roof terraces, lay the grand panorama of mountain, city, and ocean. Barnsdall christened it the "Hollyhock House" after her favorite flower, which Wright further articulated in the abstract cornice sculpture.

This was all a far cry from the sterner, crisper, more relaxed Shubui qualities of Wright's earlier Prairie period. Could this, Wright wondered, even be called "modern" architecture? Indeed the Barnsdall experience, Wright later admitted, was an exotic respite "at that [bad] time" when he felt "on the rocks economically, publicly, emotionally. . . . I called it," he later wrote, " 'a California Romanza,' this time being frankly on holiday." He admitted it was "a bit sentimental." In other, less gifted hands, he asserted, "this quest for sentimental bosh in architecture . . . has wasted billions of perfectly honest dollars, done spiritual harm, more or less violence, to millions of otherwise pretty good people," who in seeking romance got the "pseudo-romantic . . . of neo-Spanish . . . quasi-Italian, stale . . . Renaissance, dying or dead, of English half-timber and Colonial." Perhaps Wright's fear of being neo-anything accounts for his reluctance to credit his pre-Columbian references. "Perhaps better to say," he wrote, "as I have said of Taliesin, Hollyhock House was to be a natural house . . . native to the region of California as the house in the Middle West had been native Middle West. Suited to Miss Barnsdall and her purpose, such a house would be sure to be all that 'poetry of form' could imply, because any house should be beautiful in California in the way California herself is beautiful. She wanted no ordinary house did Aline Barnsdall."[19]

Wright lamented that "our nice word 'Romance' is now disreputable because implying escape from life rather than any realization of . . . life. Either by inheritance or as evil consequence, it is a loose attempt at illusion. . . . So 'Romance' lies loose in the heart, askew in the mind, something fanciful. Unlifelike. Results, at best, exotic. At worst, idiotic. So Romance in the United States becomes a sickly simpering mask for a changed new life." Here he suggested more than he may have realized about his own great need for escape and romance.[20]

The canonical puritanism of the burgeoning Modern Movement indeed made him wonder if the Hollyhock romanza was itself close to the edge. "Conscience troubled me a little," he admitted. "That 'voice within' said, 'What about the machine crying for recognition as the normal tool of your age?'" "Well my critics," he then answered drolly, "one does weary of duty. Even of privilege. . . . I again told the still-small voice to 'go to' for a time. Hollyhock House was to be a holiday for me. The plans joyfully traveling this fascinating upward road . . . delighted Miss Barnsdall. I could scarcely have keyed the romanza too high for her. . . ." But Wright's peripatetic client lived only briefly in Hollyhock House, giving it away ultimately in the best communal spirit as an art and pleasure park to the people of Los Angeles.[21]

Through the Barnsdall and other Los Angeles connections, Wright met other clients in search of both modernism and California romance, and he built four more great houses in the spirit of Hollyhock. All of these were constructed with beautifully molded concrete blocks. His own favorite was "La Miniatura" in Pasadena (1923), built "as the cactus grows," for another strong single woman, a widow, Alice Millard, who had been an earlier Prairie client in Illinois. She typified, Wright observed, the "folk from the Middle-Western Prairies" who "when . . . prosperous came loose and rolled down there into that far corner to bask in eternal sunshine." The Millard house in its lush ravine sat erect and tall, as did the Storer, Ennis, and Freeman houses, all perched grandly on their Hollywood hilltops.[22]

There were similar qualities in the simultaneous achievements of Wright's oldest son, Lloyd, who had migrated west to work for Irving Gill and whose work of the twenties strongly echoed his father's. His Sowden House (1926), was a great Cyclopean Expressionistic rock. The urbane house and studio Lloyd build for himself echoed strongly, with its concrete blocks, the aesthetic of his father's whole Los Angeles period. His house for the silent screen star Ramon Novarro (1928) had many of the features of the high Modern or Moderne Movement labeled "Art Deco" after the prominent display of works in this style at the 1925 Paris Exposition of Industrial and Decorative Arts.

The general term "Moderne" covered both phases of the movement, the Zigzag Moderne, or Deco, which was especially prominent in the twenties, and the more voluptuous Streamlined Moderne, especially popular in the thirties. Of the two, the Zigzag Deco was more synthetic and eclectic, drawing on a wider variety of sources: the pre-Columbian forms that Wright had used more explicitly in the twenties; the vivid geometry of even more recent American Indian designs, especially rugs and pottery of Navajo and other Southwest Indian groups; various Egyptian motifs in that early wave of Tutomania after the excavation in the early 1920s of King Tut's tomb; and finally the more rectilinear phases of Art Nouveau itself.[23]

The best Art Deco monument in Los Angeles, Bullock's Wilshire Department Store, was built in 1929 by Parkinson and Parkinson, interior design by Jock Peters. Its social significance in Los Angeles's history was marked by the placement of the main entrance, not on the street side, but at the rear facing the parking lot. Also important in Los Angeles's late 1920s Deco galaxy—surely along with New York's and Miami Beach's, the greatest in the world—were Morgan, Walls, and Clements with their black and gold Richfield Building, and their green terra-cotta Pellisier tower at Western and Wilshire, housing Lansburgh and Heinsbergen's

Parkinson and Parkinson, Bullocks Wilshire, 1929.

Deco masterpiece, the great Wiltern Theater. And though it contained other, perhaps more dominant, references, Bertram Goodhue's splendid Los Angeles Public Library (1925) had definite Art Deco elements.

The other side of the modernistic mode was the Streamlined Moderne, which drew its inspiration from the more curvilinear features of the International Style itself and especially from the imagery of transportation carriers—the train, the auto, the ocean liner, the airplane, the blimp, the spaceship—strongly suggesting the spirit of flight, of movement, of "getting away," if not on a rocket at least on the Super Chief. The Coca-Cola Bottling Company of Robert V. Derrah (1937) was a nautical remodeling of an older group of buildings. The green and white pylons of Wurdeman and Becket's Pan-Pacific Auditorium (1935) seemed to be great engines pulling the rest of the huge building forward. At the more popular, commercial level, Morgan,

Wurdeman and Becket, Pan-Pacific Auditorium, 1935.

Walls, and Clements did a number of stores for Ralph's supermarkets in both Deco and Streamlined Moderne. Their store from the 1930s on Wilshire in Beverly Hills suggested to weary shoppers as they stopped in for the milk and eggs that they were somehow embarking on a great modern adventure.[24]

The Moderne picked up many of the forms and effects of the high Modern Movement though usually without the essence of this spirit. Less open, more massive, the Moderne was more concerned with mass, with stuff, with bulk, with packaging, than with definition of space. It was in fact the International Style "in drag." Still, it was highly significant in the social history of architecture as the image of modernism for most ordinary people. It was a cunning compromise with modernity. While Richard Neutra and the Museum of Modern Art labeled it pejoratively as "decorative" and "modernistic," meaning "false modern," the people "out there"

seem to have loved it. Like the higher-art architecture of
Frank Lloyd Wright, it consciously infused modernity with
romance.

As opposed to Romantic Modernism, the greatest Los Angeles exponent of Machine Modernism, Rational Modernism, and the International Style of the high Modern
Movement was undoubtedly Richard Neutra, the quintes-
sential Los Angeles modernist. Born in Vienna in 1892 and
growing up in that city's turn-of-the-century cultural ferment, Neutra imbibed from his mentor, Adolf Loos, a great
enthusiasm for American architecture, especially for the
Chicago School of Louis Sullivan and the Prairie work of
Frank Lloyd Wright. Neutra's love for Wright's Prairie
School was confirmed by the German publication of
Wright's work in the Wasmuth Folios of 1910–11, which
revealed to Neutra "the fantastic living culture of . . . people
in another world." He made rough sketches in his diary of
the plans of Wright's Middle Western "Wohnhäuser." Loos
and Wasmuth convinced Neutra that "I would have to see it
with my own eyes; no one in Europe was doing anything like
it. Whoever he was, Frank Lloyd Wright, the man far away,
had done something momentous and rich in meaning. This
miracle man instilled in me the conviction that, no matter
what, I would have to go to the places where he walked and
worked." When Neutra finally got to America and then to
California and began his own practice, his work would show
greater affinities with Wright's sober, sharp-edged Prairie period then with his more florid and romantic California
work.[25]

But before Neutra could get to America, Europe exploded
and the Great War began, removing him from architecture
altogether for four years except for a small, primitive officers'
teahouse in the Balkans, that would give a sense of the pavil-

ions he was to build all his life. Until 1923, when the United States finally concluded its peace treaty with Austria, Neutra was unable to get a visa, and while awaiting this moment, he worked in Switzerland and then in Berlin with Erich Mendelsohn. He had good experiences in both places, but in cold, destitute postwar Europe, he yearned even more to get away and stretch himself. The bitter Swiss winter of 1919–20 depressed him tremendously. "I wish I could get out of here," he wrote in his diary, "and get to some idyllic tropical island, where one does not have to slave, can find time to think, or even more important, can have a free spirit." His friend Schindler was not on a tropical island but he was in America. His position with Wright in Chicago and his plans to move to sunny California to supervise Wright's projects there tantalized Neutra and rekindled his desire to migrate. A travel poster in a Zurich train station showing palm trees and ocean beaches and reading "California Calls You" stayed in his mind. Later in 1920, his *Sehnsucht nach dem Süden*, the ancient Germanic yearning for the South, made him fleetingly consider a job offer in Java. But in 1923 he finally began his pilgrimage to "the land where the lemon blooms," a line he remembered from Thomas's opera *Mignon*. After a year in New York, Chicago, and Taliesin, he and his wife Dione and their small son Frank, named for Frank Lloyd Wright, made their way to Los Angeles.[26]

Encouragement from Rudolph and Pauline Schindler had kept his spirits up. In January 1924, while Neutra was still in New York, Schindler wrote that "as far as your trip to the far west is concerned, I should think you should not hurry into it as long as you can make a living in New York. The 'season' there is no doubt more interesting than the one in Los Angeles would be. However, I believe that Los Angeles provides a better starting point to develop an independent future. The building activity is phenomenal and life is agreeable." He suggested that Neutra come in the spring of 1924, but Neutra was determined to work at least briefly in the Middle West with Wright. Schindler agreed that "a year in his studio would be worth any sacrifice." The autumn and winter with Wright at Taliesin were splendid beyond belief, but California still called and the Neutras left in early 1925.[27]

Schindler continued to offer encouragement. "Do you have a clear picture of the West," he had written earlier, "or is it as it is for so many a romantic urge? In any case, here you can make a living just as well as in Chicago and for a foreigner with better auspices for a future and an agreeable way of life. I would be very pleased to receive you and help you over the initial difficulties; as far as it is in my power, we shall not starve." The Neutras crossed the country by train the first week in February 1925, stopping en route briefly at the Grand Canyon. Schindler welcomed them at the Los Angeles station and drove them to his Kings Road house, where they would rent an apartment. It was raining, Dione remembered, and the house seemed dark—but wonderful.[28]

With the Schindlers, the Neutras began exploring Southern California: "ocean, forest, desert, snow, palm trees, South Sea fishes," Neutra wrote to a friend, "all in 2–3 hours driving." They visited all of Wright's California buildings, especially Hollyhock House, which had brought Schindler —and then Neutra—to Los Angeles in the first place. Together, they designed for Aline Barnsdall a fetching pool and pergola west of the main house. But Neutra's happiest new discovery was the work of Irving Gill. The crisp, abstract, cubistic geometry of Gill's buildings, with their flat roofs and ribbon windows, aligned him in the eyes of Neutra's generation with the Modern Movement. Reflecting these qualities a block up the street on Kings Road was Gill's handsome Dodge House (1916) and out near the beach in Santa Monica, his Horatio West Court (1919)—both of which Neutra photographed avidly and published in his book *Amerika: Neues Bauen in der Welt* (1930). It was in fact such avowed modernists as Neutra that pulled Gill into the modernist orbit. Yet Neutra was *also* impressed with the stark Hispanic Los Angeles buildings that had inspired Gill as well as with the even earlier Indian pueblo references that they had all long admired.[29]

The first major building in California that Neutra designed alone, after collaborating with Schindler on several projects in the middle twenties, was the Jardinette Apartments (1927), near the intersection of Western and Melrose in Hollywood, one of the first predictions in all the United States of what would come to be called the "International Style." When Walter Gropius visited Los Angeles in 1928, he expressed great delight in Neutra's apartment house.

By 1928, however, Neutra was hard at work on what would become his masterpiece, the house in Los Angeles for Philip and Leah Lovell. He had met them through Schindler, who had encountered them in the early 1920s. Leah was the sister of Harriet Freeman, a Los Angeles client of Frank Lloyd Wright, and it was through the Wright connection and through various mutual left-wing social and political interests that the Freemans, and then the Lovells, got to know the Schindlers. Leah, a native middle westerner, was a disciple of the liberal educator Angelo Patri and ran a kindergarten with Pauline Schindler based on free association, learn-by-doing methods. A reserved, gentle person, she stood in sharp contrast to her dynamic, athletic, and extroverted husband.

Philip Lovell, a native of the New York area, was a practicing naturopath, an antidrug physician, who advocated "natural" methods of healing and preventive health care with an emphasis on exercise, weight lifting, massage, heat and water cures, open-air sleeping, regular nude sunbathing, and most important, reliance on a natural, fresh-food vegetarian diet. Palpably proud of his fitness and virility, an advocate of free and uninhibited sexual expression, he wrote a widely followed column in the *Los Angeles Times* called "Care of the Body." Indeed, Lovell exemplified the popular image of what was already becoming—in myth and reality—the "Southern California lifestyle." Yet his buoyant élan co-existed comfortably with a Spartan avoidance not only of drugs but of alcohol, caffeine, and tobacco. He enjoyed expressing his opinions in rough, blustery street talk—with New York–accented Jewish chutzpah. He considered himself a "radical" in health and dietary matters and liked to associate with radicals in other areas—politics, economics, the arts, and architecture.

In the mid-1920s, Schindler built three vacation houses for the Lovells in three widely differing Southern California environments. Two were modest, a cabin in the mountains at Wrightwood and a ranch house in the desert at Fallbrook, near Palm Springs. The third was the epochal Newport Beach house. To ensure better views, as well as privacy from the public beach, Schindler lifted the main floor on ferro-concrete piers a story above the ground, allowing the beach environment to filter beneath the house. Interior balconies around the large double-storied living room led to open sleeping porches later enclosed as bedrooms. The specially equipped kitchen and bathrooms were designed to the Lovells' dietary and therapeutic needs. A decorative patterning in the window mullions recalled Frank Lloyd Wright. Schindler had apparently done preliminary designs for the beach house as early as 1922, but the later-designed mountain and desert houses were completed first. The beach house was finished in 1926. Neutra did the minimal landscaping.[30]

Schindler and Lovell had also discussed a larger city house and Schindler had apparently done preliminary sketches. But in 1927, when Lovell awarded the commission, it went to Richard Neutra. There were aspects of Neutra's and Lovell's personalities that *should* have attracted them to each other. Both were ambitious and filled with a sense of mission. "I liked him *despite* his aggressiveness," Lovell asserted in the early 1970s. But it might have been more accurate for him to say that he liked Neutra, not *despite*, but *because of* this. Neutra no doubt cultivated and ingratiated himself with Lovell as he did with most people who interested and impressed him. And it was likely this tendency and personality trait that Schindler remembered when he later suggested that Neutra had "taken" the commission from him. As Lovell had gotten to know Neutra, he had become increasingly impressed with the precision of his design methods—a quality he found notably missing in Schindler. He had already commissioned Neutra to remodel his downtown medical office and attached gymnasium with highly satisfactory results.[31]

Whatever the motivation for Lovell's giving Neutra the commission, the house was the turning point in his career. It is difficult to imagine Neutra's life and oeuvre without it. Schindler would no doubt have built a beautiful and significant house, but it is hard to believe it could ever have been as significant in his career—or in the history of modern architecture—as the Neutra design became. The undeniable fact is that Neutra got the job and designed a remarkable house—both for his clients and for the cause of modern architecture.

The Lovell commission bore out Neutra's later contention that in "southern California, I found what I had hoped for, a people who were more 'mentally footloose' than those elsewhere, and who did not mind deviating opinion . . . where one can do most anything that comes to mind and is good fun. All this seemed to me a good climate for trying something independent of hidebound habituation. . . ." Aline Barnsdall had told Wright she wanted no ordinary house, and Lovell contended: "I was not going to build my house the same as the woman from Peoria." In both the beach and city houses, the two radical young architects had "complete

Richard Neutra, Lovell Health House, 1927–29.

freedom of design. . . . They found in me [Lovell] a very easy mark—as long as they conformed to my [programmatic] idiosyncrasies," particularly open sleeping porches, private areas for nude sunbathing, and special provisions in the kitchen and bathing areas for dietary and therapeutic needs.[32]

Considerably more demanding and challenging for Neutra than the clients' personal "idiosyncrasies" was the difficult site, which Lovell had already chosen and acquired. Situated on a cul-de-sac at the end of Dundee Drive in the Hollywood Hills, it abutted, to the north, the beautiful, natural city-owned Griffith Park, with views of the city to the south and glimpses of the distant ocean beyond. Just across the canyon to the west lay Frank Lloyd Wright's Ennis House and a half-mile to the south, his Barnsdall Hollyhock House. Upon receiving the Lovell commission, Neutra later recalled, "I then went up to the so fateful, spectacular and precarious site . . . and lonely in the midst of all my worries, fell in love with it. I told myself that mankind, with a new health and population swell in store, would one day run out of level ground. It will have to build on steepness and on prefabricated stilts, with the living area pendant from the roof! Dr. Lovell wanted to be a patron of forward-looking experiment. He would be the man who could see 'health and future' in a strange wide-open filigree steel frame, set deftly and precisely by cranes and booms onto this inclined piece of rugged nature. . . ."[33] It was the ultimate expression of the idea of the "machine in the garden."

Neutra spent most of 1928 designing and planning the house. Unable to find a contractor he believed sufficiently competent and motivated, he became the general contractor himself, directing the subcontractors via detailed specifications and day-to-day supervision. Contracts were awarded in late 1928. The house was constructed during 1929. "Long before sunrise," he later remembered, "I started to check every one of the thousand prepunched bolt holes and shop-cut coverplates of my steel window-bearing I-beam columns." The concrete Gunite was "shot" onto the wire lath by long hoses extending from the mixers on the street. Above the heavy ferroconcrete foundation, which harbored the pool, rose the light steel frame, which supported the building. It was the first such use of steel for a residence in America. Prefabricated, with an eighth-inch tolerance, in portable elements transported to the site, the bolted steel frame was assembled in less than forty work hours. The myriad sections of standard clamped-on casement windows were neatly slipped into place as integrally moduled parts of the surface skin. Interstitial areas of thin steel panels and concrete bands alternated with the larger, predominating stretches of glass and heightened the effect of industrial assemblage. The bands, furthermore, moved beyond the enclosed volume into the landscape as walls and screens. This proved to be an especially effective element in the play yard east of the living room. On the pool side of the house they terminated in stunningly articulated upturned edges. Open-web steel floor and ceiling joists harbored plumbing and wiring. Extended balconies and sleeping porches were suspended—not cantilevered—from the perimeter of the roof frame.[34]

Indeed, as "filled" and "covered" with light concrete, steel, and glass, the frame became the essence of the building. Rhetorically echoing its Chicago School origins, the frame was the house; the house *was* the frame. Structurally and aesthetically, it gave the house its meaning. Before Neutra decided to defer to programmatic themes and call it the "Demonstration Health House," he labeled it on an early plan a "steel, glass, and shot-concrete residence in Los Angeles." Particularly on the main, image-giving southwest elevation, Neutra assembled those materials into a memorable composition. The balanced asymmetry of its rectangular geometry echoed the patterns and proportions of the abstract canvases of the contemporary Dutch painters Mondrian and van Doesburg. Few modernist images attained such a cool and complex elegance.

The news of his disciple's adventurous undertaking elicited a letter from Frank Lloyd Wright: "The boys tell me you are building a building in steel for [a] residence—which is really good news. Ideas like that one are what this poor fool country needs to learn from Corbusier, Stevens, Oud, and Gropius. I am glad you're the one to 'teach' them."[35]

After several preliminary variants, Neutra planned the house on two-and-a-half levels. A cut in the hillside just beneath the street furnished the base for the main, middle level. Another cut, one level down, harbored the bottom half-floor of laundry, utility, recreation, and dressing rooms, opening to the pool. The main entrance to the house was at the top street level, which contained the family's sleeping porches and enclosed bedrooms. The entrance terrace off the Dundee cul-de-sac opened to a hallway leading west to the sleeping quarters and south down the stairway to the main, middle floor. Enclosed by a wall of ceiling-high casement windows looking out on the city, and gently and wittily illuminated by opaquely glazed Model T Ford headlights, the Lovell stairway became one of the grandest and most exhilarating spaces in the Modern Movement. An expanded, modernist version of a fireplace inglenook offered comfortable lounging near the fire beneath the stairs. A library area, east of the stairs, nestled cavelike back into the excavated hill. The living and dining areas, west of the fireplace, soared out over the hill, completing the south half of the main, middle floor. The northern half of the middle level included guest rooms and baths on the northeast side, kitchen and service areas in the middle, and a screened eating porch on the northwest corner, later enclosed as the main dining room. Planned in consultation with the Lovells' indispens-

able housekeeper-cook-factotum, Mrs. Westerman, the
kitchen had, for the time, extra-large cutting, washing, and
draining areas for the preparation of the family's vegetarian
meals. At the foot of the main stairs, a doorway opened to a
patio and play yard, leading to the garages and to Leah's
kindergarten.

The architect designed most of the furniture and super-
vised the landscaping. Successive layers of low concrete retaining walls followed the contours of the steeply sloping lot.
Subsequently overcome by the rampant foliage, the curving
walls furnished a pleasantly lyrical counterpoise to the sober
orthogonal lines of the house. Green shrubs and trees were
balanced with flowering plants in the blue/purple palette to
complement the white/gray/blue/black hues of the façade
and the interiors. Wisteria covered the "constructivist"
front pergola. Lovell's carefully placed exercise and gym-
nastic equipment took on the character of abstract garden
sculpture.[36]

Though Lovell would later recall it as being considerably
more, the total cost of the house and its furnishings, not
counting Neutra's fee or the initial cost of the land, was
$58,672.32. His fee of 10 percent for designing the house and
supervising its construction made the total, exclusive of land
cost, come close to $65,000.

As the house neared completion, Lovell could hardly contain his enthusiasm and devoted one of his "Care of the
Body" columns to its description and celebration. "For
years," he began, "I have periodically written articles telling
you how to build your house so that you can derive from it
the maximum degree of health and beauty. . . . Always at
the end of each article was the thought, 'If I ever build a
house myself—' " He was pleased to announce that "at last
the day has arrived. We have built such a home—a home
premised on the fundamental health principles and construction ideas which I have presented in my writings. . . ."[37]

He especially relished the impact the house would have on his three young sons: "It is really a social school," he wrote, "in which they will learn their life habits." He hoped that Neutra's example would "introduce a modern type of architecture and establish it firmly in California, where new and individualistic architecture is necessary." Because he believed that such architecture was replicable on a more modest scale than that of his own house and because so many of its features could be "incorporated into the humblest cottage," he invited his readers to visit the house and see for themselves. He and Neutra would be present on four successive Sunday afternoons to conduct personal tours and explain the building's multiple meanings. Officials of the Auto Club would be on hand to conduct traffic up and down the steep, narrow road.[38]

The response to his invitation was overwhelming as thousands of amazed Angelenos poured through the house. For most of them, in 1929, it was simply too much to begin to comprehend. "Moon architecture," Neutra heard someone mutter in a mixture of shock, admiration, and skeptical apprehension. To counter such reservations, Lovell wrote a testimonial to Neutra and posted it so prominently that all visitors saw it. The public tours helped to make the Lovell House a major local news item. With obvious encouragement from architect and client, the Los Angeles papers promoted it intensely, presaging the acclaim it would soon begin to draw from the national and international trade and public press. It prepared the way for Neutra's successes of the thirties, forties, and fifties.

A series of commissions connected with the movie industry illustrated his mature achievement. It was fitting that this industry, which not only survived the Depression but thrived on Americans' needs for escape and elevation, should provide major props for Neutra's fortunes of the thirties. The earliest of these was an office building for Universal-

International Pictures at the prestigious corner of Hollywood
and Vine (1933). High atop the structure on either side of
the sleek corner clock tower were integrally attached repeti-
tive billboards advertising Universal's current releases. The
rear service yard was an elegant essay in minimalist geometry, achieved by the repetition of L-shaped door and window
bands in a mirror-image effect as those spare, simple elements moved outward from the corner. By making the vents
above the second-floor windows exactly the width of the first-
floor doors below, Neutra used a functional element to effect
a striking decorative pattern. In addition to the upstairs offices for the Laemmle dynasty, Neutra designed a multi-use
building with a handsome café and chic income-producing
stores on the busy street floor. These shops, as well as the
Coco Tree Restaurant, were trimmed and highlighted with
reflecting metal and mirrored surfaces.

The first large house that Neutra designed after the Lovell
House of 1929 was for the film star Anna Sten and her husband, the film producer Eugene Frenke, overlooking the
ocean in Santa Monica Canyon. Sten had recently arrived
from Russia via Germany, imported by Samuel Goldwyn as
the hoped-for rival to Greta Garbo and Marlene Dietrich.
Sten never became the "Russian Garbo" as prophesied, but
she and her husband did build a great house. It was chiefly
Frenke who wanted a modern building and who decided that
Neutra was the best man on the scene. The elegant off-white
stucco house with its glistening silver-gray trim was efficiently sited at the rear of the lot. A wall tied subtly to the
entrance pergola and street-side garage assured privacy without obstructing views of the ocean and mountains. The garage unit contained showers and dressing rooms for the pool
which lay between them and the house. The house was essentially a large rectangular block, textured by attached
porches and constructivist pergolas and by a large curving
bay off the front of the living room. The Sten house won

first prize in the 1934 *House Beautiful* competition—the first modern house ever to win that award. It was one of Neutra's finest achievements.

An even greater triumph, however, was Neutra's country villa in the San Fernando Valley for the German-American director Josef von Sternberg. Schindler had tried to engage von Sternberg in 1929, but in the mid-1930s, when the director decided to build a house, he turned to Neutra. They sat up one whole night, Neutra's wife, Dione, recalled, talking of Germany, California, and modern art—particularly their own worlds of modern film and architecture. "I selected a distant meadow," von Sternberg recounted later, "in the midst of an empty landscape, barren and forlorn, to make a retreat for myself, my books, and my collection of modern art. . . . I chose a comparatively unknown . . . architect to carry out my ideas of what a house should be." Designed in 1934 and completed in 1935, the house itself was a story and a half with a double-height living room surrounded by a picture-gallery balcony. Von Sternberg's exotically mirrored bath and bedroom looking out on a rooftop pool were the only other rooms on the small second floor. On the downstairs level east of the living room were a studio, kitchen, servants' rooms, and garages. The latter were divided between the garage for regular cars and the slightly larger space that would house the Rolls-Royce. The basic shell for these exotic internal functions was a series of straightforward juxtaposed rectangles, clad in aluminum.[39]

To match and complement the client's personal and programmatic eccentricities, and to liven the otherwise simple industrial façade, Neutra designed in the best Hollywood manner a series of remarkable special effects, which in layered vibrations reached out into the landscape. The first and most significant was the high, curving aluminum wall, which enclosed the front patio leading from the living room and which gave the house its "streamlined" personality. An ad-

Richard Neutra, von Sternberg House, 1935.

vanced sprinkler system around the curving wall produced the varied effects of a gentle mist or a battering rainstorm. Surrounding the wall and in broken stretches, the entire house was a shallow "moat" or reflecting pool for fish and water lilies. An actual ship's searchlight over the porte-cochere imparted, with the help of the moat and front wall, a wittily nautical ambience to the scene.

The house was widely published in the international press and evoked virtually unanimous praise. It prompted Wright's and Schindler's old client Aline Barnsdall to talk to Neutra about his building for her. They had apparently been discussing the idea for some time. "I fear you are wondering," she wrote on February 15, 1939, "why you haven't heard from me regarding the house. *All* the reasons are too complicated to write but the essential one is this: I want to build just one more house, as a home, and I want time to make it contain all that I need and no more and I want to be certain that it is a place I shall want to live the rest of my life. One reason I left Olive Hill was because I always felt weary and under-vitalized there. . . . I want you to see my land at Palos Verdes. I want a house like von Sternberg's. In talking with Wright about it a few weeks ago, I told him that while his houses are like a St. Bernard, or perhaps the more recent ones like an eagle, von Sternberg's is like a greyhound. It taught me a lot that few minutes there, it was a new world of elimination and a lot of other things. I don't mean I want to copy it; just get the feeling of it, the steel, aluminum and elimination, even to the vegetation. So you will hear from me again when I am ready." With the beginning of the European war that year and Barnsdall's own declining health and energy, Neutra never got to design her sleek "greyhound" house.[40]

The war also touched the von Sternberg house itself as its shiplike ambience appealed to the Air Corps, which exploited it mercilessly as a mock bombing target. The zoom-

ing planes on the one hand and the rural isolation on the
other prompted von Sternberg to sell his San Fernando castle. It passed through several hands before Ayn Rand acquired it. Though Sullivan and Wright were the apparent
prototypes for *The Fountainhead,* her throbbing novel
of architectural heroics, she admired Neutra greatly and
was pleased to own the house. "I don't know where Miss
Rand got her political ideas," Neutra enjoyed observing in
cocktail-party banter, "but it's obvious she used me as a
model for Howard Roark's sex appeal." In 1971, a developer
bought the property for a condominium tract and quickly
demolished the modernist castle—moat, Rolls garage,
imaginary rain, and all.

Many of the features of the Sten and von Sternberg
houses were conveyed to Neutra's other Hollywood houses
of the thirties, for the director Albert Lewin on the Santa
Monica beach and the film music composer Edward Kauf-
man in Westwood. A smaller house in North Hollywood for
the film editor Leon Barsha demonstrated the same ideas on
a more modest level—an important example of Neutra's insistence that the same design priciples be applicable to modest as to expensive commissions.

Since its earliest tenants included major movie personalities, Neutra's Strathmore Apartments also had Hollywood
connections. Long impressed with the elegantly stepped megastructures of the Southwest Indian pueblos and of the
more recent bungalow apartment courts of Southern California, Neutra designed Strathmore as a modernist version
of both vernaculars. The first tenants at Strathmore were
Dione's sister, Regula Thorston, and her parents, Alfred and
Lilly Niedermann, who had emigrated from Switzerland to
retire in Los Angeles. Regula remembered, however, that
for some months they were the only inhabitants as other
prospective early tenants found the buildings too "cold,"
"austere," and "industrial" for their tastes. "Hospital archi-

tecture," she remembered hearing them utter. But slowly the apartments attracted a number of interesting people including the film stars Dolores Del Rio, Orson Welles, Luise Rainer, and her husband, Clifford Odets. Lilly Latte, companion of Fritz Lang, kept a Strathmore apartment as her private retreat from the social whirl of Hollywood and her demanding life with Lang. The designers Charles and Ray Eames produced the first of their famous chairs at Strathmore. Later John Entenza, editor of *Arts and Architecture*, was a Strathmore dweller, as was the photographer Eliot Elisofon. Several of the celebrities wrote appreciative testimonials, Rainer and Eames insisting that living there had changed their lives. Strathmore indeed predicted Neutra's later successes with multiple-family dwellings in his Landfair, Kelton, and Elkay Apartments in Westwood and in such public housing projects as Channel Heights near the Los Angeles harbor in San Pedro, designed in 1942 to house wartime shipyard workers.

Aline Barnsdall's images of Wright's handsome but heavy "St. Bernard" buildings versus Neutra's leaner, more streamlined "greyhound" suggested a great deal about their different approaches to the California experience. But the canine metaphor did not fully get at the even more fundamental difference in their attitudes toward light. Like Gill and the Greenes and indeed many purveyors of the California Craftsman tradition, Wright saw the elements, including the sunlight, as not always benevolent in their fullest exposure. Indeed, in this land of "eternal sunshine," one might long for more shade and shadow and even occasionally for subdued romantic darkness. Hence the protective bulk of Wright's and Gill's creations and the shaded darkness of Greene and Greene's houses. But literally and metaphorically, Neutra and his postwar Germanic generation had had enough darkness and cold poetic gloom. Consequently, they compensated and sometimes overcompensated by opening their buildings to the light, aggressively encouraging the indoor-outdoor life.

If Wright and the earlier craftsmen built monuments evoking California romance, including the romantic landscape and climate, Neutra's school used those elements for a new kind of expression. As "romantic engineers" reverently and poetically evoking the machine, they certainly were not oblivious to romance. Indeed, they consciously exploited the machine to achieve a minimalism of structure and form that framed and emphasized and highlighted nature, almost, at times, to the downplaying of architecture—at least in its more traditionally formal elements. Nowhere in the history of modern architecture was the modernists' ideal of the "machine in the garden" more convincingly realized than in Southern California.

Throughout the forties and the postwar fifties, and even to a certain extent into the sixties, Neutra and his generation made vital contributions to the California landscape and to the history of modern architecture. The Nesbitt House, Brentwood (1942), reflected client tastes and wartime scarcities in its warmer, more woodsy materials. The postwar Kaufmann House, Palm Springs (1946), looked back to Neutra's sterner mode of the thirties, while the less formal Tremaine House (1948) predicted his more relaxed style of the fifties as developed in hundreds of buildings. This would be a handsome, lyrical, less tense, and less dramatic architecture, without that edge of exhilarating angst that had made the thirties work seem so much more avant-garde. And this aesthetic shift was accompanied not surprisingly by a subtle change of both cause and effect in the nature and character of clients. Those of the early period had seemed more intellectually intense, more socially sophisticated, more generally avant-garde—as opposed to the typical clients of modern architecture in the fifties who, by comparison, would come to seem more and more middle class. Neutra's houses of the fifties had become "shelter magazine" material, not radical anymore—the clients or the buildings. The *best* label now seemed to be "Good Old Modern." In fact, the UCLA linguist Edward Tuttle once remarked that these late Neutra houses seem so aggressively informal that if one lived in them, one would feel constrained to sleep in a necktie.

If Neutra and Schindler were the leading pioneers of California modernism, they were joined by a highly significant array of followers and contemporaries. Raphael Soriano's stern and austere architecture showed the greatest literal allegiance to Neutra. Gregory Ain, who had worked in Neutra's office in the thirties, reflected his and Schindler's influence in a large and significant body of work. Harwell Harris, an early apprentice of both Neutra and Schindler, revealed his debt to Neutra in a 1937 house for John Entenza, editor of *Arts and Architecture*, but eschewed the machine image in his later work as he drew more on the examples of Greene and Greene and the architects of the San Francisco Bay School. These references and Neutra's later houses of the fifties would also be important to such architects as Quincy Jones and Raymond Kappe. And the old man himself, Frank Lloyd Wright, was influenced by the Los Angeles School, particularly in such buildings as his redwood Sturges House (1939) in Brentwood. Charles Eames obviously learned from the California machine modernists, with their veneration of off-the-shelf *Sweet's* catalogue building parts. He had lived in Neutra's Strathmore, but in his own house in Santa Monica Canyon (1949) he also evoked Mies and Mondrian as well. Later variants of his high-tech modernist commitment would appear in the work of such architects as Craig Ellwood, Helmut Schulitz, and Peter de Bretteville. A different kind of modernist expression, a more voluptuous concrete plasticism, would ripen in the work of John Lautner, a former student at Wright's Taliesin. In the late 1970s, after a decade of "Post-Modern" ascendancy, another strong variant of Los Angeles modernism would appear in the work of Frank Gehry and his followers in the movement known variously as "Deconstructivist" or "Mineshaft Modern."

Throughout the twentieth century, there has been an often expressed regret that the Nobel prizes included no category for architecture. To fill this gap, the Pritzkers of Chicago, a family long interested in architecture, established in 1979 the Pritzker Architecture Prize. Throughout the 1980s, the announcement of the annual Pritzker laureate became a much anticipated event in the world of architecture, and the $100,000 stipend became almost secondary to the honor and prestige of the designation. The rotating jury included luminaries from the world of art and architecture. The first winner in 1979 was Philip Johnson, while the next ten laureates included Luis Barragan of Mexico; Kenzo Tange of Japan; Hans Hollein of Austria, Aldo Rossi of Italy; Oscar Niemeyer of Brazil; and the Americans Richard Meier, Kevin Roche, and I. M. Pei. Most of these had established their reputation as designers of mainstream modernism. The choice in 1989 of Frank Gehry of Los Angeles was, to that point, the Pritzker Committee's most avant-garde selection.

"In an artistic climate that too often looks backward rather than toward the future," the jury citation read, "where retrospectives are more prevalent than risk taking, it is important to honor the architecture of Frank O. Gehry. Refreshingly original and totally American, proceeding as it does from his populist Southern California perspective, Gehry's work," the jury believed, "is a highly refined, sophisticated and adventurous aesthetic that emphasizes the art of architecture. His sometimes controversial, but always arresting body of work, has been variously described as iconoclastic, rambunctious and impermanent, but the jury, in making this award, commends this restless spirit that has made his buildings a unique expression of contemporary society and its ambivalent values. . . . His designs," the citation concluded, "if compared to American music, could best be likened to jazz, replete with improvisation and a lively unpredictable spirit. . . . His buildings are juxtaposed collages of spaces and materials that make users appreciative of both the theatre and the backstage, simultaneously revealed."[41]

Of the world's leading architects, the name most conspicuously missing from the Pritzker list at that time was Robert Venturi, of Philadelphia, whose achievements in practice, but especially in theory, had challenged modernist orthodoxy in a way that affected modernists, postmodernists, and neomodernists all. Venturi helped make possible the later breakthroughs of such architects as Gehry, who remarked after winning the Pritzker that in earlier *fantasizing* about winning it, he had vowed he would bravely refuse the prize if Robert Venturi had by that time not received it. Being human, Gehry was ultimately not able to make such a sacrifice, but he recognized that Venturi's achievement was tantamount to his own. His conscience, moreover, was considerably relieved when Venturi won the prize in 1991.[42]

"I am for messy vitality over obvious unity," Venturi had proclaimed in 1966 in his famous manifesto, *Complexity and Contradiction in Architecture.* He then juxtaposed a series of adjectives, the first in each case a statement of his own position; the second that of the Modern Movement he was attacking: "I like elements that are hybrid rather than 'pure,' compromising rather than 'clean,' distorted rather than 'straightforward,' ambiguous rather than 'articulated,' perverse as well as impersonal, conventional rather than 'designed,' accommodating rather than excluding, redundant rather than simple, vestigial as well as innovating, inconsistent and equivocal rather than direct and clear. I am for

messy vitality over obvious unity."[43] The left-hand side of
each of those dualities would ultimately define Gehry's architecture as well.

At about the same time, Venturi's contemporary Charles
Moore was decrying what he believed to be the cold, bland
sterility of modern architecture, which had usually attempted a "forgetting of things past." Moore now called for
"architecture with a memory," for design that remembered
the best of the past and was not afraid to mix it with ideas
from various eras, including the present, the 1960s, and
achieve in this new architectural dialectic an architecture of
and for the 1960s. This shocking new synthesis was given
several names from "radical eclecticism" to simply "Post-
Modern."[44]

Still, it was not, in the beginning, an attack on modernism
as such. "Since we have criticized modern architecture,"
wrote Venturi and his wife and partner, Denise Scott-
Brown, "it is proper here to state our intense admiration of
its early period when its founders, sensitive to their own
times, proclaimed the right revolution. Our argument lies
mainly with the irrelevant and distorted prolongation of that
old revolution today."[45]

In the 1960s and early 1970s, such buildings as Venturi's
house for his mother in Chestnut Hill, Pennsylvania, and
Moore's Sea Ranch Condominium, north of San Francisco
(1965), illustrated beautifully the movement's populist commitments to a celebration of the American vernacular and
to a tense, ironic merging of forms, ideas and styles from the
recent and distant past, modern and premodern. At its best,
Post-Modernism was an edgy fusion of "something modern
and something else."[46] It lost its way and became both sad
and silly when it jettisoned its "modernist" components and
became exclusively "something else." When it began to
mime the past too literally, it produced a deluge of historicist
kitsch. In cloning the grand works of earlier times, it ex-

ploited a permissive nostalgia for an earlier, presumably more luxurious, era. It was, in short, the perfect architecture for the age of Reagan.

Frank Gehry's triumph was: first, in avoiding the trap of moribund historicism or of Disneyesque "hokeytecture"; second, in remembering the strengths of modernism, especially its neglected Expressionist and Constructivist traditions; third, in not forgetting the power of the folk and industrial vernacular; fourth, in learning from the art of the leading contemporary painters and sculptors, many of whom were his personal friends; and, fifth, in never losing sight of the early breakthroughs of Post-Modernist theory and practice that had challenged and opened modernism to new possibilities.

Frank Gehry was born in Toronto in 1929 and grew up and finished high school in Canada before his family moved to Los Angeles in 1947, largely because his father's declining health demanded a warmer climate. His parents were of Russian and Polish-Jewish ancestry and his mother's parents, Sam and Leah Caplan were especially crucial in his early development. Both Caplans were politically leftist, coming from families that had devoted considerable time to union organizing. But Sam, as president of his synagogue, was foremost a Talmudic scholar and he and Frank took long walks together discussing Judaism and its implications for their lives. Frank attended Hebrew school and spoke with his grandparents in Yiddish.[47]

Equal in importance to his grandfather's spiritual and political guidance was the fact that he also owned a hardware store, where between the ages of ten and seventeen, the grandson had a part-time job. Stocking the store's shelves with the usual hardware inventory of nails, screws, bolts, hammers, saws, pliers, pipe, chains, fencing, roofing, paint, and glass, young Frank acquired his lifelong fascination with the "nature of materials," an interest that would strongly affect his work. The store also had an appliance repair department with a changing display of radios in surgery and a gasoline pump out on the sidewalk where Frank dispensed gas to Toronto motorists.

Grandmother Caplan had not only a strong visual sense but a knack for fun and play as well. On the floor of the store's "fixit department," she and her young grandson would gather scraps and shavings from the lathe and take them home to the living room floor as the raw material for futuristic cities and giant connecting causeways. Later in Los Angeles in his depressed early twenties, while driving a truck, attending night school, and thinking about what he wanted to be, Frank recalled scanning the past for clues. The hardware store and the cities of shavings on the floor were among his most vivid recurring memories and helped to confirm his direction toward architecture. In Canada, moreover, Frank's father had been in the pinball and slot-machine business—an influence some critics would find embedded in Gehry's work. But it was his mother who especially encouraged his and his sister Doreen's artistic and intellectual interests.

In the late 1940s, after his family moved to California, Gehry became a part-time student at Los Angeles City College and worked as a truck driver to support himself; and some have argued that there remained in his work something of the truck-stop aesthetic as well. But he had always been drawn to the visual arts, and a ceramics teacher, Glen Lukens, convinced him that he should become an architect. Lukens was a friend of architect Raphael Soriano, a disciple of Neutra's, who further encouraged Gehry, and, in 1950, Gehry entered the school of architecture at the University of Southern California, graduating in 1954. As an architecture student, he began to explore Los Angeles as he never had before, and to admire the work of Irving Gill, Frank Lloyd Wright, Richard Neutra, and Rudolph Schindler, particularly Schindler for his ad hoc "constructivism" and for his interest in "cheap" building materials.

In 1955, Gehry was drafted and at Forts Benning and Hood, he absorbed the "Army Barracks aesthetic." He then studied urban planning for a year at Harvard, but found planning theory, then and later, too abstract for his tastes. He did, however, sit in on the courses of John Kenneth Galbraith and Arthur Schlesinger, Jr., and he got to know the venerable Joseph Hudnut, who introduced him to the history of architecture. After Harvard, Gehry returned to Los Angeles where he worked for several years in the large offices of Victor Gruen and Luckman and Pereira. From 1960 to 1962, as a bilingual Canadian, still restless and unsettled, Gehry and his wife Anita and their two young daughters lived in Paris, where he worked in several offices and savored as a tourist the architecture of Europe. In 1962, he returned to Los Angeles and started his own office, with important support from a former USC classmate, Gregory Walsh.

The best example of Gehry's early work was a studio for the graphic designer Louis Danziger (1964), in which the architect expressed his growing admiration for the work of Louis Kahn. In contrast to the windowless Melrose Avenue façade, the north and east sides opened to the light with large, high, factorylike windows. A cluster of bold, rectangular cubes read as virtually separate structures and, as such, predicted future directions of Gehry's work in the 1970s. In the 1980s, moreover, he would return to the Danziger motif of plain, stuccoed, juxtaposed cubes in the larger-scaled Frances Goldwyn Library in Hollywood (1986).

By the early 1970s, Gehry's architecture was obviously changing, and this was due to a number of things in his personal and professional life: first, the ending of his first marriage and his second marriage to a Panamanian-American, Berta Aguilera, who became a decisive figure in his

office, as in his life; second, the arrival in Los Angeles of
Charles Moore, which somehow, Gehry felt, gave a lift to
the whole L.A. scene, combined, of course, with the challenge Moore and Venturi and others were offering the Modern Movement in their writings and buildings; and third, the
growing impact upon Gehry's thinking of his close friendships in Los Angeles and elsewhere with the leading painters
and sculptors of the day, and his growing willingness to
transfer to architecture many of their commitments and
their ways of making art.

This era of transition in the early 1970s was best characterized by his studio-residence for the painter Ron Davis, a
trapezoidal structure of corrugated metal on the rolling hills
above the Malibu coast (1972), reflecting the aesthetic and
the expressed wishes of the artist/owner for a large shell over
spaces divided by movable partitions that could be easily
changed and rearranged. Here Gehry used the "painterly"
devices of distorted perspective and cubistic layering of space
to achieve the desired effects.

Two unbuilt designs of the late 1970s also allowed him to
experiment with new materials and building processes. In
the Gunther project, a vacation house that called for high
security when the owner was not there, Gehry solved aesthetic as well as programmatic functions with sheets of heavy
chain-link fencing, constituting forms inside forms that cast
dramatic shadow patterns against the simple box of the
house. Though the owner balked at Gehry's solution, chain
link would henceforward become one of his trademarks.

The Familian house was to be for an art collector whose
sensibilities were clearly not ready for the Gehry aesthetic of
"buildings under construction." The house was an attempt,
Gehry recalled, "to make a simple container more simple by
cutting into it with raw framing, the kind of balloon framing
that housing is made of in Los Angeles. I was interested in
the immediacy of the raw framing before it was covered up.
It had a quality that paintings have, like the brush stroke

that's just been placed. . . . Most frame buildings look great under construction, but when they're covered, they look like hell . . ."[48]

In these designs of the late 1970s, Gehry learned to sublimate the anger, pain, and fear of existing in a hostile world to architectural statements about those tensions. Frequently via irony and a somewhat dark humor, there crept into his work elements of light and hope. In that favored aesthetic of "buildings under construction," his work would suggest "unfinished business" or the poignant incompleteness of all human existence. It would also suggest *arrested* decadence in a world continually dying and being born. His buildings of the late seventies with elements "tossed" and "frozen" just before the "explosion" could be read as a metaphor of the end of the world or could be seen conversely as "disaster averted," with things pulled back to safety "just in time."

That the Gunther and Familian houses were never built was a great loss to architecture. Yet much of their spirit made their way into an important built structure in 1979— Gehry's own fantastic house, a renovation and enlargement of an old 1920s Santa Monica Craftsman-style cottage of salmon pink shingles and densely mullioned windows. Gehry recalled that his wife Berta "found this beautiful . . . anonymous little house, and I decided to remodel it, and . . . since it was my building . . . explore ideas I'd had about the materials I used here: corrugated metal and plywood, chain link. . . . And I was interested in making the old house appear intact inside the new house, so that from the outside you would be aware always that the old house was still there, and some guy had just wrapped it in new materials, and you could see, as you looked through the windows—during the day or at night—you would see this old house sitting in there. And my intention was that the combination of both would make the old house richer and the new house would be richer by association with the old. . . ."[49]

Frank Gehry, Gehry House, 1979.

Here, more than ever before, Gehry revealed in a built structure another side of his nature, or as the favored pun of the day put it, the old, straight Frank Gehry of the Danziger Studio period met the new, kinky Cali-Gehry of acute angles and distorted shapes. The work contained unexpected collisions of materials from the old and new house: corrugated aluminum, unfinished plywood, and chain link, used both as ornament and as protective enclosure on the upper roof decks which his two small sons used as a play area.

To mesh with the fragmented and newly constructed rim-like outer shell, the interior of the old two-story gambrel-roofed house was selectively gutted, peeled back, and literally and metaphorically "deconstructed" to the basic elements from which it was formed—studs, joists, beams, and rafters—combining the effects of an architectural strip-tease and a didactic museum of the carpenter's trade. Thus the old interior, as well as the new exterior, was made to look raw and unfinished and in the process of being built. The new outer kitchen and dining room addition was a half level lower than the old inner spaces of living rooms and bedrooms and was paved with asphalt like a street or driveway so that it could be washed down with a hose. These effects were softened and enriched by Gehry's use throughout the house of his handsome, durable, and surprisingly comfortable corrugated cardboard furniture of the late sixties and early seventies, complemented by masterworks of contemporary art from Ed Moses to Ellsworth Kelly to Chuck Arnoldi to Larry Bell.

UCLA students of the early 1980s writing papers on "punk culture" in history or sociology courses, with varying degrees of innocence in the history of architecture, liked to include Gehry's house as an example of "punk." And it was indeed a kind of punk updating of good, old-fashioned German Expressionism and Russian Constructivism: Caligari with Purple Hair.

It was therefore appropriate that in the 1980s Gehry was invited to design the installations at the Los Angeles County Museum of Art for several important exhibitions of German Expressionist and Russian Constructivist art. He also used the same forms and materials in an enlargement/renovation of the Gemini G.E.L. galleries on Melrose Avenue, not far from the Danziger Studio of nearly two decades earlier. The same aesthetic pervaded a small group of three connected studio houses of the early 1980s in a very poor section of the Venice district of Los Angeles, where a large number of artists have always lived and worked. Located literally next to a junkyard and rising from a sea of modest L.A. bungalows, the buildings expressed and evoked the neighborhood without proclaiming too loudly their own superior artfulness. One was sheathed in green asphalt shingles, another in natural plywood, and another in gray stucco. Built well, though looking like poorly built ramshackle throw-ups, the Indiana Street houses combined the roughness and the tenderness of the soft-edged side of Gehry's Expressionist village aesthetic. In the same year, a much more upscale version of the same idea appeared as a swanky Beverly Hills penthouse for the designer Miriam Wosk. Built atop an already existing structure, the Wosk house, with its self-consciously glitzy decor, became another version of the Gehry village.

In 1981, the architect moved successfully to the larger, institutional scale with a saltwater aquarium for the Los Angeles Department of Parks and Recreation near the harbor in San Pedro. In this tightly connected cluster of structures, Gehry's favorite materials of corrugated metal, rough wood, and chain-link mesh took on the appropriately nautical connotations of ships, docks, traps, and fish nets. The separate though connected buildings housing exhibition spaces, laboratories, offices, auditorium, and museum store resembled a fishing village with a "street" dividing its various functions. Inside, Gehry's love of pipes and ducts found ultimate expression in the necessarily complex needs for different kinds of aquarium water with varying degrees of temperature. In retrospect, it seemed an almost inevitable matching of architect, site, and building program.

In the mid-1980s, Gehry broke from the "heavy metal" aesthetic and designed a group of connected spaces for the Loyola Law School near downtown Los Angeles, a few blocks from Gehry's family's first home. The yellow east wall of the main three-story building for faculty offices and student activities, with its deeply recessed windows, its explosive central stairway, and its central gabled cottagelike "greenhouse," recalled a panoply of Italian references from classical Rome to the seventeenth-century Baroque to the twentieth-century Rationalists. The benign California climate made it feasible to place the somewhat "constructivist" stairways outside. The smaller chapel and classroom structures clustered east of the main building, featured freestanding columns supporting nothing—a surrealist homage to the ruins of classical antiquity. The otherwise obliging clients vetoed the architect's proposal that some of the columns should be broken or recumbent as in Rome. Gehry designed Loyola the way he did because of the need to do something "that looked like it had something to do with the legal profession. . . . I had just visited Rome as I was working on the design, and I got interested in the Roman Forum, with all the columns, broken, lying around, and I came back and I had that kind of idea for this . . ."[50] But later he admitted, "I get my inspiration from the streets. I'm more of a street fighter than a Roman scholar." At about the same time, Gehry transferred the idea of the exploding center of the main Loyola building to the nearby, even larger, Aerospace Museum in Exposition Park. There, he maintained the effect of a connected cluster of structures within a more consolidated grouping.

Gehry's best Los Angeles work of the late 1980s was his Edgemar Complex on Main Street in the Ocean Park district of Santa Monica, commissioned by the adventurous developer, Abby Sher. Housing an art museum, a theater, a restaurant, and several stores, the cluster epitomized Gehry's continuing penchant for the urban village. As adornment, moreover, for the individual buildings of varying colors and textures, Gehry returned to his favored materials of galvanized metal and chain link, the latter now assuming more than ever before a glistening jewellike texture. The open areas off the street between the obliquely sited structures became, especially when filled with people, one of Gehry's liveliest public spaces.

By the late 1970s and into the 1980s, the impact of Gehry's work was making itself felt on a younger generation of Los Angeles architects, some of whom worked in his office be-

Frank Gehry, Edgemar Complex, 1988.

fore moving on to their own careers and who proudly confessed their debts to him. Other young designers simply developed in his aura, their unconscious debts to him perhaps
stronger than their conscious ones. "How could one be a
young architect in Los Angeles in the seventies and
eighties," one of them, Julie Eizenberg, admitted, "without
being touched by Gehry?" The vibrations, she acknowledged, were simply "in the air."[51]

In those same years, Gehry's reputation and influence also
moved beyond Los Angeles as he acquired commissions in
Boston, Dallas, New Haven, Germany, France, and Japan.
Yet while the work outside California took on appropriately
regional attributes, Gehry's image and reputation retained a
"California" character.

"You sort of posture yourself in a way that can read as

comical." Gehry has observed. "People have called my work inordinately playful, or not serious. 'You're the California architect who does all that goofy stuff,' and I think I play somewhere in that region. Time will tell whether it was or not." Yet "time" has already celebrated the seriousness and profundity of Gehry's architecture. Indeed, his work, more than that of any other twentieth-century Los Angeles designer, has teetered, precariously and beguilingly, on the edge between the comic and tragic. As such it reflects Los Angeles itself, which in certain lights and poles *is* comic, tawdry, glossy, goofy. Yet Los Angeles is also poignantly sad as it shapes and reflects the unrealized dreams, the pot of gold that was *not* found at the end of Judy Garland's rainbow. Still, throughout all of this, the city has continued to foster the spirit of experimentation, of risk taking, and of hope. Perhaps better than any other architect's, Gehry's buildings have captured and reflected those elusive L.A. qualities. His power has derived from his ability and courage to achieve an original synthesis from two distinct impulses: the strength, toughness, texture, and power of modernism and of the machine vernacular that inspired it, and the wit, whimsy, and color of Post-Modernism—before that movement began to clone the past too literally and to lose its sense of edge and ironic contemporaneity.

Critics of the 1970s and 1980s insisted on labeling Gehry a "rule breaker." Yet, if he was breaking rules, they were rules of a different order from his own. He obeyed his own rules, the rules he had forged over a lifetime of experience: "Why should we honor those who die upon the field of battle?" William Butler Yeats had asked. "A man may show as reckless a courage in entering into the abyss of himself."

A curious quartet of modernists: Gill, Wright, Neutra, Gehry. They had come to Los Angeles seeking some of the same things: health, the sun, better fortunes, a new life. And they also found there the one thing they knew they needed: the oft-noted quality of virtually boundless freedom. Freedom to make mistakes and to lose one's way occasionally, and the corresponding freedom to find one's way and to find one's self. Despite occasional self-doubts and doubts about Los Angeles, they wrestled creatively with the dualities of time and place, of modernism and regionalism. Yet ultimately, they all knew *where* they were and *who* they were. And they should all have understood the lines of the poet Peter Viereck: "Art, being bartender is never drunk; And magic that believes itself must die./Being absurd as well as beautiful,/Magic—like art—is hoax redeemed by awe."[52]

That describes them and the comic/tragic City of the Angels.

Notes

1. Specific references will be cited throughout the notes, but I must acknowledge here my broader debts to Carey McWilliams, Reyner Banham, Esther McCoy, Dione Neutra, Pauline Schindler, Regula Fybel, David Gebhard, Robert Winter, Randall Mackinson, Charles Moore, William Jordy, Robert Sweeney, Alan Onoye, Kurt Forster, Gene Waddell, Thomas Jimmerson, Dorothy Hines, Richard Weinstein, Ann Bergren, Sylvia Lavin, Birgitta Wohl, and Richard Longstreth, who have stimulated and informed my interest in Los Angeles and architecture through informal and enjoyable conversations over the years. Portions of this essay were first given as a lecture on the occasion of the Los Angeles Bicentennial at UCLA's William Andrews Clark Library, April 25, 1981. Joining me on that occasion to deliver a companion lecture was Robert Judson Clark. Our lectures were published in *Los Angeles Transfer: Architecture in Southern California, 1880–1980* (Clark Library, UCLA, 1983).
2. Leslie Heumann, "The Architecture of Irving Gill: Two Case His-

tories" (Research paper written while Heumann was a student in my UCLA graduate seminar in "The History of Los Angeles," ca. 1980), p. 1.

3. José Ortega y Gasset, *The Dehumanization of Art, and Other Essays on Art, Culture, and Literature* (Princeton: Princeton University Press, 1968), pp. 12–13.

4. Robert M. Adams, "What Was Modernism?" (Faculty Research Lecture delivered at the University of California, Los Angeles, 1977).

5. Ibid.

6. Eloise Roorbach, "A California House of Distinguished Simplicity," *House Beautiful*, 49 (February 1921): 94; Thomas Jimmerson, "Regionalism, Primitivism, Modernism: The Reductive Impulse in the Work of Irving Gill" (Research paper, written while Jimmerson was a student in my UCLA graduate seminar in "American Cultural History," 1991), p. 1.

7. Lewis Mumford, *The Brown Decades: A Study of the Arts of American Civilization, 1865–1895* (1935; reprint ed., New York: Dover, 1955), pp. 175–76; Henry-Russell Hitchcock, "Frank Lloyd Wright and His California Contemporaries," *Architecture: Nineteenth and Twentieth Centuries* (Baltimore: Penguin Books, 1963), pp. 334–35.

8. Esther McCoy, "Irving Gill," *Five California Architects* (New York: Reinhold, 1960), pp. 58–101.

9. Irving Gill, "The Home of the Future: The New Architecture of the West: Small Homes for a Great Country," *The Craftsman* 30 (May 1, 1916): 141.

10. Ibid., p 151.

11. McCoy, "Irving Gill," *passim*; Jimmerson, "Regionalism, Primitivism, Modernism," *passim*; Gill, "The Home of the Future," p. 147.

12. Gill, "The Home of the Future," pp. 141–42.

13. William Jordy, "Craftsmanship as Reductive Simplification: Irving Gill's Dodge House," *American Buildings and Their Architects: Progressive and Academic Ideals at the Turn of the Twentieth Century* (Garden City. N.Y.: Doubleday, 1972), p. 261.

14. McCoy, "Irving Gill," pp. 85–87, 100; Bertha H. Smith, "Creating an American Style of Architecture," *House and Garden*, July 1914,

pp. 17–20, 46; Kevin Starr, *Material Dreams: Southern California Through the 1920s* (New York: Oxford, 1990), pp. 219–21.

15. Thomas S. Hines, "Saving a Masterpiece: Irving Gill's Horatio West Court in Santa Monica," *LA Architect*, July 1976, pp. 2–3.

16. Jordy, "Craftsmanship as Reductive Simplification," p. 274.

17. Though specific and conscious debts have become somewhat blurred over the years, my thinking on Frank Lloyd Wright has been influenced by numerous people, including Henry-Russell Hitchcock, *In the Nature of Materials, 1887–1941: The Buildings of Frank Lloyd Wright* (New York: Da Capo, 1973); Grant Carpenter Manson, *Frank Lloyd Wright to 1910: The First Golden Age* (New York: Van Nostrand Reinhold, 1958); Vincent Scully, Jr., *Frank Lloyd Wright* (New York: Braziller, 1960); Norris Kelly Smith, *Frank Lloyd Wright: A Study in Architectural Content* (Englewood Cliffs, N.J.: Prentice-Hall, 1966); Robert C. Twombly, *Frank Lloyd Wright: An Interpretive Biography* (New York: Harper & Row, 1973); and H. Allen Brooks, *The Prairie School: Frank Lloyd Wright and His Midwest Contemporaries* (Toronto: University of Toronto Press, 1972).

18. Frank Lloyd Wright, *An Autobiography* (New York: Horizon Press, 1977), pp. 248–57; Kathryn Smith, "Frank Lloyd Wright, Hollyhock House, and Olive Hill, 1914–1924," *Journal of the Society of Architectural Historians* 38 (March 1979): 15–33.

19. Wright, *Autobiography*, pp. 530, 248–57.

20. Ibid., p. 250.

21. Ibid., p. 251.

22. Ibid., pp. 262–77.

23. Cf. Bevis Hiller, *Art Deco of the 20s and 30s* (New York: Dutton, 1968).

24. Cf. David Gebhard and Harriette Von Breton, *Kem Weber: The Moderne in Southern California, 1920 through 1941* (Santa Barbara: Art Galleries, University of California, 1969).

25. Richard Neutra, *Life and Shape* (New York: Appleton-Century-Crofts, 1962), pp. 171–73. Photographs of designs as well as a treatment of Neutra's whole career, can be found in Thomas S. Hines, *Richard Neutra and the Search for Modern Architecture: A Biography and History* (New York: Oxford, 1982).

26. Neutra, *Life and Shape*, pp. 206–7; Richard Neutra, unpublished

diary, 6, 26 October 1919, bk. 8, pp. 26–27, 44–45, Richard Neutra Archive, Special Collections, University Research Library, University of California, Los Angeles.

27. Rudolph Schindler to Richard Neutra, January 1924, Dione Neutra Papers, Los Angeles.

28. Schindler to Neutra, November 22, 1924, Dione Neutra Papers; Dione Neutra, interview by Lawrence Weschler, July 14, 1978, Oral History Program, University of California, Los Angeles.

29. Neutra to Verena and Ruben Saslavsky, 1926, Dione Neutra Papers.

30. Cf. David Gebhard, *Schindler* (New York: Viking Press, 1971).

31. Philip Lovell, interview by author, Newport Beach, California, February 16, 1973.

32. Ibid., Neutra, *Life and Shape*, pp. 207, 220–26.

33. Neutra, *Life and Shape*, p. 221.

34. Ibid., pp. 222–24.

35. Frank Lloyd Wright to Neutra, ca. 1929, Dione Neutra Papers.

36. Neutra to Philip Lovell, May 15, 1930, Dione Neutra Papers.

37. Philip Lovell, "Care of the Body," *Los Angeles Times* Sunday Magazine, December 15, 1929, p. 26.

38. Ibid.

39. Josef von Sternberg, *Fun in a Chinese Laundry* (New York: Macmillan, 1965), pp. 270–72.

40. Aline Barnsdall to Neutra, February 15, 1939, in possession of author.

41. "The Pritzker Architecture Prize, Frank Owen Gehry, 1989," brochure in possession of author, n.p.

42. Frank Gehry, conversation with author, Los Angeles, April 10, 1989.

43. Robert Venturi, *Complexity and Contradiction in Architecture* (New York: Museum of Modern Art, 1966), pp. 22–23.

44. John W. Cook and Heinrich Klotz, "Charles Moore," *Conversations with Architects* (New York: Praeger, 1973), pp. 218–46.

45. Robert Venturi, Denise Scott Brown, and Steven Isenour, Preface to *Learning from Las Vegas* (Cambridge: MIT Press, 1972), n.p.

46. The "something modern, something else" is Charles Jencks's phrase as developed in a lecture he delivered at UCLA, ca. 1984.

For a fuller development of his ideas, see his *Language of Post-Modern Architecture* (New York: Rizzoli, 1977).

47. Many of the details of Gehry's biography as recounted in the following pages were revealed to me in a series of taped interviews with him in Los Angeles in the spring and summer of 1984. These were developed in my essay "Heavy Metal: The Education of F.O.G." in Mildred Friedman, ed., *The Architecture of Frank Gehry* (New York: Rizzoli, 1986), pp. 11–21. I am also indebted to the other contributors of essays in this catalogue of the exhibition of Gehry's work at the Walker Art Center, Minneapolis. My explications of Gehry's buildings are largely based upon my own observations of them.

48. Gehry quoted in Rosemarie Haag Bletter, "Frank Gehry's Spatial Reconstructions," in Friedman, *Architecture of Frank Gehry*, p. 56.

49. Ibid., p. 32.

50. Ibid., p. 44.

51. Julie Eizenberg, conversation with author, Los Angeles, September 1986.

52. Peter Viereck, "A Walk on Snow," from *Terror and Decorum: Poems, 1940–1948* (New York: Scribner, 1949), p. 53.

MOVIES

David Thomson

UNEASY STREET

I t is midday, and you could hear a fat leaf fall on the smooth road.

A blind lane negotiates a steep hill, feeling out the contours in the ground. You can see thirty yards ahead, before the road twists up and away, out of sight or reckoning. Behind the dense hedges and groomed fences, in the hidden houses, anyone asleep or sunbathing, but listening in their stupor, would hear every car in the same low, prowling gear. How would one tell a cop from a lover coming, or television repair from a criminal searching out openings?

Still, it is a pretty, dappled lane, with the trained heads of trees hanging over the fences, like heads in shampoo ads.

Every household keeps its back to the road: that posture does somehow permit the light tread of invasion. This is a slope where fortunate people live, or people who cling to luck the way their houses hook into the unstable earth.

Not one house assists an estimate of who lives there, or what kind of life it is. The air of satisfaction, and worry, is answer enough. The sheerness of the land arranges for the secrecy; that is why the art of construction has picked on so perverse a site. To the right is that part of the hill climbed already. The land drops so fast nothing but Mission-style roof tiles show above the fence line. To the left are cypress cigars, higher fences, and an occasional slice of façade, too looming or close to be understood. With so little to see, watching feels as precious as secrecy.

This is an address on Hollywood Boulevard. Behind the fragrant silence of this lane, you can feel the buffeting of traffic on those beeline streets supposed to be Los Angeles. They would feel as close as they are but for the incline and the abrupt, muffling growth of the foothills. Surely the charm and half the rent here are in being lifted above that grind and from boulevards where only the shimmer of congealed parallel lines stops one seeing from the 8000 block to the 6000.

That is one explanation for foothill residence in Los Angeles, for most palaces and arbors in the lopsided rectangle of Sunset, the Hollywood Freeway, Mulholland, and Beverly Glen. But this stretch of poised, uneasy road is close to where the straight of Hollywood Boulevard goes into a shock of wriggles, and sidewalk stars are replaced by ground-covering plants as wiry, glossy, and patient as the women at Beverly Hills parties.

I have a friend who has just moved here. He is in his twenties, lately promoted in the picture business (he is only an executive), and separated from the woman with whom he moved to California from the East. This is the first place he will have found to live on his own. The foothills offer so much gratifying isolation: private roads, sun-traps, nude pools, close-up patios, and inner courtyard atmospheres where the self can unwind—strongholds for escape or doing what one likes so long as no one is damaged, or runs screaming down the hill.

This is not an allusion to my friend, or what he might become. It is my response to the dramatic stance of foothill life, a mix of wanting to live there while wondering about the hostility aimed at the very few foothill people by all those fixed in the interminable grid to the south. This sounds like paranoia, and Los Angeles does make a blatant contrast of aristocracy and abject Americanness. Indeed, even the contrast is glamorous and provocative—like a great cut. Not that paranoia is simply undesirable or unhealthy; it is also the energy ready to find stories everywhere; it has been water for the picture business.

There is no obvious way of finding my friend's place. A set of wooden steps leads down through the bottle-green shade between two houses. The ground is so steep one follows the steps down to gain entrance to any of the building's three stories. It must be a strong set of steps—thick pine boards stained to a coppery color. But already its crisp edges have been softened by ivy and creepers.

My friend is all the way down, where the steps become a small stone terrace. I am not sure this is the place, so I look in the windows on the last tack of steps. Then, from the terrace, through an artful hole in the trees and bushes, I can see all the way to the smoky towers of Downtown. None of the adjacent structures can be seen, and yet a view is available, a gray mirage by day, glittery and romantic at night. Someone might sit on the terrace and feel authority—or authorship—creeping on.

This house was built in the 1930s. Glass doors look out on the terrace: once a way of bringing light into the house, this is now my friend's front entrance. As he let me in, I realized his "apartment" was just the lobby of the old house—that and twin curving staircases up to the next level, a shelf that swells at either end into small windowed platforms, his bedroom and his kitchen. Once, it would have been the threshhold where people were greeted or sent out into the night. Now a clever designer has made it a rental, wrapped into being by the glass that separates it from the outside.

The sleeping area seemed especially blunt and anecdotal, like a bed in a stage spotlight where death and a seduction occur every performance. I imagined my friend bringing a woman home, sitting her down in one of the leather chairs, letting her absorb the presence of the bed with a scant margin of floor around it. But floor-to-ceiling window is only an arm's length from the bed. One could hardly retreat there without first drawing down every blind in the apartment—or sitting there in the dark seeing shapes in the moonlight.

"The odd thing is . . ." said my friend. He'd told his boss about this new apartment, and later in the day the boss came back to check the address. The boss is a movie producer, a man who gave my friend his first big opportunity in the industry. ". . . and, apparently, one of his former girlfriends had lived in this same place. He had insisted she keep a gun."

When we had surveyed the new apartment, we went outside onto the terrace. I looked at the ground, and thought I saw security devices buried in the plants; but perhaps it was only the bullet hardness of blooms still in bud beneath the leaves. He told me animals come sliding down the hill some nights—raccoons, rats, and others he did not name—so that he gets used to movement in the undergrowth.

We went to lunch, and as I walked back up the wooden steps I saw an azalea bloom on the rim of one step. Half of it was as flat as wet tissue: I could see the grain of the wood through the veins of the flower. But the other half remained perfect, frilled and brilliant pink. I did not want to alarm my friend. The flower was like a clue, or a warning. But I had heard and seen no one else on the steps, and I was sure I had not trod on the flower myself. Blooms must fall or fade in the foothills, but must they land with the aplomb of a gardenia in Billie Holiday's hair?

This happened several years ago. My friend has moved, and he is married to someone he never knew at the time. He has produced a picture himself, and he has a child. So it all passed over. But I've never forgotten, or solved, that half-crushed bloom on the step. There must be a story—the sight was so acute, so ready, such a hook. If I'd had a camera with me I'd have taken its picture. I'm sentimental about such sights in L.A.

Los Angeles became a city through the act of seeing and its industrial transmission all over the world. Because so many pictures were shot in L.A., we were seeing its streets, its ocean and desert, its cars, trees, and light. Before ordinary people ever dreamed of traveling vacations, L.A. was the ideal of a place to go to.

Of course, most people never went. They stayed in their seats in the theater. Yet L.A. felt as if they had come. In a hundred years, the population has gone from about 150,000 to something like 5 million, depending where one draws the boundary. Its sprawl is physical, yet if L.A. always reckoned on a getaway drive to Palm Springs or Agua Caliente, so its promise reaches far beyond Mexico. In that direction, L.A. is "El Norte." In Las Vegas—once a set erected in the desert —L.A. remains the subtler, parental place for gambling with one's life. Death Valley could hardly bear that minatory title without some metropolis at hand, a factory city for Westerns and parables about *Greed*. To the north, L.A. reaches as far as San Simeon, where William Randolph Hearst built his

weekend dome and kept jars of mustard—taxi-bright—on
the authentic baronial table beneath tapestries filched from
the Renaissance. L.A. goes all that way, yet further still—
into our thoughts.

Some factories make gimmicks, rivets, or screws that
change thinking. Long before I had seen anyone dead, I
practiced the gay tumble (and it was gay then) of death as
seen in action films. Where could we study kissing, smoking,
or the most alluring toss of hair but at the movies? (If one
watched anyone in life with such staring scrutiny, one would
be warned off or challenged. But at the movies no one knows
we are watching in the dark.) Movies showed us the look of
sincerity—and made it available for lying; they taught us the
elements of beauty and the necessities of decor; and they
schooled us in consequences—in plot construction and ed-
iting logic—in ways that are fluent, beguiling, and generally
unknown in real life.

But life came later, after a childhood in the dark, and the
dark's effect is beyond educated control. For the lesson of
the movies may be that, yes, there is light or enlightenment,
but it is not here, not ours. It is there, on the screen, while
we are here in our dark. In ninety-minute movies, we see
129,600 photographs (think of the drip-irrigation of looking
at that many separately). In a year, I saw 100, then 200, then
300 movies . . . all before the outline of career set in. It is
said that the American college freshman has seen 20,000
performed killings in movies and TV—which is dutifully regarded as ominous. But no one observes the possibly greater
delusion in the certainly greater numbers of love scenes.
The factory has been at work—and we are all members of its
mechanical age.

There has developed a way of seeing and "knowing" a
thing without contact, experience, or responsibility. Being
in the dark, and watching the light; being granted the privilege of voyeurism, but having to recognize the impotence
and even the absence that go with its advantage; being there

and yet having no presence. The voyeur has to accept nullity for what he gets to see. Millions abide by this alienation; many are filled with hope, happiness (and the hope of greater happiness, the American pursuit) because of it. Only a few, like John Hinckley or Ronald Reagan, act out the wonder and terror it affords. They are kindred ghosts who needed each other. Yet most of us have a buried understanding of the dislocation and its urge to be on the public screen.

And if we know how close we are to such famous unreality, then to live in Los Angeles is to be within the most futile reach of The Story, The Show. It is grisly yet lulling that the waiters in L.A. are waiting to be actors, that valet parking attendants have script projects, and that the kids in the mail room have board-game plans for taking over the studio. There is so much scrambling, smiling readiness to be convincing. People in L.A. think in scenes and give you lines; the city is like a daytime talk-show. Its great urban and civic problems may slip past if it plays well.

What prevented me from facing the drabness of L.A. was that ghostliness was very near. For the accumulation of movie stories lingers in the acrid and clouded air. The real smog is deplorable and dangerous. Yet it is also a cue for nostalgia, a way of saying, "Remember when Los Angeles" —with the hard, Spanish "g"—"was rural, with fields, farms and the smell of eucalyptus and pepper trees, with bright, clear, hot days—in 1920, 1930, and 1940 even?"

And even if smog is poison (and it *is*), it makes for a colored, vapored view, a painter's ferment: in movies, we see without collateral damage, without organic participation, don't we? I hear you coughing, but this fog is like the one put down on sets before "Camera!" to make a mood of intrigue and suspense. The events of L.A. are sooner or later absorbed by the tropes of scenario. L.A.—Lies Allowed. Consider Mulholland Drive . . . is that road *there*, in geography, as well as in the imagination?

Mulholland is a drive and a highway, running east-west,

the best vantage point for Los Angeles and the San Fernando Valley to the north. Imagine the spirit of Marilyn Monroe, fifty miles long, lying on her side on a ridge of crumbling rock, the crest of the Santa Monica Mountains, with chaparral, wildflowers, and snakes writhing over her body. You'd need a certain height to recognize that intricate course as a body—and you need to be movie-minded. But I use the metaphor for two reasons: to help you feel sensuousness in the land, and to suggest the air of death up there in the jasmine sunlight. For Marilyn has meant more dead than she ever did alive. Death fixed her image—the concept was settled.

Her toes twitch at the Hollywood Freeway, sleepily disturbed by the traffic. From the knob of her ankle you can look down on the Hollywood Bowl or see Downtown trembling in its steam. As the legs become thighs, Mulholland enters its richest stretch, full of designer security systems for houses hidden from the road, of sprinklers sighing over bougainvillaea and the blinding roses, of golden real estate, some with views north and south, of San Fernando's pimento suburbia and the rubber-colored daytime swell of L.A., which puts on black fur and jewels at night (this is realtor language).

There are those who only think of this Mulholland, who would not go beyond the belt that is the San Diego Freeway. But there's much more to find. A little west of the freeway, Mulholland becomes a dirt road for nearly eight miles, as far as Topanga Canyon Boulevard. In a minute of driving, you give up the serene sway from one curve to another for a jolting surface and roadside weeds so dusty their short green season looks like old dollars.

There are no houses or telephones, none of the tidy firehouses from the wealthy, worried section. If you broke down, you would be stranded. To the north you can see the sharkskin surface of Encino reservoir, but to the south there are only folds of hillside where hawks spin in the mauve dust of sunset. You could lose a Live Aid Concert down there in Topanga State Park. How much easier for a few desperate characters to lurk there. The dirt road section is eerily empty on weekdays, a bikers' track at weekends, and a place for furtive love and dealing. You can come upon a packed car with talk too delicate to approach. There are mattresses dying in the brush where trysts were enjoyed, or exhaustions lived out, how long ago?

Just as you think you are lost, the hard-top resumes and you slide into a patch of community before the last long section. This rolling countryside contains a distant dewdrop golf course, a ranch where stunts are filmed, riding trails, the homes of solitaries and artists, a mock Alpine section, a rough trailer park, the satellite dishes of a Jewish recreation center, hillsides burnt black by the latest fires, and, at last, the highest number of Mulholland, 35375, a camp for blind children set among eucalyptus trees. Then there's the sea, past Malibu, a beach named after actor Leo Carrillo, side-kick to the Cisco Kid, and platinum surf like Marilyn's hair in her last pictures.

Some say the road was built for that journey, so that the sweaty poor of Bunker Hill and Fairfax secretaries could get to the sea for relief. There are faster ways now, on the freeways or Santa Monica Boulevard. And even in 1923–24, when Mulholland was built, the road was as much a gesture of triumph and philosophy as a means of transport.

That's why it was named after William Mulholland (1855–1935), the superintendent of the L.A. Water and Power Department, who designed and presided over the scheme that sucked water from the Owens Valley, 250 miles away, to make L.A. fertile, flush-friendly, and be-pooled. He is regarded now as a robber baron and ecological rapist. But that label is the "Bless me, for I have sinned" the Angeleno murmurs whenever he enters the shower or drops into the copper sulphate pools that fill every navel and armpit along Mulholland. No one is sending the water back to the desolate Owens Valley. They're keeping it, along with the casual guilt.

The eighties were a decade of drought and increased use. But no one has discarded Mulholland's estimate of the water: "There it is—take it." His Drive still lives on that principle, just as Hollywood taught us to be fascinated by scoundrels and people who, in life, would repel us. Men like Noah Cross in *Chinatown* or Michael Corleone in *The Godfather*. From the screen, those black souls have one reassurance for voyeurs: they whisper to us that crime *is* organized, the wicked world is under control, the story has an author.

Mulholland begs for story and a moment when Noah Cross can point at the chaotic wilderness and the amenities of the city and say, "Look! See what power does accomplish!" This is the edge where the desert touches Gucci and Mercedes, where pet chihuahuas can be eaten by coyotes. There is even a Manson Avenue that runs off Mulholland: one wonders whether it was scripted tribute or ghastly impromptu, for Cielo Drive, where the Mansons came in at night, is only a stone's throw beneath Mulholland.

There are Brancusis in some groomed gardens and beer bottles shattered from target practice a few miles farther on. The Drive is meant to contain that contrast: it is a highway that says, "Look at me—tame me—if you can." The road thrills to the way man has commanded power and beauty here, and turned them into a property or a story. That HOLLYWOOD sign at the eastern end, white letters fifty feet high, is a title, a caption. Nature has been sold out to the culture of cute ideas.

In Hollywood and Los Angeles there have always been signal words or phrases. There were the titles in silent pictures, not just the things characters were saying but morals for the tale, all so forthright that those with poor English might keep up. To say nothing of the titles of the films, slogans and inducements, and phrases that might be more cogent and magical than the films themselves. Consider the trash poetry in just a brief selection: *Hearts of the World*; *The Age of Desire*; *The Salvation Hunters*; *Sunrise*; *Madame Satan*; *Trouble in Paradise*; *I Am a Fugitive from a Chain Gang*; *It Happened One Night*; *The Awful Truth*; *Only Angels Have Wings*; *Suspicion*; *Since You Went Away*; *Leave Her to Heaven*; *Out of the Past*; *They Live by Night*; *The Bad and the Beautiful*; *The Searchers*; *The Sweet Smell of Success*; *Splendor in the Grass*; *The Way We Were*; *Rocky*; *Apocalypse Now*; *On Golden Pond*; *Fatal Attraction*; *Pretty Woman*.

Now read that list again and judge how many would fit a good photograph of Mulholland Drive near sunset, showing wilderness and culture in the same frame, *or* a new perfume. I have not tricked you, for the secret of movie titles is to give access to all kinds of wonder and sensation. The best American movie titles do not promise us *one* film; they assure us of being in the world of movies with *all* dreads and dreams and the comfort that knows just about everything in life can be rendered in a few words so profound they will transcend the humiliating idiocy of being put up as fifty-foot tin cutouts on the side of a hill.

That HOLLYWOOD sign is so endlessly funny, and dreadful —and L.A. is proud of it. The sign was falling down once, and luminaries got together to restore it. Seeing signs in the texture of everyday existence is a fictional urge; it is like seeing a stranger and guessing he is a villain—or seeing a flower and fearing plot. The paintings of Edward Ruscha tease this cult with wondrous wit and elegance. Just as many TV commercials now compress the fuss of full-length movies into sixty or thirty seconds, so Ruscha makes pictures like haiku, road signs, and fortune-cookie mottoes for foothill

L.A. Incidentally, he has found eccentric but delicious media that allude to the prevailing haziness of L.A. For example, in this work the letters are cherry-juice stain on the swirl of dusty pink moire:

WORD PAINTING	VERY ANGRY PEOPLE

Or, pastel on paper:

WORD PAINTING	HONEY, I TWISTED THROUGH MORE DAMN TRAFFIC TODAY

Ruscha concentrated on such works in the mid-1970s just before a term made its way to the fevered surface of industry attitudes in Hollywood: HIGH CONCEPT, or it may have been HI, CONCEPT at first. This is the idea for the ad of a film before the film, a way of marketing that is the most creative act. High concept could say of *Pretty Woman:* "Chilly tycoon meets lovely whore and teaches her to shop and dress nicely, but she gives head without help." Yet, really "Julia Roberts in *Pretty Woman*" is concept enough now. In May 1991, Hollywood considered changing the "downer" title of her next picture, *Dying Young.* One executive proposed renaming it "Another film with Julia Roberts" as a sure way of grossing $50 million. The highness in concept here is not loftiness of an aesthetic or social kind. No, this is the highness that must be viewed from below, so that the enforced crouch of awe or worship obscures the sham (as in giving head). It is not unlike the heights of Mulholland.

But the discovery of "high concept" was a landmark in the

rare, absurdist brutalism that drives L.A. If I could just get high-concept enough, I might get that experience I thought I had in the foothills into development . . . the azalea on the step. I'm not sure azalea makes it, but gardenia? THE BRO-KEN GARDENIA? Not quite. What about FALLEN FLOWER? Julia Roberts in *Fallen Flower?* Julia Roberts *is* FALLEN FLOWER! I can see those words, months in ad-vance of the film, on the huge signboards over Sunset. They could do it in bloodstain on crushed silk. It seems to me so *right*, I don't know that we're going to have to actually make the film.

Jeremy Larner

RACK'S RULES
The Mechanics of Morals in Movieland

O
ne day in the Age of Reagan, I find myself sitting at a wooden table in a West L.A. mock-up of a railway diner with my friend Wysteria, whose ambition it is to produce a feature film. She is paying for lunch, which gives her the privilege of telling me the trials of her life and trying to talk me into writing a script on an "important property" which she has optioned. We both know she can get a studio to hire me on a "development deal," whereupon my work will be sent to a star and/or director, who, if they are "interested," will promptly make the project their own by firing both Wysteria and myself and getting the script restudded with hunks of dialogue like hardened Jell-O. Then, and only then, can they possibly "commit."

Wysteria has raised a small stake to develop two scripts in hopes of attracting bankable names, but she must be very careful. She has already spent more than half her funds on a perverted murder script with social overtones, and still owes the writer a payment for a rewrite, which she has stalled by convincing herself she is dissatisfied. And in truth, how could she be satisfied, till her judgment is stamped by coins descending?

Yet with a week's work on the telephone, Wysteria has managed to get "her" murder script to several well-placed "readers," and has had ten-minute meetings with junior agents of CAA, ICM, and William Morris. She even got a return call from Rack Rookstein, the Rooker, the Rock of Malibu, superpackager most lately known as the man who brought in the Japanese money. Rack read the two-page summary known as "coverage" and said he would send the script to one of his star clients, Modesto Megalo, whose thrillers chill and whose horrors redeem themselves with love. Rack has not called Wysteria for three months, but she never fails to mention Megalo's "interest" when sending the script to directors.

But what is this! None other than Rack himself comes sliding through the restaurant, actually bends and bestows a smart kiss on Wysteria's lips. "Hi, kid," he says to me, for we have known one another since the sixties. From behind Wysteria, Rack shoots me his gorgeous grin. He loves to encounter me in social situations, where he never fails to spot that I am once more making a disastrous blunder. His raised eyebrow conveys as much about my judgment in lunching with Wysteria. "But look," he says to her, "I've got some news for you, sweetie. Come back with me to the office."

Wysteria's heart pounds—the Megalo deal! But after three months of unanswered calls, she's not going to let him think he owns her.

"Rack!" she cries. "I'd follow you to the ends of the earth, but as you see I have a meeting here."

Why sure, Rack wouldn't dream of interrupting. Maybe Wysteria could just pop up to his office afterwards?

He leaves Wysteria with the heady feeling she has seized movie power in the course of a lunch. Rack needs her. Her tone changes. If I don't have faith in her project, she may have to take it to hot Screenwriter X, who has been calling every day and panting over the phone like a puppydog.

Forcing herself to walk slowly down Wilshire, Wysteria arrives at Rack's building twenty minutes later. She is about to enter the elevator when the receptionist calls to her. Whom does she wish to see? Does she have an appointment? Unbelievably, this robot lobby lady scans the daily printout looking for Wysteria's name. Wysteria frosts her with New York ice. Rack is expecting her, will the lady take responsibility when he learns she was detained? The lobby lady wearily picks up her phone and calls the penthouse floor. "There's a person here who claims she has an appointment with Mr. Rookstein." She listens, turns to Wysteria with the slightest hint of a smirk. "I'm sorry, Mr. Rookstein is in a meeting."

No, says Wysteria firmly. She just saw Rack, he asked her personally to come. The lady shrugs, punches more digits, hands Wysteria the phone. Going through the same routine, Wysteria gets the upstairs receptionist to fetch Rack's secretary. A five-minute wait, with the lobby lady keeping an eye on her, as if Wysteria were about to steal a potted palm. The secretary comes on the line, hears the story, hesitates, sighs, and ask Wysteria to hold. An even longer pause ensues, giving Wysteria plenty of time to imagine her approach to the deal with Megalo.

Hello? I'm sorry, but Mr. Rookstein is booked solid. He said he'll call you."

An air-conditioned chill sweeps up Wysteria's legs. As the

sun falls into the Pacific, it reaches her heart. She calls Rack every day for the next two weeks, with no reply.

Now the question, dear reader, is not what happened to the Megalo deal. The question—the one Wysteria obsessively thrusts upon me and her other friends, thus slipping further in their regard—is why did Rack bother? Why did he lie when the truth would be far less trouble? When he could merely nod and leave the restaurant, go about his business?

Could it be, she wonders, that Wysteria was simply the closest woman whom Rack wanted to command for the benefit of someone else in the room? No, Wysteria is over thirty with no major credits and no illusions about her sexual drawing power in a garden where teen bubbles are available like grapes. Now she must fight madly to kill her fear that Rack has canceled the big meeting with herself and Megalo just because she wouldn't abandon her lunch. Wysteria is an intelligent woman, she graduated NYU with a *magna* in Communication Arts, but her tendency to torment herself second-guessing people's motives is a sign she can't really play the game, and prefigures her humiliating return to public television.

When I ask Rack, he honestly can't remember. He was merely improvising—like a Laker star he had seen in the men's room, throwing his wadded-up paper towel behind his back across the room and into an ebony urinal. Spotting the two of us pretending we had something serious to discuss, Rack couldn't resist. He broke up the play as offhandedly as Magic Johnson steals a pass, and forgot his little move the moment he strolled off the court.

Rack's Rule: Work out, stay loose. You are the moves you make.

Rack's Rule: Forget about rules already. Make up your own, or else play by some other guy's.

Why should Rack walk by with a hello like every other

schmuck? Rack doesn't play audience for people like me and
Wysteria, he takes control.

Rack's Rule: Power is no accident. It depends on total
freedom.

"You fooled with her," I say. "You drove her nuts."

"Sorry, kid. I didn't do a thing to her. She did it to herself."

Rack's Rule: No one does anything to anyone. What people get is what they really want. Give it to them.

But wait a minute! Have I caught the legendary Rack in a
social error? Hasn't he handed Wysteria an unpleasant story
to tell all over town? Rack grabs my head, rubs his knuckles
through my hair. This is why he loves to talk to me. He loves
a guy who prides himself on reading and vocabulary and so
forth, and who gets all the rules wrong.

Rack's Rule: All you learn from stories is who has the
power.

Wysteria's story will hardly underrate Rack's importance.
Who cares whether Wysteria thinks she likes his behavior?
Her thoughts are just miniparticles of dying energy in the
great game in which we all are players, know it or not, like it
or not. Since she keeps on calling. Rack knows at bottom
Wysteria accepts the universe as he views it. In a way he
does need her, but only as a country's ruler needs guys who
take him seriously on TV. Never mind what she thinks she
thinks, she will leap faster next time it occurs to Rack to snap
his fingers.

Rack became a kind of patron for a while when I came to
L.A. at the end of the sixties. After a few years working for
his father's network in New York, he had come West to
produce the first late-night acid rock concert TV shows.
Meantime he raised funds for his first feature—a film about
a rebel psychedelic guitarist who runs from the cops and
discovers America, which beats the shit out of him but

doesn't kill him, leaves him in fact a hipper, cooler guy. The movie was a wild success. The film critic of the *New Republic* announced the creation of a secular religion. Rack got rich as the producer who could make the real goods for the youth culture. Rack himself was sold on his gut-level feel for how this country was changing and what it needed. He passed out joints at meetings with studio heads. He was in touch with underground revolutionaries, and drank champagne when the Isla Vista branch of the Bank of America was torched. He was an early discoverer of Timothy Leary, and played tapes of Baba Ram Dass chanting "that too, that too," on the cassette deck in his Porsche 911-S.

Rack hired me to rewrite a script based on a novel of youth rebellion, *Hell's Bells*. The novel took place at a prep school where Rack and the writer—whom Rack called "Weenie"— had been students. Rack, to his pride, was thrown out, while Weenie took highest honors—but the situation was reversed now that Rack had bought Weenie's obscure novel and induced him to write the first draft of a screenplay for less than union scale. Both Rack and Weenie agreed that Rack had rescued this would-be hard-bitten ironist from the nonworld of the Iowa Writers Workshop. They agreed that movies were the great art form of the Twentieth Century. But Weenie had a list of black & white films he cherished and studied, and thought he was a natural for Hollywood— whereas Rack knew his language and attitude were hopeless. "By definition," I heard him tell Weenie, "You *can't* know what I do about people—because you're writing all day while I'm dealing with one person after another."

True enough, Weenie couldn't write scenes or dialogue. His novel was written in proto-postmodern expressionist style, with precious bits of observation and obscure scraps of conversation, going nowhere in the supposed mode of our time. It was the subject Rack wanted to buy—and he assured me only I could really write it. He hired me as his assistant,

instructing me not to refer in Weenie's presence to my re-
writing his script, because of Weenie's "ego problems." This
left Weenie to assume he was sole author, just as I secretly
regarded myself, though before I had finished my third draft
at trainee wages Rack had, unknown to me, hired a comedy
team to inject laughs and a rock lyricist to write a voice-over.

When I found out, after the movie was shot, I asked Rack
why he hadn't told me. "It would have discouraged you," he
said. "You might have pulled out and never made your con-
tribution. I thought I handled you pretty well. If it weren't
for me, you'd still be passing out your poetry in Washington
Square."

"Don't you remember," I said, "standing by that window
and telling me I would have a chance to go over the shooting
script?"

Rack laughed—oh, how I amused him! "There never was
a shooting script. The kind of director I deal with thinks he
makes it up as he goes along. Besides, what is this business
of remembering what people say?"

Rack said this with no malice. He was trying to help a
stranger in a strange world.

Rack's Rule: Don't get scripted on what you're going to
say. Let your instinct fit your words to the moment you say
them. Remember whatever's best to remember at the time
you remember it. Your relations then take place entirely in
the present. *Be here now,* as Leary said.

After a screening of the first rough cut of the movie, I
witnessed a confrontation between a sobered, stiffened
Weenie and Rack the wonder-producer high on creative
pride. Rack announced he'd made a book deal to publish the
script.

Weenie: "You mean my script?"

Rack: [defender of cinematic art] "I mean a transcript of
the film."

Weenie: "Under what title, may I ask?"

Rack: *"Hell's Bells,* of course."

Weenie: "Rack, old boy, it happens a book by that title already exists, and I am the author by U.S. Copyright. Isn't it the usual practice to release a new paperback, with stills from the movie on the cover?"

Rack: "You want your sales to ride my movie."

Weenie: "Your movie of my book. And my contract gives you a piece of the book action."

Rack: "I can't permit it."

Weenie: "Why not?"

Rack: "For the same reason you can't permit me to publish *my* book."

Weenie: "That's totally different!"

Rack: "That's your illusion, that you're different. But in reality it's purely a matter of your ego versus my ego."

Weenie attempted a sarcastic laugh. He looked to me for validation, but that's a mistake in a movie office. I was watching Rack, waiting for some shift, some payoff, but he continued to bear down on Weenie with high moral intensity.

Weenie: "You're sick."

Weenie left, shaking his head in amazement. I thought sure Rack was bluffing. Why should he pass up his chance for a book tie-in? But it turned out he meant what he said. Weenie's new edition came out without a movie cover, and Rack shrugged off his 20 percent.

In his office sauna, Rack stretched out on his back, thrusting his abnormally large genitals in the air. "You'll notice," he said, "Weenie was the one who resorted to name-calling and manipulation. With him, it's U.S. Copyright. With me, it's a matter of principle."

"Principle?"

Oh, the elementary stuff Rack had to explain to me! It was the birds and bees of show business.

Rack's Rule: In a business deal, everything is negotiable, nothing is personal.

Rack's Rule: Every ego wants all it can get. All egos are

equal. The difference between people comes out when someone is honest enough to admit it—and to act on what he knows.

Rack's Rule: You get only what you're entitled to, by virtue of the power you take for yourself. To try for more than you're worth by lecturing someone worth more is self-delusion and hypocrisy. Things are as they should be, and as they change will remain exactly as they should be. That too, that too.

One way Rack could tell Weenie's ego was just like anyone's was the way Weenie stared at the ingenues who would arrive at Rack's office for auditions. Rack—again from principle—was heavily engaged in stretching the definition of the "R" movie, and if the part he was casting called for a nude scene, the rest of us would have to leave for half an hour.

Sex in Rack's mind was a vast territory. He thought he knew, or could tell with a glance, how any person behaved in bed. In my case, he informed me, I might not really like to fuck. I disagreed, but Rack demanded proof. What, for instance, did I consider my greatest achievement in the realm of sex?

Under pressure, and partly to save my bourgeois sense of privacy, I made up something harmless and nonrevealing. When I was eighteen, I almost made love with a girlfriend in a bunker at night on a midwestern golf course. At least, I thought of it. Some intrusion—perhaps passing headlights from the highway—startled us and sent us back to our car. Telling the story to Rack, I converted thought to deed, changed night to day, and backdated eighteen to fifteen. I even invented some approaching duffers. Did I prove Rack right in his concept of the honest man?

What Rack told me in exchange, I still don't doubt to this day. On a Sunday visit from his best friend and his best friend's wife, Rack screwed the wife while her husband and his own wife took afternoon naps. *In the same house,* Rack emphasized.

That story, I objected, had nothing to do with enjoying sex.

Rack's Rule: Everything relates to sex, even sex itself.

Rack's continuing relations with Weenie had a lot to do with sex in this sense. Weenie grew unbearably excited as the release of *Hell's Bells* drew near. He must have thought he was going to be let in on the only real action he had ever dreamt of, the life of celebrity. Though even he knew by now he had no voice in decisions, Weenie brought friends to the screenings of each new cut, explaining at length how his script had been changed. He also showed up at the office to look over ad layouts, as if this were essential to safeguard his interests. Rack greeted him cordially, following his rule never to take things personally. Then, too, Rack relished an appearance by Weenie in his home territory. Rack had further plans for Weenie.

One day Rack said, "Weenie, my man, you know my wife Samantha has a thing for you." Ignoring Weenie's stunned expression, he went on casually, "Hey, I'm going to take the film to the Venice Festival next week. Why don't you drop by the house, keep Sam from getting too lonely?"

Weenie didn't answer, embarrassed at what he thought a show of naïveté or perversion. Sam was one of those impeccable Beverly Hills wives who was mysteriously silent, surly, and gorgeous. Some instinct innate to such women leads them to disregard my presence entirely, so that no word I addressed to Samantha Rookstein ever received a reply. I remember only her perfect tiny teeth, the sharp curl of her mouth. I'm sure Weenie was amazed by the announcement of her interest. From that moment, Weenie was thinking about Sam at poolside in her thong rather than making annoying demands that he, too, should be flown to Venice. He left the office without once looking Rack in the eye, as if already guilty of adultery.

Rack's Rule: Look everyone in the eye. That way, what you say is always the truth.

But it seemed to me Rack was giving his wife away.

Rack's Rule: Sex is a natural human activity, which should never be restricted in any way. Again, the difference between people lies in who is honest about it.

Rack himself never concealed his desires or stinted on them; he would freely answer any question. He had no desire to restrict his wife—his only requirement was that she tell him all about it. After all, what was marriage without intimacy?

In fact, I found among many of the people I worked for in L.A., a democratic willingness to share or talk openly about their sex lives. Often they would bring it up, so to speak, on first meeting. Five minutes after shaking my hand, the director Greg Mussolini, hailed by buff reviewers as the true American novelist of our time, buzzed in his middle-aged secretary and asked me if I agreed she was "very fuckable." He explained she was feeling low after a breakup and he was trying to reassure her. Greg felt she was painfully aware that he himself had never slept with her—and there followed the story of his recent arrest when his girlfriend locked him out of his own beach house, his subsequent divorce, the desires that came up during his psychoanalysis, the kind of party he preferred when in New York, etcetera. He bounced around the room as he spoke, snapping off and on his beloved machines, charming me in the manner of a four-hundred-pound teddy bear. He told me he had never met anyone who understood these matters as I did, and embraced me as we parted . . . never to meet again.

The head of a studio once scheduled a script meeting in a hotel room occupied by his mistress, with a special hot tub installed on the verandah. The young lady was just leaving as we arrived, and I wondered why we were dispossessing her, since the lot was only five minutes away. But as we watched her charming bottom wave good-bye, I caught a glint in the boss's eye. He was turned on, and if we ate our hearts out, he would be all the more so.

Rack certainly did not conceal his various lady friends, liked in fact to have them up to the house. On such occasions, Sam kept to the background like an exotic flower, handling the servants while Rack was the affable host. Not that she'd mince words, if it came to that—but Rack was disappointed in her honesty. She told him about Weenie, of course—apparently Rack's boyhood friend had had quite an unnerving experience. Still, Rack suspected Sam of keeping other affairs secret. Furtiveness didn't anger him, just aroused his pity.

He only felt sorry when Weenie slunk back to Iowa, from whence he now and then wrote accounts for *belles lettres* quarterlies telling the ironic tale of how his script for *Hell's Bells* had been vandalized—though if someone liked the movie, Weenie was more than willing to take credit.

When I drove him to catch his midnight flight to Des Moines, Weenie tried to tell me the details, but all he could get out was that Sam had said Rack would fuck a snake. Somehow the circumstances made Weenie feel unmanned that he himself would not, could not, fuck a snake. Not even if his sex life, future fame, and success in Hollywood depended on it—as they seemed to that night.

I tried to tell him Sam would have said the same thing, in the same tone, in front of Rack and a roomful of guests. Rack enjoyed Sam's comments in the same way he enjoyed Wysteria's complaint. Still, he hadn't guessed when he married this rich beauty from Bryn Mawr that she would have so much trouble around the sexual revolution. Yet neither her discontent nor her divorce action perturbed Rack in any way, until Sam sued to void their contract and claim profits from future film projects.

Then Rack was furious—he mobilized his lawyers to do

her in, "by whatever means necessary"—his favorite phrase from Malcolm X. Even in his fury, Rack enjoyed himself. His moral fervor was unblemished by a smidgen of self-doubt. He loved getting calls from his lawyers, which he would take "on the box," so whoever was in his office could listen. I remember one day his chief litigator advised him a minor actor had a good case that Rack had stolen a long-cherished movie idea the actor had pitched to him, and made a movie of it without the actor's involvement. Rack was delighted. "Let him sue!" he crowed. "Sue me! Sue me!"

Another time Rack was sued by an animation lab he had brought in on a film. Rack's deal was to keep a 10 percent commission from the fee the studio paid through him—but he actually kept 20 percent. The animators were friends of Rack and first tried a personal call. I could see that look of happy outrage brighten Rack's face. "That's the way I do business!" he shouted to the speaker box. "Sue me!" They did, and settled out of court for 15 percent.

In fact, the only time Rack ever got angry at me was over a matter of money. I was spending the weekend at his ski lodge, and he overheard me giving my personal charge number to the long-distance operator. He tore the phone out of my hands. I was his guest, what did I mean by attempting to buy something in his house?

Rack's Rule: He who pays has power. To be treated is a sign of vassalage, or, in modern terms, a constraint on freedom.

What happens, I wondered, when Rack dines with someone like Roy Tucker, the star who has all his belongings furnished, and is on total expense account everywhere he goes, every minute of his life, yet likes to pass the check to whomever he eats with, on the grounds that everyone in his presence is by definition trying to get something from him? For Roy, the payer, not the payee, was the vassal. Simple, said Rack. Tucker takes, that's his power. Rack pays, that's

his. Each can think of it how he likes, therefore each remains free.

In all the years I've known Rack, he's never let me take a
check, nor ever set foot in my house, or even my hotel room.
Nonetheless, every time he owes me something for a rewrite,
I have to have my agent call his bookkeeper, then wait a
month for the check. Rack will gladly explain to me how
each case reflects his principles. But when I asked him once
just what his percentage was and how much he made on a
film I worked on, he was shocked and indignant. What made
me think I could intrude upon his privacy?

Question: Why is sex so freely discussed in L.A., while
money is secret?

Rack's Rule: Openness in sex and privacy in money feel
right because they are both forms of power. Each permits
maximum freedom and leverage for those who can conceive
of and afford such things. The only exception to the money
rule is the selected announcement of profits, about which
one always lies, so as to keep control.

I have known both a star and a senator who each lie about
their age by one year—as a means of control. Rack himself
never answers when someone asks his age, height, or weight.
But after his divorce, when Rack was running a studio, he
didn't hesitate to tell me of his campaign to seduce his pu-
bescent daughter. He would never have approached her in
her early years, but now he wanted to express his love and
admiration by getting her started on the right foot. He was
scornful of my fear that his attentions might harm her.

Rack's Rule: The expression of sincere feeling is intimacy in action. Repression leads to hostility, distrust, confusion, and death. Repression is the sure sign of a loser, the
last thing you'd want to pass on to a child.

A Rodeo Drive shrink confirmed to me that planning to
fuck one's daughter is widespread among powerful men in
the vicinity. They like to think, he said, they are above the

rules of human nature. But Rack maintained he was Natural Man, one of the few who survived the civilized oppression of what was known, in those days, as "The Society."

Rack's daughter was a match for him, and I don't think he had his way with her, though it was not a point he would insist on. He was nothing if not an accepting father. Rachel Rookstein eventually came to live in the cabana by Rack's pool with her punk boyfriend, Mick. Sometimes at night father and daughter would be screwing back to back in the shallow water. Or Rack would position his date so he could watch, and enjoy the eye contact. This was a favorite way with him, and he would have relished it if Samantha had dropped in now and then to join the party—but Sam, finally, maintained the traditional view of sex as property.

Rack's live-in woman at the time was a friend and classmate of his daughter's. Snowflower stuck with him from thirteen until she went off to college. Rack swore he had never known a woman so uncompromisingly independent. "By the time she was ready to leave, she knew she was queen pussy." They remain friends to this day, and Rack is friendly, too, with her parents, who are Reichian therapists. Even Samantha stayed on friendly terms with Snowflower, knowing how un-hip it would be to express the obvious—which Rack thrived on anyway. He loved nothing better than obtaining the reaction and not reacting to it.

Rack's Rule: To be disturbed by anything is to be a loser.

Not being disturbed was a special advantage at social events, where Rack could observe people like myself. I never did get used to seeing my fellow guests gaze past me, as if my status and income were printed on my forehead. The words of people lower than oneself are literally unheard at movieworld gatherings, as what advantage would it give one to hear them? Nor should one expect laughter to greet a witty remark.

Rack's Rule: Laughter is a form of social tribute.

Rack always laughed at me, never at anything I said. He only acknowledged humor on those occasions when he wanted to assure a powerful person he was recognized. My compensation was that I had access to Rack, or rather, he gave me access. *Rack's Rule:* Access flows downward only.

A corollary was that if someone more important than myself entered Rack's office—or passed by at a party—Rack would abandon me in the middle of a sentence. Rack called this "the walk-away." It was practiced by everyone in show business, so that the recipient might experience the warm glow of private friendship—which for brief periods can be better faked than the real thing—followed immediately by the chill of obliteration.

The young producer (now chief of production) Regina Speare was a master of this technique. When I entered her office to discuss the script I was doing for her, she would shoot me an adoring look and rush into my arms. Within a minute, she would be telling me of her disillusion with her current boyfriend. Though I knew better, I was convinced each time she had been in love with me for years and was about to arrange a consummation. But should a director or a studio executive enter, she would not even introduce me. She and her visitor would perform a conversation in front of me, as if I had ceased to exist. Or she would draw the visitor down the hall for a private word, without either of them glancing in my direction. At parties, she would pass by without the slightest sign of recognition. Rack called this "the walk-on."

Rack's Rule: One-on-one conversation is a gift wherein the more powerful person permits the less powerful person to try a number on him. To continue that same number in public is an attempt to force a favor into an obligation. Social position is earned only by success, one can't charm or impress one's way into it. After all, that too is nothing personal.

———

It didn't surprise me to discover that Rack, in his Greenwich Village period after he dropped out of Yale in the late fifties, had been an early reader of Norman Mailer's essay "The White Negro." Mailer energized the jaded literary world with his argument that the urban black man—in response to surroundings of unremitting danger—learns to rely on his instinctive reaction, not merely to survive, but to turn the threat of paranoia into a dance of pleasure and triumph. The existential hipster, Mailer said, takes this style as a model, shrugs off the mediocrity of middle-class morality—which leads to dictatorship, war, and cancer—and permits himself to operate in a larger room of possibility—where he is aware of options screened out by the square who enters each scene with fixed limits to his personality. On occasion, the hipster might do anything at all to sustain the calculus of his personal growth, even partake of the refreshment of murder.

It turned out that, insofar as Rack bothered with what he called the "linear word," Mailer was his favorite author. But Rack insisted I had Mailer all wrong. His work, properly read, was an elegant put-on, just what the market called for at the beginning of a revolution. The point was that Mailer took the freedom to write his fantasies of extreme violence, and to connect them with sex, marriage, money, and fame. Powerful stuff, but words, all words, less influential than Rack's own movies, which spun these fantasies into the all-embracing world of the image. The truly hip individual could think and do anything he wanted, perhaps lead an actual political upheaval. But there was no need for personal violence. The point about Mailer—or Rack's hero Fidel Castro, for that matter—was not violent words, but personal freedom and success based on the audacity to command the public imagination.

Sure, but what would Rack do if he were confronted, say, by a jealous, murderous pimp, as is Mailer's protagonist in *An American Dream*, where he summons the instant imagination to throw the pimp down a stairwell?

"I would never be in that situation," Rack said. "I would signify to the man, and he would see our common advantage. That's what I do, what I'm all about."

But what if, I pressed absurdly, some crazy person assaulted him before he could speak or think? Was Rack saying he could not die? "I'd close my eyes," Rack said, in the language of his psychedelic Buddhism, "and float downstream." He was ready for death, he thought of it as the Great Adventure Flick. But once more I missed the point, Rack informed me. When Mailer spoke of entering the mindframe of the psychopath, he wasn't advocating death or craziness, just a freer, expanded definition of the truly sane. If you read the conventional literature on individuals The Society labels "psychopaths," they turn out to be addicts, con men, thieves, and whores, who deceive everyone they meet and fall back again and again to prisons and asylums. Whereas the people Mailer was writing about were people like Rack and his friends: the chosen few of our era, the people who through their command of communications skills were running the world, taking responsibility for nourishing, protecting, and inspiring future generations.

Though Rack at that time regarded Ronald Reagan as a political enemy, he became Reagan's special-events producer in the late seventies. Rack is fond of pointing out that he probably leads the list in combined contributions to the Weathermen in the sixties and the Reagan campaigns of the eighties. Rack now sees Reagan as a pioneer who laid down the dialectical groundwork for a new order to come. Though Reagan comes from a more traditional expression of the American Dream, he turned out, when his karma was ripe for Rack to meet him, to be a man not unlike Rack himself: "a man of principle, but effortlessly flexible. He lives in the present, handles whatever is happening, does exactly what he wants, and is totally serene. And he's a spiritual person, too. He likes himself, he exudes that quality and it makes the whole country feel better."

Rack's Rule: You can't love anybody until you love yourself.

This corresponded with Rack's great discovery in his ultimate peyote session, the one which put him on the final path to his spiritual destiny: "that basically my life is all about serving other people, and it always has been. Truly, I love everyone."

Rack's Rule: The people who get real power in L.A. are happy people—much happier than you are. They lead peaceful, constructive lives, inventing in every generation new ways of loving America. That's what movies are all about. That too, that too. Power from movies is no coincidence. It is exactly as it should be.

In the eighties Rack moved leisurely around the globe, operating as an American diplomat without portfolio as he put together business structures to consolidate new communication technology, with the goal of bringing video, film, news media, and print publishing under a single, enlightened, planetary management system.

As he foresaw, his life has taken a religious turn, and Rack frequently visits the lodge he set up on a mountain above a sprawling desert resort he owns, which serves as the headquarters for a worldwide spiritual institute. I can't precisely describe the institute's doctrine, because its profoundest teachings are a secret known only to an inner elite which has paid a great deal of money. The idea that has trickled down through classes and books to the dues-paying membership involves a past civilization on the earth of a much higher order, destroyed by laserlike alien weapons. The Ancestors live among us, guiding our incarnations, slowly letting us develop into what we will ultimately be . . .

This is a perfect religion for Rack, the logical extension of his tripping in the sixties, because it is exclusive, elusive, and provides the distinctive calling card of social shock he likes to leave behind him on his journey through our dreamlike but satisfying world . . .

Despite his ever-increasing sphere of influence, Rack is no snob, and when he bumps into me he greets me as an old friend. He has even stayed in touch with Weenie, who manages to get five minutes with Rack every time he's in L.A. Weenie shamelessly fawns upon Rack, still hoping to share what he considers the only real action in our culture.

Weenie has an arrangement with a slick magazine, wherein he writes in high literary style an annual "profile" on the "new woman of the year," a starlet chosen by Rack's conglomerate (which also owns the magazine). The task allows Weenie to get away from Iowa for two weeks, to attend discotheques and what he describes as "real coke parties," and to worship at the shrine of a worldly young beauty, whose marble-eyed boredom he takes for profound intuition. In his five minutes with Rack, Weenie feverishly pitches movie ideas. Recently he proposed to turn Wagner's Ring Cycle into a trilogy of mythic Latin dance movies, and Rack actually got him a development fee to write a treatment. Rack didn't go so far as actually to read what Weenie wrote, but back at the Writers Workshop Weenie arouses a stir of jealous excitement as he ironically recounts the adventures of a veteran screenwriter . . .

As for myself, I last saw Rack in the city where I live, at a preview of the year's most expensive film, for which fifteen top writers had been hired in succession to express the movie's great theme—the genius of its director. I came up to Rack in the theater lobby, where we exchanged a few words. Rack was draped in loose costly clothes, still handsome, smart, tanned, relaxed, and slender, traveling with Brazilian twins he met at his institute's retreat near their Swiss finishing school. I asked him if he had arranged Reagan's $2 million post-presidential trip to Japan, and he admitted he had.

Rack wanted no publicity for it, he had taken no fee, done it purely for his commitment to world harmony. Besides, he anticipated the mutual sharing that would come his way when the studios were transnationalized with Japanese capital. As I started to reply, he turned away, catching an eye that gave him greater glee, and murmured, "Fall by the house, any time you're in L.A. . . ."

"But you," I barked, overwhelmed a final time by my desire to cling on to his ease, his charm, his knowledge, "could come to my house tonight!"

Rack's raucous Zen laughter rose up the staircase to the balcony as he did the walk-away.

CONTRIBUTORS

EVE BABITZ is the author of *Sex and Rage, Slow Days, Fast Company,* and *L.A. Woman.*

ALEXANDER COCKBURN is a regular columnist for *The Nation,* the *Los Angeles Times,* and *The New Statesman,* and contributes to numerous other periodicals. He is the author of *Corruptions of Empire,* and with Susanna Hecht, *The Fate of the Forest: Developers, Destroyers, and Defenders of the Amazon.*

MIKE DAVIS has taught at the Graduate School of Architecture and Urban Planning at UCLA and also at Cal Arts. He is a member of the editorial committee of *The New Left Review* and a frequent contributor to its pages. He is the author of *Prisoners of the American Dream* and his most recent book, *City of Quartz: Excavating the Future of Los Angeles,* was a finalist for the 1990 National Book Critics Circle Award.

LYNELL GEORGE is a staff writer at *L.A. Weekly,* where her series "Sometimes a Light Surprises: The Life of a Black Church" was nominated for the 1990 National Association of Black Journalists' Award.

THOMAS S. HINES is a professor at UCLA, where he teaches cultural, urban, and architectural history. A co-curator of the Neutra Retrospective at the Museum of Modern Art in 1982, he is the author of *Richard Neutra and the Search for Modern Architecture: A Biography and History* and *Burnham of Chicago: Architect and Planner*. The recipient of National Endowment for the Humanities, Guggenheim, and Fulbright fellowships, he is currently working on a book to be called *Modernism and Regionalism: A History of Los Angeles Architectural Culture*.

JEREMY LARNER, a screenwriter, poet, and essayist, is also the author of the novel *Drive, He Said*. In 1973 he received the Academy Award for the best original screenplay for *The Candidate*, which starred Robert Redford.

RUBÉN MARTÍNEZ, a contributing writer for *L.A. Weekly*, is at work on a book about Los Angeles and the border country.

DAVID REID is coeditor, with Leonard Michaels and Raquel Scherr, of *West of the West: Imagining California*. He is currently at work on a book about New York City and the American Empire from 1945 to 1950.

CAROLYN SEE'S most recent novels are *Golden Days* and *Making History*. A regular contributor to the *Los Angeles Times* and *New York Newsday*, she has received a Guggenheim Fellowship in fiction and a National Endowment for the Arts grant. She teaches at UCLA.

DAVID THOMSON is the author of *Suspects*, *A Biographical Dictionary of Film*, and *Warren Beatty and Desert Eyes*. His most recent book, *Silver Light*, was published in 1990. He is a frequent contributor to the pages of *Film Comment* and *The New Republic*. He is currently working on a biography of David O. Selznick.